FRONT-PAGE GIRLS

FRONT PAGE GIRLS

WOMEN JOURNALISTS IN AMERICAN CULTURE AND FICTION, 1880–1930

[JEAN MARIE LUTES]

Cornell University Press
Ithaca & London

First published 2006 by Cornell University Press

Printed in the United States of America

Library of Congress Cataloging-in-Publication Data

Lutes, Jean Marie, 1967–
    Front-page girls : women journalists in American culture and fiction, 1880–1930 / Jean Marie Lutes.
        p. cm.
    Includes bibliographical references and index.
    ISBN-13: 978-0-8014-4235-3 (cloth : alk. paper)
    ISBN-10: 0-8014-4235-4 (cloth : alk. paper)
    1. Women journalists—United States—History.   2. Women journalists in literature.   3. Journalism—Social aspects—United States—History.
    4. Journalism and literature—United States—History.   I. Title.
    PN4888.W66L88 2006
    071'.3'082—dc22
                                                                2006014454

Cornell University Press strives to use environmentally responsible suppliers and materials to the fullest extent possible in the publishing of its books. Such materials include vegetable-based, low-VOC inks and acid-free papers that are recycled, totally chlorine-free, or partly composed of nonwood fibers. For further information, visit our website at www.cornellpress.cornell.edu.

Cloth printing   10 9 8 7 6 5 4 3 2 1

To Robert Blaine Lutes
in loving memory

Contents

Acknowledgments

This book has its roots in the career I left when I decided to pursue graduate studies in literature. My experience as a reporter was quite different from that of the women whose experiences are chronicled here, but my first acknowledgments must go to the newspapermen and women who introduced me to the profession—the student editors at the *Daily Tar Heel* who taught me how to write, especially Janet Olsen and Grant Parsons, and the late Jim Shumaker, the legendary journalism professor at the University of North Carolina who assured me that going to graduate school would ruin me as a writer. (I tried to prove him wrong.) I am also grateful to my professional newspaper colleagues at the *Pittsburgh Post-Gazette* and the *Miami Herald*. The memory of their wit and dedication remains vivid, even after years away from the city room.

My research was supported by an American Fellowship from the American Association of University Women; a Villanova University sabbatical; a National Endowment for the Humanities Summer Stipend; a Mellon Fellowship from the Harry Ransom Humanities Research Center; a fellowship from the Gilder-Lehrman Institute of American History; and two awards from Manhattan College, a Summer Research Grant and a Mahony Award. A grant from the University Seminars at Columbia University helped me to prepare the manuscript for publication. I am especially grateful to Villanova University, which provided me with a supportive community, time off from teaching, and able research assistance in the person of Jana Diemer, who corrected many of my mistakes. The staff at Villanova's Falvey Library, especially Judith Olsen, often came to my aid with grace and efficiency; Donna Blaszkowski and Bernadette Dierkes in the graphics design office provided critical help with the illustrations.

Portions of this book have appeared elsewhere, and I thank the original publishers for permission to reprint. In somewhat different form, chapter 1 was published by the Johns Hopkins University Press as "Into the Madhouse with Nellie Bly: Girl Stunt Reporting in Late-Nineteenth-Century America" in *American Quarterly* 54, no. 2 (2002): 217–53, copyright The American Studies Association, and chapter 3 was published by Oxford University Press as "Sob Sisterhood Revisited" in *American Literary History* 15, no. 3 (2003): 504–32.

My editors at Cornell University Press have been models of professionalism and patience. I am especially grateful for Sheryl Englund's early enthusiasm about the project, Alison Kalett's guidance through its final stages, and the generous and instructive commentary I received from the press's anonymous readers.

As a scholar, I have been blessed with kind and stimulating colleagues, first in graduate school at the University of Wisconsin–Madison, then at Manhattan College and again at Villanova University. For their support from the earliest days of my graduate career, I thank Katherine Adams, Emily Hall, Kirsten Jamsen, Robert Kachur, Erin Smith, and Edie Thornton. Since then, I have benefited from the insights of many other readers, including Rachel Adams, Michael Berthold, Matt Bivens, Scott Black, Ellen Bonds, Jon Connolly, Julie Crawford, Ashley Cross, Kathleen Diffley, Kim Donehower, June Dwyer, Maria Farland, Heather Hicks, Barbara Hochman, Patrick Horner, Valerie Karno, Seth Koven, John Lowney, Crystal Lucky, Rocco Marinaccio, Susannah Mintz, Hugh Ormsby-Lennon, Evan Radcliffe, Lisa Sewell, Mary Beth Simmons, Vince Sherry, Lauren Shohet, Mark and Anya Taylor, Jennifer Travis, and Liza Yukins. Rick Delano provided generous support at a crucial moment. I also appreciate the suggestions of those who heard me present my work in progress to the Columbia University Seminar on American Studies, the New York Americanist group, the Philosophy Colloquium at the University of North Dakota, and panels at meetings of the Modern Language Association, the Society for the Study of American Women Writers, and the American Literature Association. During my stay in Austin to use the Ransom Center collections, Martha Campbell was an ideal host, offering both warm hospitality and the gift of genuine curiosity about my work.

Among the many people who helped me during the years I worked on this book, two require special mention. Ashley Cross read all my early drafts, forced me to be clear even when I didn't want to be, and made me snort with laughter while sitting in the New York Public Library Reading

Room. Rachel Adams responded to my work with patience and rigor, pinpointing its weaknesses even while she urged me on. She also cooked gloriously excessive dinners and weighed me down with leftovers for my subway trips home.

Although this book is not a revision of my dissertation, that work served as a critical foundation for what came next. I owe special thanks to Dale Bauer, who directed my dissertation, who has served as my mentor and helped me more times than I can count, and who continues to inspire me with her intellect, energy, and courage. Gordon Hutner has long been an invaluable source of professional wisdom and incisive commentary. The late Sargent Bush Jr. was an important reader, advocate, and scholarly role model. I sorely miss his integrity and wry humor.

The love of my family and friends has made my work possible and enriched my life beyond my powers to express. For this I thank Patricia Dolan; Alice, Elena, and Vivian Dueker; Nick Simon; Erin Smith; my mother, Mary O'Neil Lutes; my brothers, especially Christopher Lutes; and my sister, Beth Hillman, my earliest and most profound inspiration. Beth read every word of this book, more than once, and she has supported me in every way possible for as long as I can remember. Finally, I note my great debt to my father, Robert Blaine Lutes, who died while I was finishing the book. In recognition of his love and kindness, and because he always read the newspaper, this book is dedicated to him.

FRONT-PAGE GIRLS

Introduction

By the time a 1901 *Ladies' Home Journal* article asked "Is the News-paper Office the Place for a Girl?" it was almost too late to bother posing the question.[1] At the turn of the century, women reporters were already a visible subset of the nation's newspaper journalists. Ishbel Ross called them "front-page girls" in her 1936 history *Ladies of the Press*.[2] The description was not entirely accurate: they were rarely "girls" (although many were teenagers when they entered the business), and their stories did not always make it to the front page. But Ross's phrase—in its simultaneous celebration of women's access to the power of publicity and disparagement of them as young and silly—captures the defining charac-teristics of the newspaperwomen who elbow their way through the pages of this book. They compel serious attention and attract ridicule almost at the same time. They qualify as professional pioneers, but they often appear to be looking backward instead of forward, clinging to tired nineteenth-century ideas about women's roles and, perhaps worse, all too willing to profit from the modern press's interest in their shock value. And they left behind a newsprint trail in which they personally figure more prominently than any story they told. "The front-page girl had better know her stuff," warned Ross, a former reporter herself, "if she wants to function under the garish lights that burn down on the city room, revealing the flaws in her equipment with shocking candor."[3] This warning makes it difficult to tell whether "equipment" refers to newsgathering skill or bust size, and that is precisely the point. No matter how well she knew her stuff, the front-page girl could not escape those garish lights; the best she could do was to func-

1

tion under them. Newspaperwomen thus crafted a journalistic legacy by subjecting both themselves and their news reports to the stark glare of publicity. In this book I argue for the cultural and literary significance of that legacy, which intertwined the bodies of news writers with the news itself.

In the 1890s, novelist and critic William Dean Howells, frustrated by what he perceived as a feminization of American literature, complained that only women read books, while men read nothing but newspapers.[4] But Howells was voicing an assumption, not a fact. By taking him too much at his word, literary historians have misread news writing as a masculine antidote for women's influence on fiction and distorted the gender dynamics of turn-of-the-century journalism. Although historians have long noted that a rapid increase in the numbers of newswomen occurred in the decades after the Civil War, existing scholarship on journalism and literature dismisses women as deviants from a culture that tied newspaper work to male identity.[5] This dismissal has rendered invisible the intrepid women who flocked into city newsrooms in the late nineteenth and early twentieth centuries. This group—which included stars in the making such as Willa Cather and many lesser-known writers—produced a volatile mix of publicity, sensationalism, and professional and literary anxiety that shaped American print culture in striking ways. By failing to attend to newspaperwomen, we have lost more than an adventurous chapter in the history of professional women. We have lost a key index of modern publicity, a means of unlocking some of the deepest contradictions of the American public sphere.

By the early twentieth century, the metropolitan newspaperwoman was one of the most recognizable popular images of the woman writer in America. More likely than her male counterparts to be pictured along with her stories, more likely to inspire controversy by her physical presence at an event, the newspaperwoman was a conspicuous anomaly, hard to ignore even by those who wished that she would go away. Stunt reporters, following the lead of daredevil Nellie Bly, had insinuated themselves into prisons, hospitals, asylums, circuses, and brothels, joined caged animals in zoos, kicked up their heels with cabaret dancers on stage, and caught rides in newfangled vehicles from automobiles to airplanes. Although newsmen occasionally staged stunts—Stephen Crane's "experiments" in misery and luxury come to mind—they were not defined by those stunts in the way newspaperwomen were.[6] For men, participatory journalism was a choice; for women, it was one of the few ways to break out of the women's pages. Even women writers who avoided stunts and covered unstaged "hard" news, such as murders, fires, train wrecks, and political conflicts, often found themselves in the spotlight. Nicknamed "sob sisters," they were assigned to provide the so-called woman's angle by reporting on their own sympathetic reactions to news events. Their reports were expected to express the conventionally emotional responses of women, documenting not just the news but the femininity of its tellers.

This on-demand outpouring of emotion could turn back upon itself, devolving into a weary repetition of pro forma feeling, a phenomenon that potentially undermined the authenticity of all women's reportage, even those who resisted the formula. Although sob sisters were not stunt reporters per se, performing sympathy and registering the emotional impact of the news for readers took its own mental and physical toll. The hard-working title character of "The Sob-Lady," a 1915 short story published in *Good Housekeeping,* is a young newspaperwoman who describes her occupation with chilling resignation: "Splashwork—word splashes. Violent, screaming, red and black splashes. For example, take tonight: four burning elevated cars, packed end to end with working men and children. Someone else does the news; I go over and write the picture. I tick down the stuff, red-hot, just as I see it: men and women shrieking, raving, cursing, clawing, fighting to escape alive from that burning pen."[7] This sob sister's matter-of-fact recitation sounds startlingly hardboiled. Moreover, she acts as a mechanical medium, ticking off horrors in service to her newspaper's demand for "splashwork"; her writing is not crafted but somehow automatic. She splashes words like tears, her language as unformed as the water that wells up in her eyes. This notion of women writers as word-splashers indicted them not just as hypocrites whose emotional extravagance belied their own lack of feeling, but also as careless writers, unable to recognize the power of well-chosen words. Sob-sisterhood transferred the loss of bodily control associated with bursting into tears into a vision of authorship that was equal parts sappy and slapdash.

In many ways formulaic and unreflective, the narratives of the stunt reporters and sob sisters were not known for deliberation and depth. Yet does it necessarily follow that they exerted no significant influence on print culture in the United States? If newspaper reporters and literary critics have anything in common, it might be the shared desire to take a closer look, the suspicion that initial impressions are not the most accurate, the commitment to looking further, harder, longer. And the longer one looks at these newspaperwomen, the harder it is to dismiss them as flash-in-the-pan opportunists without real power or impact. Newspapers were taking on new roles in this era, spurred by advances in printing technology and the expanding, diversifying readership of fast-growing cities. The number of daily newspapers in the United States quadrupled between 1870 and 1899.[8] More people, of more varied socioeconomic, ethnic, and racial backgrounds, were reading more newspapers than ever before. Turn-of-the-century newspaperwomen, still thoroughly entangled in conventional notions of womanhood, nonetheless blazed a path in an unprecedented venue. Enacting a daily drama in a medium that was previously unthinkable, they appeared both defiantly public and defensively feminine. The obscurity that descended on them in subsequent decades contrasts sharply with their prominence in the mass-circulation newspapers of their day. By 1900, bylines for women were more common than for men.[9]

It may have been that very prominence that consigned newswomen to the historical shadows. With the professionalization of journalism came a new commitment to objectivity that privileged a detached reporting style which was out of sync with the modus operandi of the sensational journals most likely to hire female reporters.[10] Caught up in the extravagant self-promotion that distinguished the era's "yellow journalism," newspaperwomen made easy targets for press critics scornful of the excesses wrought by competitions such as the epic circulation battle between William Randolph Hearst and Joseph Pulitzer.[11] If, as one influential media analyst has argued, late-nineteenth-century journalists underwent a "conversion downwards," shifting from independent interpreters of events to producers of news as a commodity, the attendant rise of the newspaperwoman could be readily identified with, and even blamed for, this troubling trend.[12] It is no accident, then, that the newspaperwomen featured in this book share little in common with the era's most esteemed female journalist, the muckraker Ida Tarbell, whose famous investigation of John D. Rockefeller's business practices was published as a series in *McClure's* magazine in 1902 and 1903 and then issued as a book, *The History of the Standard Oil Company,* in 1904. Even her most forceful critics would have been hard-pressed to call Tarbell's reporting "splashwork." Her early love of microscopes presaged her scrupulous attention to detail as a reporter; she rarely used the first person, scorned sensational tactics, and made a point of corroborating her personal observations by consulting other sources. After witnessing the horrifying conditions endured by textile workers, for instance, Tarbell reviewed the reports of social workers to confirm what she had seen.[13] As Tarbell's case makes clear, the phenomenon of the daily newspaper "girl reporter" did not include all women journalists. Yet the stunt reporter and sob sister models of reportage crossed over into American fiction and helped to shape public responses to women writers as a group, influencing their representation in a way that Tarbell, despite her stature as an investigative journalist, did not.

Even if Howells was correct in asserting that novels had lost male readers in the course of the nineteenth century, he was most certainly wrong to suggest that newspapers lacked female readers. In fact, they were courting women more aggressively than ever before. The woman-centered model of news reporting that emerged, however, was not embraced by the American literary establishment. At a time when arbiters of literary taste like Howells were seeking to elevate the artistic reputation of American writers, the woman reporter who surveyed the city with tearful eyes was of little use, especially for advocates of literary realism. The image of a fraternity of newsmen, manly reporters who cast a cynical look at the world around them, offered a better corrective to the nineteenth century's woman-identified model of sentimental authorship.[14] It also gave male novelists—a notoriously anxious group when the question of sexual identity arose—a convenient way to distinguish themselves from sentimental writers and from British contemporaries such as Oscar Wilde, whose aestheticism and flamboyant homosexuality interfered with attempts to promote authorship as a respectable and manly profession.[15]

Yet women's intensely personal, corporeal reporting exerted as much influence on fiction as the male-defined model of journalism most often cited by American literary historians. Tracing the figure of the female reporter, both real and imagined, in the late nineteenth and early twentieth centuries reveals that the commonsense connection between news writing and literary realism, between the skills of the reporter and those of the realist novelist, has obscured other channels of influence between journalism and literature, ties based not on claims of realism, neutrality, and authenticity but on the celebration of bodily particularity, personal bias, and easy reproducibility. Newspaperwomen renovated conventions of nineteenth-century sentimentality to suit the rapidly evolving mass media and developed controversial new models of self-reflexive authorship that involved not just reporting the news but *becoming* the news. Women's newspaper reportage—anchored in the physical, defined by its appeal to the masses, distinguished by its failure to transcend its moment and its obvious entanglement in anxieties about sex, class, and race—was both too old-fashioned (in its sentimentality) and too modern (in its mass-market public venue) to fit into the story of American literature that people such as Howells were beginning to tell.

This book revises that story, both to deepen our understanding of the role of journalism in American fiction and to suggest that the spectacle of the female journalist offers crucial insight into the broader dynamics of turn-of-the-century mass culture. Analyzing women's reportage, fictional portrayals of women journalists, and the literary careers of female reporters-turned-novelists, I show that newspaperwomen forged a vibrant tradition of sensation journalism that reverberated from grubby city newsrooms to exclusive literary circles. Female reporters offered to ease the uncertainty and alienation of urban life by using their bodies as conduits for the news, projecting themselves into their stories and thus into their readers' lives. Cast as representatives of the emerging public that the era's newspapers sought to cultivate, female reporters took center stage as mass culture came to be identified with women and "the masses" came to be understood—and denigrated—as irrational and over-emotional. They fashioned a model of authorship that influenced the public reception of other women writers, even those who never wrote for newspapers. That authorial model countered the realist shift toward objective—we might even say disembodied—narration.[16] Instead, it promoted an image of the woman writer as both body conscious and deeply enmeshed in the mass-market media.

Newspaperwomen's bodies, circulated through the pages of the papers that employed them, became emblems of publicity. Publicity in this sense is not simply the state of being on display but rather, as the theorist Michael Warner puts it, "the use of media, an instrumental publicness."[17] As emblems of publicity, female reporters were identified with and through the process of making public their images and their words. They functioned as both agents and pawns in this process: to participate in it, they had to subject themselves to its imperatives—its demand for texts and visuals that could be easily apprehended, its reliance on the shorthand of cultural convention, its goal of disseminating information in the most emphatic form to the widest possible audience. Male reporters, of course, were equally subject to these imperatives. But unlike women, they were not primarily identified with and through them. Newsmen could at least profess to be participating in a public sphere that featured disembodied reason and deliberation; newswomen—whose access to that public sphere often depended on their willingness to discard all pretense of neutrality and to write from an intensely personal perspective—could not. In the self-reflexive nature of their writing, female reporters came to embody the practice of publicity, a practice that was changing how Americans understood themselves and their relation to the communities in which they lived. By eschewing disinterest and using their own experiences as sources of news, women reporters enacted as individuals what mass-market newspapers were doing on a broader scale: creating a media cycle that redefined publicity as an end in itself, in which the ability to attract attention carried inherent value. This cycle addressed itself to the mass public, an imagined community of readers that, as Warner has argued, includes everyone in general but no one in particular.[18] Newspaperwomen were asked, in effect, to stand in for that mass public, to represent it in their own persons and to serve its various interests. This role appeared to come naturally to them because they were assumed, by virtue of their gender, to be incapable of deliberating rationally, transcending their personal interests, or making neutral judgments.

Thus newspaperwomen acted as both standard-bearers and scapegoats as the national literary imagination adapted to a new era of mass-market publicity. Female reporters, writing for the world's first mass-circulation papers, served as focal points for debates on the necessity of objectivity, the propriety of women's public roles, the dangers of sexual desire, even the national passion for publicity. These debates extended from daily newspapers through some of the era's most powerful fiction, written by authors as varied as Charles Chesnutt, Abraham Cahan, Theodore Dreiser, F. Scott Fitzgerald, Edith Wharton, and Anzia Yezierska. Female reporters also modeled a new kind of authorship for their readers, synthesizing sentimental tropes of female authorship within a self-consciously professional version of the modern literary woman. They advanced a model of the woman writer as unapologetically, even triumphantly embodied, a writer whose physical presence at an event became an integral part of the news, a writer who was on display first when she was gathering the news and again in the text of her reports.

Inevitably caught up in cultural attitudes toward women's bodies, particularly those involving racial identity and sexual propriety, newspaperwomen were called upon not only to be professional reporters but also to be professional women, to fulfill a middle-class model of femininity that revolved around assumptions of racial whiteness and sexual inviolability. Thus they offer insight into a telling moment in the history of race and sexuality in the United States, a moment when the city room's preoccupation with the flaws in what Ishbel Ross called newspaperwomen's "equipment" betrayed mainstream society's urgent need to protect an increasingly fragile vision of the inviolable, native-born white female body. That vision was being threatened by a rising tide of ethnic and racial diversity, particularly in the urban areas where most reporters worked. The mainstream newspaperwoman's whiteness and respectability, repeatedly displayed through her physical interventions in the life of the city, promised to absorb and even neutralize cultural tensions. The strain of managing such expectations altered women's news narratives, shaped fictional characterizations of female reporters, and exerted pressure on the authorial vision of women journalists who went on to write fiction.

Two strands of scholarship inform my discussion of newswomen's cultural impact. On the one hand, literary critics have argued for the importance of journalism to emerging forms of literary fiction; on the other, journalism historians have recovered the writings of early women reporters whose work has been long neglected.[19] I bring these strands together to explore the conjunction of publicity and femininity embodied by female reporters, who achieved a special iconic status in both fact and fiction. I focus primarily on members of a select group, the defiant few who wrote for the city desks of mainstream newspapers, Ross's "front-page girls"—the women who somehow ducked the growing demand for writers to cover fashion, society, and household topics. Although I pay special attention to the African American journalist Ida B. Wells, who crossed over into mainstream papers as the star of the black press's anti-lynching crusade, I do not address the many contributions of women who wrote for suffrage journals, socialist publications, and other alternative presses,[20] or those who wrote specifically for the burgeoning women's pages, women's magazines, and women's editions of newspapers.[21] Instead I look closely at the writings and images of women who inserted themselves directly into the male-dominated world of metropolitan newspaper reporting, who sought to cover the same news as men, on the same footing. If they rarely succeeded in attaining such footing—the ground beneath them tilted often, leaving them scrambling alongside male reporters whose right to show up at news events went unquestioned—they nonetheless garnered considerable attention while trying.

Notable newspaperwomen existed before the late nineteenth century, of course.[22] But in 1870, the first year in which the U.S. Census distinguished journalists by sex, women made up fewer than 1 percent of working journalists.[23] As the turn of the century approached, women as a group began to make a significant mark in newsrooms. The 1880s saw the launch of the first women's press associations, and by the early 1900s, some two dozen such groups had been established in seventeen states.[24] The new respectability of reporting as a profession, expanding educational opportunities for women, and newspapers' growing interest in female readers, who were highly desirable to department store advertisers, all fueled the trend.[25] By the 1880s, a half-dozen women could be found in full-time positions on the daily newspaper staffs of most cities.[26] *The Journalist,* a weekly trade publication, estimated in 1886 that five hundred women wrote or edited copy for American newspapers; two years later, the estimate jumped to two hundred women in New York City alone.[27] In 1888, *The Journalist* printed a two-column article on Chicago's best-known newspaperwomen, and in 1889 it devoted an entire issue to women journalists, including biographical sketches of fifty female writers.[28] "Women have taken to journalism like a duck to water," enthused newspaperwoman Dorothy Dix in a 1902 address.[29] According to the U.S. Census, the percentage of women journalists more than doubled between 1880 and 1900 and climbed steadily after that. Women made up 16 percent of all working journalists by 1920 and 23 percent by 1930.[30]

Public commentaries on the wisdom (or folly) of women in journalism bore witness to their growing public presence. "As a reporter I believe a lady has the advantage of the masculine reporter in many respects," journalist and advice columnist Gertrude Bustill Mossell declared optimistically in her 1894 book *The Work of the Afro-American Woman*. "She can gain more readily as an interviewer access to both sexes. Women know best how to deal with women and the inborn chivalry of a gentleman leads him to grant her request when a man might have been repulsed without compunction. In seven years' experience as an interviewer on two white papers I have never met with a refusal from either sex or race. If at first for some reason they declined, eventually I gained my point."[31]

Mossell's rosy portrayal of newspaper work, shaped in part by her commitment to encouraging African American women to seek professional employment, is almost fantastically upbeat, given the widespread discrimination faced by women—especially women of color—who sought work at mainstream newspapers. But Mossell was not alone in recognizing journalism as a legitimate career option for women. Frances Willard, the well-known leader of the Women's Christian Temperance Union, devoted a chapter to newspaperwomen in her 1897 book *Occupations for Women*.[32] A 1911 *Atlantic Monthly* article exalting journalism as a newly respectable profession foresees both men and women in the upcoming generation of professionals.[33] One of the first textbooks written for professional journalists, Edwin L. Shuman's *Practical Journalism: A Complete Manual of the Best Newspaper Methods* (1905), includes a chapter on "Women in Newspaper Work" and estimates that the average city daily employed about five women writers. Although Shuman admits that women reporters faced "special disabilities and prejudices," he opens the chapter by insisting that they now "stand on exactly the same basis as the men, and they hold their positions simply because they can do their work fully as well as men could do it." Shuman does not go out of his way to encourage female reporters, however. "Reportorial work rubs the bloom off a woman much more quickly than school-teaching or employment in a business office," he cautioned. "The paper takes all her time, all her strength, and robs her of almost all social life and of many feminine characteristics."[34]

This bloom-off-the-rose anxiety continued to appear regularly in commentaries on women in journalism. Despite impressive gains, the rapid rise in the number of female reporters did not herald a major transformation of the male-dominated newspaper business, and women remained a mi-

nority on newspaper staffs for most of the twentieth century.[35] Women
should expect no special treatment in newsrooms, they were repeatedly
warned.[36] In 1901, when *Ladies' Home Journal* editor Edward Bok asked
leading newspapermen and women if they would want their own daughters to work in a daily newspaper office, sixty-nine of the seventy-two
respondents said no.[37] In 1905, ex-reporter Helen M. Winslow shared
her woes with *Atlantic Monthly* readers in "Confessions of a Newspaper
Woman." Winslow urged young women with literary ambitions to avoid
newspaper work because the long hours and poor pay had exhausted her
so thoroughly that it ruined her talent. "There has been a great influx of
women into newspaper offices in the last decade, but I believe they will
never be so numerous as reporters again," Winslow wrote. "The life is too
hard and too hardening."[38] In a *Collier's* article in 1909, former newspaperwoman Anne Eliot detailed the difficulties of her six-year stint in journalism, complaining that she was made to feel a "tool" of a publicity system
she could not control. "It is impossible for a woman to make a success of
yellow journalism and maintain her self-respect," she proclaimed.[39] Yet by
the 1920s, entire books—not just chapters—were devoted to giving advice
to hopeful female reporters.[40] Women continued to move steadily into
newsrooms, despite admonitions against it, and sometimes, no doubt, because of them. When a young Barnard graduate named Agnes Ernst told
her parents in 1907 that she planned to be a reporter, her mother cried
and her father said he would rather see her dead. She was soon freelancing for the *New York Sun* anyway.[41]

⁘

Between 1880 and 1920 the newspaperwoman emerged as an icon of
American culture, a figure of modernity that promised to alleviate some of
the alienating effects of the mass media that made possible her very existence. The chapters that follow trace that figure through newspapers and
fictional narratives, exploring the woman reporter's role in mediating tensions between publicity and intimacy, journalism and fiction, the abstraction of literary authorship and the visceral experience of embodiment.
The first three chapters deal with three forms of sensational news writing
dominated by women at the turn of the century. Chapter 1 takes up urban
stunt reporting, pioneered by Nellie Bly; chapter 2 the journalism of anti-
lynching crusader Ida B. Wells; and chapter 3 the coverage of playboy
Harry Thaw's 1907 murder trial, during which newswomen got so much
attention that they earned the dismissive and enduring nickname "sob sisters." In each of these cases, newspaperwomen took on supercharged roles
fraught with sexual tension, and they acted as both agents and objects of

publicity. The last two chapters follow the repercussions of these acts of public embodiment through American literary culture, examining how writers represented newspaperwomen in fiction and how women's journalism altered the conditions of possibility for women seeking to establish themselves as authors. In chapter 4 I read the reporter-heroine in fiction as a marker of mass publicity, focusing on Henry James's use of Henrietta Stackpole as an authorial figure in *The Portrait of a Lady* (1881). In chapter 5 I consider how three strikingly different writers who began their careers as reporters—Willa Cather, Edna Ferber, and Djuna Barnes—grappled with the body-conscious legacy of women's journalism. Attending to the ways women authors responded to the public spectacle of the newspaperwoman illuminates an alternative reporter-novelist tradition, featuring not professional detachment and precise observation but rather the intimate, deeply subjective realities of physical experience. This tradition recognizes that those realities are often performative, caught up in the process of making bodies public which defined mainstream women's journalism at the turn of the twentieth century and continues to shape the lived experiences of women today. By becoming the news, female reporters created fictions of themselves that far outlasted—in scope, depth, and impact—the fleeting news value of the stories they covered.

Into the Madhouse with Girl Stunt Reporters

In 1887, after months of rejection from editors who refused to consider hiring a woman, aspiring journalist Nellie Bly finagled a meeting with the *New York World*'s managing editor.[1] Determined to make the most of her chance, she offered to travel to Europe and return steerage class, to report firsthand on the experiences of the immigrants then coming to the United States in record numbers. The editor rejected the idea as too far-flung for an inexperienced reporter, but asked instead if she would feign insanity and have herself committed to the infamous insane asylum on Blackwell's Island, home to most of the city's prisons, charity hospitals, and workhouses.[2] The assignment was more local but scarcely less risky. In contrast to the facilities at better-funded institutions patronized by the middle and upper classes, the conditions at the Blackwell's Island asylum were notoriously poor. It provided cheap custodial care for impoverished mentally ill immigrants. Nevertheless, Bly eagerly accepted the assignment.

It was a brilliant move. Her madhouse performance inaugurated the performative tactic that would become her trademark reporting style. With little formal education, no professional training as a journalist, and no credentials in any specialized field, Bly lacked virtually all of the commonly accepted qualifications for professional status in late-nineteenth-century America.[3] Yet she transformed her amateurism from a liability to an asset, countering bureaucratic and scientific authority with her own truths based on physical sensation. In an era that embraced scientific experts with furious optimism, Bly's reportage exulted in the concrete specifics of one individual's experience and scorned the relative abstraction of disinterested observation. By adopting the hysteric's hyper-female, hyper-expressive body, she created her own story and claimed the right to tell it in her own way. Moreover, impersonating insanity allowed her to flaunt the very characteristics that were being used as an excuse to bar women from city newsrooms: her femaleness, her emotional expressiveness, her physical—even her explicitly sexual—vulnerability. The first article in her "Ten Days in a Madhouse" series attracted so much attention that Bly's name appeared not just as a byline but in the headline of the next installment. The headlines of her subsequent stories followed the same pattern: "The Girls Who Make Boxes: Nellie Bly Tells How It Feels to Be a White Slave," "Nellie Bly as a Mesmerist," "Visiting the Dispensaries: Nelly [sic] Bly Narrowly Escapes Having Her Tonsils Amputated," "Trying to Be a Servant: Nellie Bly's Strange Experience," "Nellie Bly in Pullman: She Visits the Homes of Poverty in the 'Model Workingman's Town.'"[4]

The first and best of the gutsy late-nineteenth-century journalists known as "girl stunt reporters," Bly became a national phenomenon at a formative moment in American mass culture. Her success at masquerading as a hysteric—and, later, as a succession of other marginalized women, from factory workers to chorus girls—inspired so many imitators that girl stunt reporting became a recognizable genre in the popular press of the late 1880s and early 1890s.[5] Stunt reporters visited opium dens, joined workers who rolled tobacco for cigarettes, went begging on the streets in rags, sought illegal abortions, and fainted on the street to gain admittance to public hospitals. One even raced Bly around the world in 1890.[6] Meanwhile, Bly's name became a synonym for adventurous newswomen from the Atlantic seaboard to the West Coast. The *San Francisco Examiner*'s Winifred Black was frequently compared to Bly, while the *St. Louis Republican*'s Ada Patterson was christened "the Nellie Bly of the West" and the *Boston Post*'s Caroline Lockhart—who donned a diving suit to go to the bottom of Boston Harbor—was called "the Nellie Bly of Boston."[7] In the early 1890s, an ambitious American named Elizabeth Banks became one of London's best-known journalists when she took stunt reporting across the Atlantic and impersonated a series of British workingwomen.[8]

Despite their popularity, these news narratives have been neglected by literary historians of the late nineteenth century; the burst of scholarly interest in turn-of-the-century writers who crossed class lines has left the stunt reporters' contributions to American public culture unexamined.[9] Characterized as a fad that quickly subsided, the stunt reporters have been viewed as an awkward, even embarrassing phase of sensation journalism, out of sync with the professionalization that was transforming news writing in the final decades of the nineteenth century.[10] Indeed, current scholarship insists that news writing conventions, especially those that shaped realist and naturalist fiction, were inherently male. The no-frills newsroom environment, coupled with the city reporter's journey through the rough-and-tumble world of the streets, is said to have helped forge the self-consciously masculine identity of writers such as Stephen Crane and Jack London.[11] This characterization of journalism as exclusively male has obscured a national public venue for women's voices, created by female journalists who imagined themselves as vehicles of publicity, a dual role in which women acted simultaneously as both objects and agents. Long after Nellie Bly's byline lost its punch, women journalists continued to be identified with stunt reporting, which never went entirely out of fashion.[12]

In this chapter I go "into the madhouse" with Nellie Bly to analyze the genesis of stunt reporting and to argue for its significance in the history of journalism, women's writing, and women's access to the public sphere in America. As a hybrid of emotional "soft news" and tough-minded "hard news," stunt reporting gave women journalists a way to profit from the attention so frequently focused on their bodies. Acting, in effect, as the sensation heroines of their own stories, they redefined reporting and used their bodies not just as a means of acquiring the news but as the very source of it.[13] The stunt reporters' popularity may even have inspired a misogynist backlash against women's growing presence in newsrooms. The aggressive masculinity of the dogged city reporter—so often cited as proof of women's marginal status—can also be read as a reaction against a perceived threat from women who had begun to write the news themselves. Undoubtedly, the figure of the manly reporter was a significant factor in the explosive gender politics of turn-of-the-century news writing. That gritty masculine figure, however, arose in tandem with that of the newspaperwoman, and the girl stunt reporter offered a particularly brash counterpoint.

Stunt reporting formed an important, if lowbrow, niche for the women who had begun appearing in newsrooms in unprecedented numbers in the 1880s and 1890s. While Bly and her followers were often scorned by more traditional journalists (including well-known muckrakers such as Ida Tarbell), they were the first newspaperwomen to move, as a group, from the women's pages to the front page, from society news into political and criminal news. Frank Luther Mott observed in his classic history of American newspapers that the late nineteenth century's "New Journalism" promoted investigative efforts and encouraged reporters to write vivid accounts from personal experience. Having writers adopt a disguise and stalk the city as crusaders neatly combined reformist and sensationalist impulses. Having those writers-in-disguise be *women* made the innovation all the more daring. As Mott noted, the woman journalist's appeal extended beyond the women's pages: "Women were sent to cover the war in Cuba and in the Philippines, the prizefights, and murder trials, in order to bring to the paper the feminine point of view in the news. Papers were full of the performances of girl reporters."[14]

Although not all stunt reporters followed Bly's lead precisely, their stories rarely deviated significantly from the standard she established. To trace the parameters Bly set, I examine her asylum series in depth. Her subsequent stories and those of her imitators also figure in my analysis, but Bly's madhouse performance receives the most sustained attention. In addition to defining the genre, it inspired multiple narratives that make it possible to read her own account against the competing versions published in the *World* and in other newspapers. A critical reading reveals a strategy that transformed her own white, middle-class body into a vehicle of publicity that anchored her pursuit of "the real" in corporeal experience. In the process, Bly forged a contradictory and, inevitably, a sexually charged position. The news reports generated by Bly's stunt verify her sexual vulnerability and thus make the gaps in her own narrative all the more telling. She became an agent of publicity, empowered to inform the public and to act as the intrepid reporter. Yet this peculiar form of agency required her to become the *object* of publicity at the same time. Her performance as a mental patient operates on several levels: while she becomes the object of both medical scrutiny and other journalists' reports, she also asserts her role as primary storyteller by narrating the process of her own objectification.

By their very profession, late-nineteenth-century female journalists represented newly aggressive forms of publicity and called attention to the expansion of public roles for women. Illuminated themselves by publicity's often brutal light, the stunt reporters claimed the power to shine that light on others. By exercising this power, however, they entered into a public discourse that often managed rising class conflicts and racial tensions through a preoccupation with white women's bodies, particularly their sexual purity. This preoccupation gave particular symbolic weight to the antics of the stunt reporters, who were almost all white, middle-class women themselves.[15] Throughout the narrative of her ten days "behind asylum bars," the balancing act Bly performs is far more subtle than her prose style, as she creates a self-assured, sexually attractive but emphatically virginal self. It suited the *World*'s much-vaunted crusade of supporting the

working poor and welcoming waves of new immigrants to have a staffer impersonate them. But it also served the paper's relatively conservative political stance not to have that staffer impersonate them all that *well*.

As will become apparent in the analysis that follows, I do not seek to recover Bly's sensationalism as a shining example of cross-class empathy. The
stunt reporter's success as a crosser of boundaries depended not only on
her sense of derring-do but also on her ability to reconstruct the very social boundaries she transgressed. Yet Bly's narratives cannot be neatly dismissed as a deft way of fooling poor, immigrant, and/or female readers
into thinking that the *World* was serving their interests.[16] In "Ten Days in a
Madhouse," Bly's sensationalism wields considerable power; endowing the
female experimental subject with an agency of her own, Bly undermines
the foundation of expert knowledge itself. When the first installment of
the exposé appeared in the *World,* the story highlighted not the mistreat-
ment of asylum inmates but rather Bly's success in deceiving police offi-
cers, judges, doctors, nurses, and other journalists. By performing hysteria
and being diagnosed by experts as "most definitely" suffering from that
malady, Bly countered an expert discourse that often disempowered women.
She entered territory usually controlled by the predominantly male medical establishment, in which female sexuality was exposed, unmasked, and
interpreted by men. By turning the tables and unmasking the male experts
themselves, Bly positioned herself as an authoritative interpreter of one of
the most threatening zones of the city: the asylum.[17]

Into the Madhouse

> A modest, comely, well-dressed girl of nineteen, who gave her name as Nel-
> lie Brown, was committed by Justice Duffy at Essex Market yesterday for ex-
> amination as to her sanity. The circumstances surrounding her were such as
> to indicate that possibly she might be the heroine of an interesting story.[18]

The author of this news item was prophetic; the young woman did indeed prove to be the heroine of an interesting story. "Nellie Brown" was
actually twenty-three-year-old Nellie Bly on her first undercover assignment for the *World*. Her performance was so convincing that she merited
coverage in competing newspapers, whose reporters were not in on the
ruse. Articles like the one quoted speculated about her past and waxed eloquent over her plight, unknowingly paving the way for her spectacular de-
but as a stunt reporter. In spite of what the news item suggests, it was not
simply "the circumstances surrounding her" that aroused reporters' inter-

est in the mysterious Nellie Brown. In fact, they knew next to nothing about her "circumstances." Rather, it was the figure of Bly herself—her "modest, comely, well-dressed" appearance—that attracted attention in her case. By subjecting herself to the conditions experienced by poor immigrants, Bly revealed how unacceptable they were. At the same time, however, she protected her more privileged readers from the dangers of overidentification with the less fortunate segments of the urban population, by carefully preserving the respectability of her physical self, by reiterating her "modesty" and "comeliness"—characteristics that marked her as part of a class whose members were *not* crazy, *not* poor, and *not* ethnically different.

The *World* devoted an entire Sunday front page to the first article in Bly's asylum series. The headlines for the ten–column story and the news summary printed above the text are worth quoting in their entirety because they illustrate so clearly the central themes of the Bly phenomenon. They establish her discursive authority by countering expert authority with (presumably more authentic) sensationalism; they stress Bly's personal performance rather than the plight of those whose position she temporarily inhabits; and they reiterate her difference from the role she has adopted even while they celebrate the success of her impersonation. The news summary that follows the initial headline is extensive:

BEHIND ASYLUM BARS.
The Mystery of the Unknown Insane Girl.
Remarkable Story of the Successful Impersonation of Insanity.
How Nellie Brown Deceived Judges, Reporters and Medical Experts.
She Tells Her Story of How She Passed at Bellevue Hospital.

Studying the Role of Insanity Before the Mirror and Practising It at the Temporary Home for Women—Arrested and Brought Before Judge Duffy—He Declares She Is Some Mother's Darling and Resembles His Sister—Committed to the Care of the Physicians for the Insane at Bellevue—Experts Declare Her Demented—Harsh Treatment of the Insane at Bellevue—"Charity Patients Should Not Complain"—Vivid Pictures of Hospital Life—How Our Esteemed Contemporaries Have Followed a False Trail—Some Needed Light Afforded Them — Chapters of Absorbing Interest in the Experience of a Feminine "Amateur Casual."

A Delicate Mission.[19]

Bly's "delicate mission," not the actual subject of her investigation, was billed as the real story. The exposé angle—the references to "harsh treat-

ment" and the admonition that "charity patients should not complain"—
is buried in the fifth line of the news summary; the bold-print headlines
do not mention it at all. To point this out is not to deny that Bly's piece
evoked sympathy for the patients confined to the asylum, or that it inspired
city officials to reform the hospital; indeed, it did both.[20] The newspaper's
handling of the story, however, suggests that public interest centered on
Bly and her transgression of social and cultural boundaries rather than on
the mentally ill immigrants. It also pointed out right away that she was an
"amateur casual"—a sly jab at the experts, who were used to scoffing at amateurs, not having amateurs scoff at them.

The image of a well-bred middle-class young woman "BEHIND ASYLUM
BARS" was the driving force behind the stories.[21] The unspoken question
was, could a woman *remain* respectable behind such bars? And could a
woman manufacture hysterical symptoms without becoming hysterical
herself? Bly answers an emphatic "yes" to both questions. Her narrative es-
tablishes her credentials as sane, respectable, and relatively financially se-
cure before she gets anywhere near a courtroom or a mental institution.
In the opening of the first article, Bly distances herself from the class of
people she is scheming to join by remarking that "unfortunately for the
end I had in view, my acquaintance with the struggling poor, except my
own self, was only very superficial." Her ironic reference to her financial
straits is lighthearted; she makes a joke of her own difficulties while distinguishing herself from the masses of urban poor clustered in city slums.
By confessing that she has had "only very superficial" contact with such
people, she places her origins comfortably outside the city's poverty-
stricken zones. As Bly explains how she practiced acting hysterical, she
notes that her inexperience in such matters complicated her task: "I had
never been near insane persons in my life and had not the faintest idea of
what their actions were like. . . . I began to think my task a hopeless one.
But it had to be done. So I flew to the mirror and examined my face." Her
body, typically, is the source of her answers: it will help her to deceive others even while it signifies her difference. Yet she confesses to limited hopes
for success early in her story: "I had little belief in my ability to deceive the
insanity experts, and I think my editor had less."[22] One might conclude
that a person with some passing familiarity with mental illness would have
been a better choice for this particular stunt, but it was precisely Bly's inexperience that made her the perfect person for the job. Having aligned
herself with sanity and respectability, she could now safely take her readers
with her into a part of the city that many were unwilling or afraid to enter
on their own.

And, according to her asylum series, that is exactly what she proceeded to do. Leaving all identifying documents at home, Bly checked herself in to a boardinghouse for women. To alarm her fellow boarders, she spoke irrationally during meals and stayed up all night, making noise in her room. Her report stresses the physical manifestations of her anxiety about what would happen next; at one point during the night, she grows frightened and turns up the gas: "The weather was not cold, but nevertheless when I thought of what was to come wintry chills raced up and down my back in very mockery of the perspiration which was slowly but surely taking the curl out of my bangs." By morning, the assistant matron tried to kick Bly out, but she resisted and babbled about her missing trunks. In short order, the matron called the police, who took Bly into custody. She continued to appear disoriented during her court appearance, answering questions about her name and circumstances by saying that she couldn't remember. The *New York Times* reporter who covered the story described her as "a mysterious waif" with a "wild, hunted look in her eyes."[23]

In documenting her descent into the madhouse, however, Bly reiterates her connection to her "real," respectable self even as she describes her attempts to appear insane. As the curl goes out of her bangs, her control over her situation diminishes. Yet her physical disintegration is not mirrored by mental decline; indeed, she presents herself as more in touch with her "essential self" than ever before. When Bly describes her night in the rooming house, she explains that she grew bored after hours of watching cockroaches and rats. To keep herself from dozing off, she imagines her life story: "How strange it all seems! One incident, if never so trifling, is but a link more to chain us to our unchangeable fate. Old friends were recalled with a pleasurable thrill; old enmities, old heart-aches, old joys were once again present. The turned-down pages of my life were turned up, and the past was present." She goes on to imagine her future, then writes: "That was the greatest night of my existence. For a few hours I stood face to face with 'self'!" That "self" which Bly faces, the "past" that was "present," all work to remind her—and her readers—of her sane childhood, her sane young adulthood, and her sane future. The greatest night of her existence is spent not loosening but rather strengthening the social bonds that ensure her stable social position.

The drawings that accompany the article highlight the incongruity between Bly's "real" status and her triumphant transformation into a madwoman. Under the long list of headlines appears a drawing of a neatly dressed young woman, presumably Bly, sitting at a desk, pen in hand (see figure 1). She looks demure, dignified, even rather dull; she could be writing a grocery list. This prim image of woman-as-writer, however, is countered immediately by the next drawing—of woman-as-actress, or, more

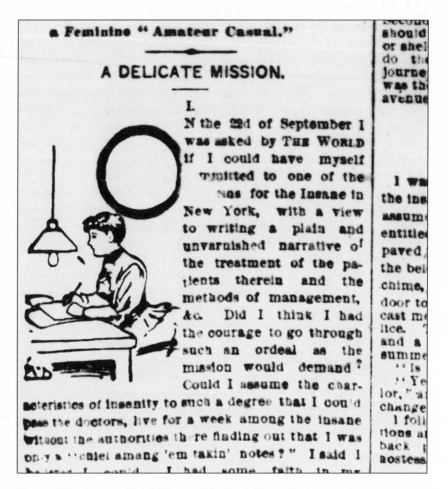

a Feminine " Amateur Casual."

A DELICATE MISSION.

I.

IN the 22d of September I was asked by THE WORLD if I could have myself ʀⱼmitted to one of the ⸺ᴀs for the Insane in New York, with a view to writing a plain and unvarnished narrative of the treatment of the patients therein and the methods of management, &c. Did I think I had the courage to go through such an ordeal as the mission would demand? Could I assume the characteristics of insanity to such a degree that I could pass the doctors, live for a week among the insane without the authorities there finding out that I was only a ··chief among 'em takin' notes?" I said I ⸺

Figure 1. The report on Bly's "delicate mission" to infiltrate the insane asylum opens with a prim image of a young woman seated at a desk. (*New York World,* October 9, 1887. General Research Division, The New York Public Library, Astor, Lenox, and Tilden Foundations.)

precisely, woman-performing-insanity. The illustration, captioned "Nellie Practises Insanity at Home," depicts a still-neatly dressed woman standing before a mirror, frowning and pulling her hair straight up with one hand; she is trying out different expressions to see just how crazy they might look (see figure 2). The juxtaposition of the two drawings links Bly's positions as writer and actress while emphasizing the disjunction between her adopted and actual roles. The images also allow readers a chuckle at the expense of the experts, who were taken in by a young woman whose only preparation for her task was an evening spent making faces in front of a

Figure 2. Captioned "Nellie Practises Insanity at Home," this image shows the reporter preparing for her stunt. (*New York World,* October 9, 1887. General Research Division, The New York Public Library, Astor, Lenox, and Tilden Foundations.)

mirror. By the late nineteenth century, according to a well-known history of professionalism, "legitimate authority now resided in special spaces, like the courtroom, the classroom, and the hospital; and it resided in special words shared only by experts."[24] Bly claims her own "special space" of authority by making herself into a vehicle of publicity, using her body to drive a wedge between those "special words shared only by experts" and the reality she represented to her readers.[25]

At the same time, Bly exploits the expert tendency to pathologize differences of race and class. Thus her story takes advantage of the way social distinctions permeated professional culture, despite its claims to the contrary. In the process of making her first and most crucial move, the transformation from free woman assumed to be sane to incarcerated woman assumed to be mad, she reveals the liability of claiming an ethnic identity in a legal system that purportedly saw beyond such distinctions. During the critical hours when she had to persuade the police and the judge to send her to Blackwell's Island, Bly pretends to speak Spanish and calls herself Nellie Moreno. Although she passes as an ethnic Other only briefly—once incarcerated, she drops the pretense and speaks in her obviously American English—she takes advantage of the ease with which cultural difference could be encoded as pathological difference. It is possible, of course, that Bly's "real" identity as native-born white American was obvious to the authorities, and that her adoption of a foreign name and tongue was interpreted as yet another sign of her mental imbalance. Nevertheless, at this decisive juncture, Bly's displaced whiteness serves her larger purpose. By distancing herself from her white privilege, she facilitates her own loss of freedom.

Perhaps because of the slapdash air of the stunt reporters' narratives, the complexity of their tactics and the boldness of their challenge to a male-dominated public sphere have been underestimated. Brooke Kroeger, author of the only scholarly biography of Bly, attributes her appeal to her straight-shooting style: "There was no mind-splitting intellectual insight or noteworthy literary finesse. Bly simply produced, week after week, an uninhibited display of her delight in being female and fearless and her joy in having such an attention-getting place to strut her stuff. . . . [E]ven her detractors found her too astounding to ignore."[26] This persistent fantasy of "uninhibited display," of un-self-conscious parading of personality, is all the more remarkable when we recognize the delicacy of Bly's mission, which required her to enter threatening situations while at the same time protecting herself from experiencing any threat too severely. Despite her many subterfuges, Bly always gave the impression that she was presenting her "true self" to her readers; a subscription to the *New York World* was a permanent backstage pass to the Nellie Bly Show. Readers could watch her trick others—people who deserved it, presumably—but she assured them that *they* were getting "a plain and unvarnished narrative" of how she did it and what she found out.[27] Kroeger demonstrates the power of the effect, even a century later, when she argues that what set Bly apart was "the way her own voice, her own personality, her essential self penetrated the page in spite of whatever she actually had to say."[28] What Bly had to say, of course, created the *effect* of her essential self; to separate the two, or to suggest that one was communicated "in spite of" the other, is to ignore how intimately connected they were. The force of Bly's personality, evinced by that physical, supposedly essential self that reacted to her environment, presents itself as so authentic that she makes it easy for her readers to make this mistake.

The commonness of this error reflects the ease with which the woman reporter's personality is conflated with her body—and the ease with which that body is accepted as an obvious and uncomplicated source of truth. This illusion of "uninhibited display" gives Bly's narratives a peculiar double edge that sharpens class and race divisions while blunting those of gender. While I agree with the scholars who have argued that cross-class investigators at the turn of the century forged a pernicious dynamic that reified class and race hierarchies under the guise of challenging them,[29] I want to suggest that this same dynamic enabled the stunt reporters to disrupt a different set of hierarchies: those of gender. By reinforcing assumptions about essential class and race difference, Bly gained an opportunity to defy narrowly drawn definitions of womanhood and to enter territory that was usually off-limits to middle-class white women. As this reporter charges through her own narratives, sharing personal impressions in willy-nilly style, she gives her readers a breathless tour of the often overlapping edges of sanity, middle-class respectability, and whiteness.

Laura Briggs's essay on the racial politics of hysteria in late-nineteenth-century science illuminates one of the "edges" on which Bly's persona teetered. Briggs argues that definitions of hysteria revolved as much around race as around gender; the figure of the neurasthenic white woman who was unable to reproduce properly, she suggests, emerged in opposition to the figure of the "savage" woman of color who was oversexed and reproduced *too* successfully. Thus the hysterical white woman functioned as an emblem of endangered whiteness.[30] As Briggs acknowledges, however, the opposition itself was fraught with contradiction: the strict division of women's bodies into two categories—white, weak, and undersexed versus racialized, hardy, and oversexed—was impossible to uphold. Bly's asylum series engages the contradictions of hysteria discourse directly by revealing how easily a white woman's body could slip into the "over-sexed" category supposedly reserved for women of color. At the same time, Bly presents a drama of endangered whiteness with a guaranteed happy ending: the reinstatement of whiteness as the dominant racial category. Despite her short-lived masquerade as an ethnic Other on her way to the asylum, the stunt girl persona she forges is emphatically native-born and white.[31] Her whiteness, like her middle-class respectability, acts as her armor. And as a woman who staked a claim to authorship on her willingness to put her body at risk, that armor was something she could not do without.

The Advantages of Looking Like "Somebody's Darling"

While her pretense of ethnic difference helped Bly to outmaneuver the court system, her narrative soon revealed that the idiosyncratic biases of expertise were not to be taken lightly. In fact, she discovered that she had more to fear than she may even have realized. Her asylum stories verify the near-irrefutable power of the interpretive categories controlled by experts. In particular, they dramatize just how difficult it was for women to preserve the aura, much less the fact, of sexual purity once they were assigned to the category of "insane woman." A drawing captioned "An Insanity Expert at Work" shows Bly sitting ramrod straight in a chair, her expression calm and her hands in her lap, while a man in a lab coat bends over her, twirling his mustache, a quizzical expression on his face (see figure 3.)

The image accompanies Bly's report of a medical exam in which a doctor determines that she does indeed belong in the asylum.[32] Like the other drawings, it emphasizes Bly's respectability and the absurdity of the doctor's status as "an insanity expert." Despite the proximity of their faces (he leans quite close to her), there is little hint of sexual threat in the drawing; the doctor appears less aggressive than confused. But Bly's transcript of the interrogation demonstrates that her prim appearance did not keep this expert from assuming that she was sexually promiscuous:

> "Tell me, are you a woman of the town?"
> "I do not understand you," I replied, heartily disgusted with him.
> "I mean have you allowed men to provide for you and keep you?"
> I felt like slapping him in the face, but I had to maintain my composure, so I simply said: "I do not know what you are talking about. I always lived at home."
> After many more questions, fully as useless and senseless, he left me to

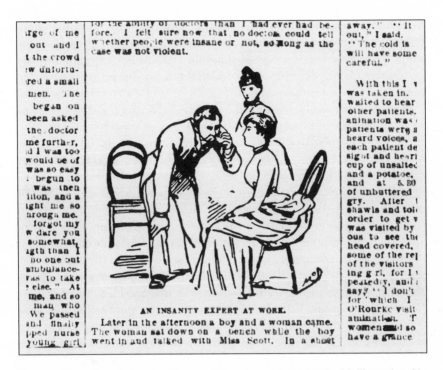

AN INSANITY EXPERT AT WORK.

Figure 3. The asylum doctor who diagnosed Bly as insane is mocked in this illustration, "An Insanity Expert at Work." Bly's report of the interview reveals that he assumed she was a prostitute. (*New York World*, October 9, 1887. General Research Division, The New York Public Library, Astor, Lenox, and Tilden Foundations.)

talk with the nurse. "Positively demented," he said. "I consider it a hopeless case. She needs to be put where someone will take care of her."

And so I passed my second medical expert.

After this, I began to have a smaller regard for the ability of doctors than I had ever had before. I felt sure now that no doctor could tell whether people were insane or not, so long as the case was not violent.[33]

Bly takes full advantage of the opportunity to disparage the authority of this "second medical expert," who labels her a prostitute and a hopeless case; he decides that she must move from being "kept" by a man (in a sexual relationship) to being "kept" by the state (in an asylum). She suppresses her first impulse—to slap his face—and pretends to misunderstand him instead. She leaves her readers, however, with no doubt about either her interrogator's implication or her reaction to it: disgust and contempt. Her pretense of misunderstanding enables her to "maintain her composure," a ladylike role that, as I discuss later on, protects her from more than scurrilous insinuations.

In diagnosing Bly as "hysterical," the asylum doctors placed her in an explicitly gendered but vaguely defined category of abnormality. They also unwittingly provided fertile ground for the formation of Bly's stunt reporter persona. Hysterics, often described as both incoherent and overly effusive, represented an extreme version of the verbally and sexually excessive woman. Nineteenth-century doctors noted that hysteria patients were more likely than other women to be independent and assertive, to show strong resolution, and to be fearless.[34] Although the medical term "hysteria" was attributed to a huge variety of causes, it was generally applied to women who were unable to express themselves except through inarticulate body language, which was then "dubbed" by a male doctor.[35] As Janet Beizer wryly notes in her study of hysteria in nineteenth-century France, "The hysteric was not, I think, a very attractive or inspirational subject for women who wrote, given that her body was defined by the absence of its woman's voice."[36] Bly, however, turns this disempowering figure against itself and takes charge of her own hysterical performance. She invites the male doctors to dub her body language, then she reveals their errors. In doing so, Bly enacts the psychiatric expert's worst nightmare. Elizabeth Lunbeck emphasizes the unstable position of hysteria within the production of expert knowledge: "To no other psychiatric category was the distinction between truth and reality on the one hand, lies and simulation on the other so critical but so impossible to determine. No other category— and no other group of patients—so stirred psychiatrists' anxiety and so unsettled their professional equanimity."[37] Thus the doctors who called Bly "hysterical" did more than set themselves up for an embarrassing incident; they also shaped Bly's emerging stunt girl persona by giving her a label that was already vulnerable to manipulation.

While her success at "faking it" may have encouraged skeptics to dismiss all women with hysterical symptoms as "fakers," it also robbed the diagnosis of hysteria of its interpretive power by proving that a patient could manufacture behavior to suit a diagnostic category. Perhaps more compellingly, it showed how tenacious even the most wrongheaded diagnosis could be.[38] Once labeled hysterical, Bly did not even have to manufacture bizarre behavior to maintain the pretense. "From the moment I entered the insane ward on the island I made no attempt to keep up the role of insanity," she insisted. "I talked and acted just as I do in ordinary life. Yet strange to say, the more sanely I talked and acted, the crazier I was thought to be."[39] Bly's critique of the medical establishment is self-serving, of course. Here, as elsewhere, she shrugs off responsibility for contributing to the medical mistakes, even though the errors are produced, in part, by the incongruities of her contrived appearance on Blackwell's Island. Nevertheless, Bly goes out of her way to avoid letting her doctors off the hook, a strategy she would later apply to a host of other authority figures.

Paradoxically, Bly's failures as an actress proved critical to her ultimate triumph. Despite the headlines' claims that she successfully impersonated insanity, crucial to this "success" was the incompleteness of her act, her proven inability to transform herself fully into one of "them." She does not fit in; that is why competing newspapers suspect her of being "the heroine of an interesting story." Her articles show that the disjunction between her middle-class self and her contrived circumstances earn her special favors throughout an admittedly harrowing experience. Despite her sexual vulnerability—an unspoken but central threat that underlies not only this narrative but many of her subsequent stories as well—Bly emerges from her adventures unscathed because her "true" social status keeps shining through, thanks to her gender identity as chaste young woman. By striking an innocent pose, she appears to discourage the sexual overtures to which she might otherwise have been subjected.[40] This strategy is readily apparent in her report, despite her general silence on the threat of sexual violation.

Maintaining her virginal self was no easy task, given that many experts associated hysteria with sexual voraciousness. Luckily for her, the experts she encounters in the process of having herself committed prove to be better readers of her class position than of her true motives. In the Essex Market courtroom, Bly reports that after the judge who will determine her fate insists that she lift her veil and expose her face, he exclaims, "I am positive she is somebody's darling," a statement he hastily amends to: "I mean she is some woman's darling. I am sure someone is searching for her. Poor girl, I will be good to her, for she looks like my sister, who is dead."[41] The judge first identifies Bly as someone's "darling," a phrase that suggests his appreciation for her sexual attractiveness. Then, in a move that protects both his own respectability and Bly's, he shifts the ground of his identification, choosing safer, less sexually charged ground; he claims that she reminds him of his sister. Either way, he has singled her out for gentle treatment.

We find even more striking evidence of how Bly's appearance protected her in an article that appeared in the *World* the day after the first "madhouse" installment.[42] The article detailed the furor Bly had caused and reported the reactions of those who came into contact with her during her journey to the asylum. In an interview, the "ambulance surgeon" who drove Bly from the hospital to the Blackwell's Island ferry insisted that he knew she was "romancing" because she did not make a pass at him. His explanation—which, curiously, was printed without comment from Bly (who recounted her ambulance ride as uneventful) or from the anonymous author of the article—offers proof of the danger of sexual violation for women in Bly's predicament. "Insane girls always make violent love to the ambulance surgeon," he declared. "I have had them jump clear across the wagon and hug me, press my hand and even fondle my knees. They make the most violent kind of love when they are demented. Now, Nellie did not even so much as press my hand. At one time I came very near subjecting her to an infallible test as to insanity in a woman, but her good bearing and general appearance were so much in her favor that I desisted."[43] There seems little doubt that the surgeon's "infallible test as to insanity in a woman" would have had severe consequences for Bly; he does not even bother to veil the sexual threat. Only her clearly visible difference—"her good bearing and general appearance"—protect her sexual purity. The surgeon's conflation of hysteria and nymphomania was by no means unusual.[44] In the same article, the reporter asked why one of the asylum doctors had put his arms around Bly's neck (an incident that Bly never mentions). One of the doctors who had diagnosed Bly as hysterical answered: "If that girl had been insane she would have liked it. All insane girls like to be treated that way."[45]

Medical experts in Bly's era frequently linked insanity and "sexual perversion." While they debated whether feebleminded males were under- or oversexed, most agreed that similarly impaired females tended toward sexual voraciousness. In the 1880s, the trustees of the New York State Custodial Asylum for Feeble-Minded Women argued that "retarded women required special care because they were 'easily yielding to lust.'"[46] Experts also documented cases in which shrewd sex-crazed women concocted symptoms that required gynecological examinations because such exams brought them sexual pleasure. One author, whose description of this pattern of behavior was published in the New Orleans Medical and Surgical Journal in 1894, referred specifically to patients at the asylum where Bly was housed to demonstrate what he called "the moral leprosy" of sexual perversion.[47] Lunbeck's study of early-twentieth-century psychiatry describes the hypersexual female as "a central player" in experts' evolving theories about human sexual natures and needs; it also shows that experts usually blamed women for male acts of sexual aggression.[48] By interpreting a woman's submission to forced sex as evidence of promiscuity, psychiatrists contributed to a climate that made incarcerated women easy targets for potential sexual predators like the ambulance surgeon who imagines making sexual advances toward Bly.

Bly's wordy asylum series is conspicuously silent on these threats. While she describes the filthy ferry, hard benches, inedible dinners, ice-cold baths, lack of warm clothes, and gruff, tobacco-spitting nurses, she mentions no sexual advances. Perhaps the risks were understood. Or perhaps the taboo was simply too strong—and the risks too real—for her to include such details in her story; they would have complicated her already vexed role as brave but innocent border-crosser. It was safer for her to let her respectable appearance speak for itself, signifying her privilege and hence her virtue. To become a victim, particularly a victim of sexual abuse, would undermine her status as swashbuckling heroine and turn her visceral reports from comic to tragic. The silences in her narrative thus point to the contradictions that underpin her physical self-presentation, despite the persistent illusion of uninhibited display. While not all of Bly's stories require her to enter a climate as sexually charged as the asylum, the contradictions of the stunt girl persona she forges there remain central to her future articles and, indeed, to the genre itself.

After the Madhouse: Bly and Her Imitators

Bly's asylum reports rely on her body to illuminate, but also to filter and sanitize, aspects of city life that were off-limits but intriguing to her more privileged readers—and that actually threatened her less privileged readers, who ran a legitimate risk of being victimized by the same judicial and medical system that so spectacularly misdiagnosed Bly. Her subsequent narratives echo this pattern. Whether highlighting the sufferings of the urban poor or debunking experts and charlatans, Bly opens with first-person expressions of curiosity and moves directly into her personal reactions to self-inflicted predicaments. In "The Girls Who Make Boxes," she starts by saying: "I had always wondered at the tales of poor pay and cruel treatment that working girls tell. There was one way of getting at the truth, and I determined to try it: It was becoming myself a Paper Box Factory Girl."[49] In "Nellie Bly as a Mesmerist," she describes her own preconceptions about mesmerism before she details the mesmeric treatments she received.[50] In "Nellie Bly in Pullman: She Visits Homes of Poverty in the 'Model Workingman's Town,'" she devotes several paragraphs to the tiring, dusty journey she undertook to reach the town before she reports the appalling conditions she found there.[51]

Some stunts involved more direct personal risk than others. In "Visiting the Dispensaries: Nelly [sic] Bly Narrowly Escapes Having Her Tonsils Amputated," Bly's wry comic tone seems designed to reassert control as she recalls a harrowing physical exam in graphic detail. The report has a typically self-centered opening: "I started out the other day to investigate some of the New York dispensaries and see for myself how the poor girls fare who are really sick and have to seek charity. Naturally I concluded before I started that only the very poor were recipients of free medical aid, so I spent some time over my make-up. When it was completed I flattered myself that I looked as poor as any of them." Self-congratulations complete, she visits the Metropolitan Throat Hospital, complains of a sore throat, and finds herself in a "glaring lit room" under the inspection of three men wearing reflectors on their heads. Once again taking readers with her into the examining room, Bly continues her matter-of-fact recitation:

> "Open your mouth wide."
> I opened it. I did not want to, but I knew I was in for it. He caught my chin firmly and ran the instrument down my throat. Just then the horrible thought came that with the same thing he had looked into the other woman's throat. And she had cancer! Ugh. . . .
> "That tonsil needs a piece cut off," he said, dropping the probing instrument and taking up another whose bright gleam gave me a chill. I'll do a great deal, I think pathologically to get a story, but I won't give up half a tonsil. . . .
> He throws his headlight into my eyes, I am blinded! With a quick movement he catches my tongue and wraps the linen tightly around it. I am by force speechless! Mercy mercy, will he cut a tonsil out and not allow me a word of explanation?

Facing a direct threat, Bly tells her readers that she has reached the limits of her bodily sacrifice; although she will "do a great deal," even "pathologically," to get her story, she will not sacrifice a tonsil. Yet in the next moment, blinded and rendered speechless, Bly seems to lose control of both her tongue and the situation. Eventually, by clutching the doctor wildly and pleading "nerves," she manages to delay the operation. Before he lets her leave, however, the doctor inserts a probe into her nose, pushing so deeply, Bly said, "I could almost feel it touch my brain."[52] As she had done before, Bly dramatizes the fearful consequences of surrendering authority over one's own body to a medical expert. It was one of her most powerful themes, common among her imitators as well.[53]

As the dispensary story suggests, Bly's stunts endangered her body in many ways, not all of them sexual. Nevertheless, she often reports the sexualized surveillance to which young working women submitted on a regular basis, and at times she openly acknowledges the connections between class position and sexual vulnerability. In the story about box factory workers—subtitled "Nellie Bly Tells How It Feels to Be a White Slave"—Bly notes that being a "working girl" subjected her to all sorts of unwelcome sexual advances: "I had more men try to get up a flirtation with me while I was a box factory girl then I ever had before." While her observation reinforces the stereotype that working-class women were more sexually active, Bly goes out of her way to assert the difference between the stereotype and the actual behavior of the women she encounters. Thus the men who "try to get up a flirtation" come under censure, not the working women, whose comportment, according to Bly, is as proper as that of middle-class women. She even credits the workers with more social grace than their social betters: "There was quite a little air of 'good form' in many of their actions. I have seen many worse girls in much higher positions than the white slaves of New York."[54] Bly's use of the term "white slave"—a euphemism for forced prostitution which also appears in the subtitle of the story— makes her insistence on their "good form" and politeness all the more contentious. Perhaps because she is on safer ground here, among hard-working factory employees rather than mentally unstable women, she encourages a direct identification with their plight. In doing so, she does not question the morality of middle-class standards of propriety, but she does turn those standards against the women they were supposed to protect, using the factory workers' "good form" to elevate them over the "many worse girls in higher positions."[55]

One of Bly's rivals on the *World* staff, Nell Nelson, wrote a "white slave" series that addresses similar topics. As "Among the White Slaves: Girls of the Cigarette Factories in Hunger and Poverty" opens, Nelson is rushing to work on a cold, gray day: "I was in the hungry, shivering throng, and my heart ached for the little martyrs I was following." She goes on to describe the unwanted sexual advances that were routine at the factory. "As might be expected the novice invariably handled the materials awkwardly, but instead of oral correction the foreman illustrated his method by getting his two arms about the pupil's neck so that while his fingers were busy with the weed and roller, his face was so very close to the cheek of his prisoner that confusion and embarrassment robbed the lesson of its value. I had watched this remarkable method of instruction for some time, and when my turn came I was ready to rebel." She dodges the foreman, but she quickly explains that other workers could not afford to resist: "That maneuver came near costing me my apprenticeship. Few of the girls about me could speak English."[56] Shifting directly from sexual harassment to the immigrant sta-

tus of the Russian, Polish, Italian, and Irish workers, Nelson presents sexual purity as a luxury of the native-born.[57]

Yet the stunt reporters were far from consistent in their representations
of female sexuality. While some stories portrayed workers as blameless victims of sexual predators, others denied the threat of sexual violation or
judged "fallen" women harshly. In "Begging as an Avocation: An Adventurous Woman Goes Out Asking Alms in the Street," Viola Roseboro concludes that being a beggar was "not a very hard business." Roseboro insists
that men simply ignored her, while women proved to be easy marks; she
gives no indication that she was ever in any danger.[58] Bly herself, notwithstanding her willingness to defend women factory workers, was not generous in judging prostitutes. "In the Magdalen's Home: Nellie Bly's Visit to
an Institution for Unfortunate Women" betrays no kind feelings for the
women Bly encounters during a brief masquerade as a prostitute. "Dressed
to suit the character I wished to represent," with whiskey splashed on her
coat, Bly shows up late one night at an institution for prostitutes who are
trying to reform. After spending a single night and day there, she tells her
readers she had learned all she needed to know: "I had but little sympathy
for these women who do wrong and have no inclination to do otherwise."
Bly reports that she met only one woman "who had the least remorse" for
her actions; "the others were as indifferent about it as if it were an honor
to them." The story ends with a grim exhortation about the wages of sin:
"I tell you the path of sin is like a toboggan slide; once we start down there
is no stopping until we reach the end."[59] Bly takes no chances here; she
does not even pretend to hop on that sinful toboggan. Although the white,
middle-class, sexually pure body that Bly constituted through her narratives could, as a rule, be relied upon to distinguish her from the marginalized women she impersonated, she shields that body from what may have
been the ultimate test. She found no safe way, apparently, to encourage her
readers to identify with the plight of sex workers. Instead, she turns her
stunt into a jeremiad.[60]

Although the *World* cultivated stunt reporters more assiduously than its
competitors, other newspapers published similar "performances." Most
are variations on the template Bly established in her asylum series. In 1888
a *Chicago Times* writer identified only as "the girl reporter" stole the lime-
light from her male partner when she posed as a desperate pregnant
woman in order to write an exposé of abortionists. Their stories made the
front page every day for nearly a month and inspired stinging criticism of
the medical profession. As co-author of what historian Leslie R. Reagan
called "the earliest known in-depth study of illegal abortion," the girl re-

porter quickly became an object of speculation, while her (equally anonymous) male partner attracted no special interest. The anonymous young woman was even attacked by the Chicago Medical Society and the Journal of *the American Medical Association,* for "sneaking around like a snake, trying to make a reputation," and for seducing doctors with "many a pearly tear trembling on her pretty little eyelids."[61] In 1890, on her first big assignment for the *San Francisco Examiner,* Winifred Black ("Annie Laurie") had a doctor friend put belladonna drops in her eyes to dilate her pupils, pretended to collapse in the street, and was admitted to a public hospital. Although Black condemned the hospital's insensitive treatment of indigent patients, the plight of the poor was eclipsed, at least in part, by the startling image of an attractive, respectable young woman being carted to the hospital in the same wagon used to transport dead bodies, forced to consume an emetic of mustard and hot water, then carelessly discharged.[62] As Black recalled years later, "Everybody in all the public institutions started to watch for redheaded girls to be sure of what happened when they were around."[63]

By the early 1890s, stunt reporting had become synonymous with women's journalism in some circles. When Ada Patterson was looking for reporting work in New York City in 1894, she heard that the *New York American* wanted "a woman's job done in a hurry."[64] The newspaper needed someone to go down in the caisson of the bridge being built across the East River, because the men who worked there were getting the bends and the air pressure was apt to cause deafness. Patterson volunteered, wrote the story, and earned a spot on the *American* staff.[65] Her triumph, however, was mitigated by the fact that the *World* had learned of the stunt and immediately sent its own woman reporter under the East River. The *World* published its version on the same day Patterson's *American* story appeared.

The authority of girl stunt reporters was already beginning to wane, however. Although Bly's self-assertive strategy had given her unprecedented name recognition and influence on the *World* staff, the newspaper's editors soon found a way to keep other women from achieving similar status.[66] They chose a catchall byline, "Meg Merrilies," and used it for any woman writer who did Bly-like stunts.[67] It was "Meg Merrilies" who wrote the story that robbed Ada Patterson of her East River scoop.[68] This new bureaucracy did more than squelch the career aspirations of hopeful stunt reporters. It also reduced the appeal of stunt reporting itself by imposing a group-think mentality on a genre that depended on idiosyncratic, individualized reportage. The byline belittled both news writers and their readers; this "Meg" was a joke, whether she was "Merrily" entering a lion's den

Figure 4. This image, "Miss Meg Merrilies in the Lion's Den at the Circus," accompanied a report on the pseudonymous Meg's day as a lion tamer. (*New York World,* April 1, 1894. General Research Division, The New York Public Library, Astor, Lenox, and Tilden Foundations.)

(see figure 4) or, worse, telling "Merry-lies" to her readers. Deprived of a singular voice, the Meg Merrilies stories were a predictable pastiche.[69] They never came close to being as popular as Bly's.

This reliance on personal physical experience, on the specific sensations of a decidedly non-sensational female body, distinguishes the stunt reporters from the better-educated Progressive Era investigators of subsequent decades who adopted similar strategies and went among the poor in order to write about them. As Mark Pittenger observes in his analysis of such writers, "Even as down-and-outers came to identify with their fellow denizens of the social pit, they found ways to inoculate themselves against the danger of infection." They did so through more literary methods than the stunt reporters', however. According to Pittenger, such writers used their genteel education (quoting Shakespeare to themselves, for instance) and the act of writing itself (sneaking off to take notes at night) to maintain their connection to their "real" positions.[70] The stunt girls, in contrast, were more likely to invoke in their narratives the inherent whiteness, purity, and respectability of their own bodies—presented as sexually inviolate against all odds—to differentiate themselves from the people they were impersonating.

Newspaper readers were more than receptive to this performative brand of reporting. The story of Bly's incarceration, for example, posed a commonsense challenge to the authority of educated experts and tapped into the anti-intellectualism of a mass public already tiring of its lowly inexpert status. This appeal to a mass reading public was central to the ambitious circulation goals of newspapers like the one that hired Bly. Historians have long recognized that the unprecedented success of Joseph Pulitzer's *World*—which became the first modern mass-circulation newspaper in the 1880s and 1890s—resulted from its appeal to a multiethnic, cross-class audience, especially its attempts to speak to the needs of the most vulnerable members of urban society: immigrants, women, the working poor, even the barely literate. While the lack of extant circulation records makes the actual readership of the *World* impossible to determine, scholars agree that marginalized groups constituted a major part of the newspaper's audience and that the *World's* sensationalism, updated and expanded from the antebellum penny papers' tradition of sensational reporting, was specifically designed to appeal to such readers.[71] The *World* actively promoted its image as an educator and uplifter of the immigrant masses.[72] But Pulitzer avoided controversial appeals for women's rights and most other calls for radical reforms; his paper's crusades for the disempowered may be best interpreted as business maneuvers. Thus it is unsurprising that the stunt reporters' stories were ambivalent toward the lowly masses whose interests they claimed to represent. Press historians may dismiss "stunts, as distinguished from useful crusades or promotions,"[73] but what they lacked in the strict journalistic sense they more than made up for in their shrewd negotiation of the carefully drawn lines between the sexually pure and the sexually profligate, the native-born and the foreign-born, the sane and the insane.

The Wages of Sensation: The Stunt Reporters' Legacy

Bly and her stunt reporting cohorts joined a long line of writers, from sensation novelists to etiquette guide authors, who offered readers strategies for interpreting and coping with the "wicked city." If the chaotic nature of the female hysteric's body seemed to require a male interpreter, then the chaotic nature of the city seemed to require a similar intervention, a male narrator who could impose a rational, unifying narrative on an irrational, fragmented community. Because sexual excess was so often represented as an indication of the city's irrationality and corruption, the need for an explicitly male (hence more rational) perspective in such narratives appeared all the more pressing.[74] Throughout the nineteenth century, controlling women's bodies was a crucial theme of popular narratives attempting to make sense of city life. At mid-century, when American sensation novelists adapted Eugène Sue's "mysteries of the city" genre, offering voyeuristic tours of the dark side of urban life, they frequently portrayed uncontrolled lust—and, specifically, oversexed women—as the center of urban corruption. The threat of the city, then, was linked to the threat of the sexual woman, a conjunction that made it difficult, if not impossible, for a woman to claim authority as an urban guide.

Yet the authority of the stunt reporters as chroniclers of urban life stems directly from this conjunction. They offered themselves as mediators between their readers and the city, deliberately embracing situations in which the female body was likely to be viewed as suspect, oversexed, out of control. Denied the position of objective urban spectator by virtue of their gender, the stunt reporters take the opposite tack and cultivate the position of an intensely interested spectator. Their stories thus evolve from the earlier explorations of the city's dark side, which implicitly suggested that through careful investigation, urban disorder could be identified and removed.[75] The stunt reporters' adventures take this structure a step further; instead of employing a third-person narrative voice to trace the downfall of unsuspecting city-dwellers, their authorial strategy puts their own bodies at risk. They confront the corruption themselves, resist it, and maintain both physical and psychological integrity. Their first-person narratives thus minister to the desire of the urban reading public to reconstruct a sense of coherence and community in an increasingly fragmented world. They literally call their bodies into the service of public reality, transforming threatening urban terrain into a manageable landscape by inserting themselves into it.[76]

As noted earlier, the medical knowledge Bly so openly mocks in her asylum series actually helps to solidify her position as respectable (hence reliable) narrator of her own experiences. The experts who had addressed the question of who can suffer—and who cannot— had, for the most part, resolved the question in Bly's favor, by suggesting that the ability to suffer marked the progress of modern civilization; not all races and cultures could suffer equally.[77] This scientific assertion strengthened the stunt reporters' authority in several ways: it gave them heroic status by suggesting that when they went outside their class, they were subjecting themselves to *more* suffering than those who actually lived in such conditions; and it gave them a surefire way to reaffirm the social hierarchy they appeared to be dismantling. The more they suffered, the more civilized and superior they appeared. Their suffering is "real," but it is recounted in such a way as to affirm their difference from the people who are *really* suffering. In the asylum series, Bly is the perfect—the "expert"—impostor for her readers precisely because her transformation is only partial. *Something*, whether her bearing, her spirit, her breeding, or her spunk, always surfaces to distinguish her from the role she is playing.

It would be inaccurate, however, to insist that stunt reporters' stories reinforce class hierarchy all the time, in every way. At emotionally charged moments in their stories, the writers' sensational suffering doubles back on their privilege and works against their careful maintenance of a coherent, respectable body. Throughout most of her asylum series, Bly cultivates an ironic distance from her performance as a crazy woman, reporting several times that she had to cover her mouth with a handkerchief to keep a straight face in front of the judge and the doctors. But at the moment of her most intense physical suffering, when she is forced into a freezing bath, she comes closest to defining herself as insane: "My teeth chattered and my limbs were goose-fleshed and blue with cold. Suddenly I got, one after the other, three buckets of water over my head—ice-cold water, too—into my eyes, my ears, my nose and my mouth. I think I experienced the sensation of a drowning person as they dragged me, gasping, shivering and quaking, from the tub. For once I did look insane."[78] Stripped of her clothes and her dignity, fearful for her safety, her typically haughty bearing overwhelmed by the indignity of being dunked in the same water as the other patients (the horror is inspired as much by fear of contamination as fear of drowning), Bly places herself, both mentally and physically, on the margins of sanity. Her difference has been obliterated, for the moment. Her narratives gain force from moments like these, from the tension created by doubt about her ability to maintain a coherent self as she crosses and re-crosses social lines: "for once" she did look insane, if only once, only for a moment, only after she has been robbed of her unflappable calm by the gross violation of a public bath.[79] Although Bly's stunt reporting persona required her to recover and reassert her respectable selfhood, her best stories flirt with the dangers of overidentifying. When she refuses to do so, as in her account of the prostitutes at the Magdalen Home, the stunts fall flat.[80]

The stunt reporters' sillier articles—Bly's stint as an elephant trainer comes to mind[81]—can still make readers cringe, even at a century's distance. Yet in a transitional moment for American journalism, these reporters asserted their interpretive power as writers in a way that the women who followed them could not. Their sensational authenticity offered a serious challenge to expert knowledge—a challenge that faded along with the stunt girl phenomenon. Pittenger's analysis of the more serious-minded impersonators who came to replace the stunt reporters suggests that in subsequent decades, female "down-and-outers" lost their special claim to authenticity, in part because of their tendency to identify with disinterested experts and, consequently, distance themselves from the messiness of physical sensation.[82] Although male down-and-outers often adopted an aggressive stance, reveling in their discovery of "authentic" experience in their travels among the disenfranchised masses, women writers often adopted, as Pittenger puts it, "the more neutral idiom of a professionalizing social science that sought only to cast light on a hitherto-unstudied realm."[83] This discourse positioned men as rational thinkers who could analyze situations and produce expert knowledge, while it viewed women as caregivers best suited to perform emotional, not intellectual, work. The decline of the girl stunt reporters, then, cannot be read as an unmitigated triumph for women's writing. The stunt reporters boldly challenged the value of experts' neutrality, insisting instead on the significance of their own bodies as sources of knowledge. Nellie Bly's sensational authenticity, despite (or perhaps because of) its excesses, took advantage of her femaleness rather than apologizing for it. Flouting the very notion of disinterestedness, Bly asserted her authorship through her own embodiment, insisting on and even celebrating her inability to transcend the concrete particulars of her own physical existence.

The African American Newswoman
as National Icon

O n a Saturday in 1883, Ida B. Wells boarded a train and found a seat in the "ladies' car." It was a familiar trip; she was leaving Memphis to return to the small town outside the city where she taught school. As an African American woman, however, she knew that her access to first-class accommodations was far from assured. Shortly after she was seated, the conductor asked her to move to the second-class car, even though she had a first-class ticket. She ignored him. He returned, picked up her bags, and again urged her to move. She refused. When he grabbed her arm to force her out, she braced her feet and bit his hand hard enough to draw blood. Other passengers then helped the conductor eject Wells, who chose to get off the train rather than sit in the second-class car reserved for African Americans and passengers who smoked. Angry at this treatment, Wells sued the railroad for damages. Although she eventually lost the suit, the incident was not a total loss. The account of the lawsuit that she wrote for the *Memphis Living Way* in May 1884 marked the beginning of her journalism career.[1] Wells would go on to become an internationally recognized anti-lynching crusader and one of the era's best-known female journalists.

Ida B. Wells and Nellie Bly, born within two years of each other, achieved professional success in the same decade.[2] While the two women had little in common other than their shared historical moment, the Memphis train episode had some stunt-like qualities: Wells placed her body at risk, sought to oppose established authority, and used her personal experience as the basis for her published report. Yet the incident was certainly not staged.

African American women like Wells, who risked racial violence even when returning home from a weekend trip, had no need to contrive dangerous situations.[3] Moreover, they were poorly positioned to write in the stunt reporting genre. Already hypersexualized by a racist culture, unable to profit from cultural norms that linked whiteness, sexual purity, and middle-class status, they were necessarily more protective of their safety than their white counterparts. Although bold writers such as Victoria Earle Matthews occasionally used their ability to pass as white to slip into segregated businesses and document discrimination against black women, none courted danger—sexual or otherwise—in the carefree style of Bly and her imitators.[4] For them to generate narrative tension over their sexual vulnerability would have been misguided at best.[5] And to make a spectacle of witnessing racial violence would have been even more ill-advised. Once, in a gruesome adaptation of the on-the-scene strategy of stunt reporting, Wells was *invited* to a lynching that was about to occur in her former hometown of Memphis. Shortly after receiving the personal summons to come south and "write it up," she learned of the killing and mutilation of Lee Walker, an African American man who apparently startled two white women by asking them for food.[6]

African American newswomen did more than avoid the stunt reporting genre: they wrote against its central premise. The drama of endangered whiteness that served as a critical subtext for white newswomen's "stunts" also fueled narratives that justified the lynchings of black men. Against the backdrop of white-defined objectivity and mainstream newswomen's sensationalism, African American female journalists embodied the black press's hope of creating an alternative to the dominant public discourse that sanctioned lynching. They became not only writers of the news but also personifications of their race's intelligence, virtue, and promise. Male writers for the black press and many other successful African Americans also served as racial representatives, of course, symbolizing the potential achievements of all people of color. During this era, black intellectuals used illustrations of both men and women to counter racist images.[7] But black female journalists garnered special notice. They served as striking models of the professional New Woman and intervened in a sexualized public discourse that sanctioned racial violence.

In one sense, simply by appearing in public as legitimate journalists, African American newswomen disrupted the lynching rationale that captured the popular imagination most successfully: the myth of the black rapist. This myth, which depended on a belief in black men's uncontrollable lust for white women, either rendered black women invisible or viewed them as contributors to a licentious atmosphere that promoted acts of sexual aggression against white women. Scholars of black history, beginning with Ida B. Wells herself, have long noted that most victims of lynching were *not* accused rapists and that white paranoia about black men's sexuality does not sufficiently explain the explosion of white mob violence.[8] Some feminists have even argued that Southern white women's support of the rape myth was a displacement of anger at their own oppression; unable to act out against white men, they targeted black men instead.[9] Yet the rape rationale loomed large in the national consciousness, referred to as fact by mainstream white newspapers and magazines and fictionalized in popular entertainment.[10] Wells biographer Linda O. McMurry argues that rape became not just a convenient excuse for lynching but "a metaphor in the white mind for any assault on white supremacy."[11]

Attacking this myth was so dangerous that black newspapers tended to treat the topic gingerly. Wells was one of the first black journalists, male or female, to violate this standard protocol so directly. The risks she incurred are evidenced, in part, by her dearth of imitators; unlike Nellie Bly, Wells inspired no flood of newswomen eager to emulate her attention-getting strategy. Few joined her in raising an eyebrow at the assumption of white women's chastity.[12] The singularity of Wells's achievement, however, has led some historians to portray her as more of an anomaly than she actually was. In this chapter I argue that the rise of the black woman reporter provided a crucial framework for Wells's ascent from Memphis schoolteacher to international public figure. Wells, as I will show, was an exemplary member of a surprisingly large group of writers who attained unique symbolic status as icons of racial equality. Although none of the era's black newswomen took up the anti-lynching cause with the same public fervor as Wells, they all played a significant role in the fight against lynching. Some protested lynching directly, challenging white society's rationale for racial violence. Mary Church Terrell attacked the practice in "Lynching from a Negro's Point of View," an essay published in the elite *North American Review* in 1904.[13] But even those who avoided volatile political subjects, focusing instead on domestic concerns or fashion and beauty tips, implicitly challenged pro-lynching discourse. Their conventionality itself contradicted the racist notions of black bestiality regularly invoked by perpetrators of racial violence.[14]

After reviewing commentary about women journalists in the black press, I return to Wells in order to read her work in light of a discourse that called upon newswomen to embody a desperately needed counterpublic. As the most exceptional newswoman of her era, Wells registered the consequences of that call most acutely. She profited from it, gaining power and stature from the symbolically charged role it assigned her, but she also bore its burden of vulnerability, as she subjected not just her writing but also her face and figure to public judgment. For a woman writer's work to be identified with or interpreted through her physical appearance was not unusual. But the dangers of exposing one's body to public scrutiny were especially significant for a black woman who was writing about lynching, a practice that turned the black body—beaten, mutilated, hanged, and burned—into a brutal spectacle of white power.

Since the bodies of women of color sustained no fantasy of inviolability in the national imagination, African American newswomen could not deploy their bodies to filter, sanitize, or authenticate their reportage, particularly their anti-lynching work. Instead, they disavowed sensationalism and sought other means to assert their authority, stressing factual accuracy, using rational argument, and drawing on sources outside their personal experience, such as previously published articles from white newspapers. Although their reformist goals precluded their striking a disinterested pose, most adopted a formal, measured writing style and an emotionally controlled tone. Thus they extended a nineteenth-century tradition that one press historian has called "a rigid and conservative style of providing straight news and opinion about racial problems without any sensational flair," seeking to invest the news "with dignity and honor."[15] Even Wells, an exceptionally bold risk-taker who addressed such taboo topics as white women's sexual attraction to black men, crafted a dignified print persona. She was less emotionally controlled than her peers, and her tone varied. Sometimes she sermonized; sometimes she wrote with scathing irony. Yet her writings often surrounded her passionate calls for action with prose more suited to a sociological treatise than a newspaper. Given the kinds of stories she wrote—documenting horrors, not recounting adventures—the choice makes sense. The gravity of her topic seemed to require, even to demand, a measure of abstraction. To report on her own sensational suffering, to testify to the details of her own bodily experience, would have trivialized not just her work but also the violence she sought so passionately to end. Some scholars have concluded that she deliberately minimized details of black women's bodily sufferings in her writings.[16]

Yet the sternest rejection of "sensational flair" could not keep African American journalists from being implicated in the racial and sexual politics of a national culture in which lynching was reaching epidemic proportions. The antithesis of stunt reporters in many ways, black newswomen nonetheless shared a significant condition with their white sisters: no matter how "straight" their news, how "rigid and conservative" their style, and how much "dignity and honor" they invested in their stories, they could not achieve the disembodied anonymity of the objective journalist. Although they practiced a less corporeal form of journalism than the spectacle-seeking white stunt reporters discussed in chapter 1, they could not escape the perils posed by their own embodiment. Their reportage may have been reserved, but their public reception was not. Their bodies inevitably came into play in their journalistic efforts, whether they were being caricatured by white newspapers as unreliable and oversexed or praised by black newspapers as models of virtue and decency.[17] Attempts to assume the mantle of respectability—such as taking a seat in the ladies' car, as Wells did on the train in Tennessee—could bring about indecorous confrontations, if not physical violence. Yet they had little choice but to persist in making such attempts.

In doing so, they sought to transform their embodiment from a source of vulnerability to an advantage, using the attention they attracted as a means of countering racist stereotypes circulated by the white-dominated press. This process of transformation was collective, a characteristic that marked it as strikingly different from the strategy of the white stunt reporters, who performed independently and whose shared racial privilege remained an unspoken bond. Each "stunt" was reported as an individual's triumph, told from the idiosyncratic standpoint of an audacious woman. Black newswomen, in contrast, did not celebrate their personal experience as exceptional. Their bodies served not as sources of sensation, as they had for the stunt reporters, but rather as vehicles for racial uplift. They repeatedly marked their membership in a group, whether they were writing in a restrained style, cultivating self-consciously proper self-presentations, or arguing, as they frequently did, that the black press offered black women better professional opportunities than the white press offered white women.

African American women journalists acted as conduits for and representatives of a black counterpublic that was being nurtured by an abundance of black newspapers in the late nineteenth century. A counterpublic acts as an alternative forum for a group whose members have been denied access to the dominant public sphere; it functions, as the theorist Nancy Fraser has explained, as a "parallel discursive arena where members of subordinated social groups invent and circulate counterdiscourses to formulate oppositional interpretations of their identities, interests, and needs."[18] At the turn of the twentieth century, African Americans urgently needed to formulate such oppositional interpretations. Damaging stereotypes about the licentiousness, laziness, and ugliness of people of color were circulating widely in American culture. An 1894 article in the *New York Times* could assert casually that raping white women was "a crime to which negroes are particularly prone."[19] During this brutal era, African Americans

faced more racially motivated violence than in any other period in U.S. history.[20] This was especially true in the South, a region that produced most
of the era's African American newswomen.

Driven by a sense of urgency and a passion for justice, African Americans founded more newspapers during these years than in any subsequent
historical period. According to one study, 1,219 black newspapers were
started between 1895 and 1915. The pinnacle was 1902, when 101 papers
were launched.[21] "Negro weeklies make no pretense at being newspapers
in the strict sense of the term," wrote James Weldon Johnson in 1914.
"They have a more important mission than the dissemination of mere
news. . . . They are race papers."[22] Johnson's term applied not only to
newspapers but to African American women journalists as well. They
were never simply reporters in the strict sense of the term; they were race
women. The black press aimed to create a new audience of readers and to
form an active counterpublic.[23] In the process of cultivating that counterpublic, black newspapers developed a complex relationship to the institutions of the white majority. Struggles over competing meanings and values,
Thomas C. Holt contends, "gave shape to the separateness of black publicity even as they forged intrinsic and inescapable links between the spheres
of dominance and of opposition."[24]

That "separateness of black publicity" came to be reflected in the
iconography of the African American woman reporter, and its contours
emerge most clearly when we read the black journalist's image along
with—and against—the white images she contested and resisted. Like the
stunt reporters, black newswomen acted in a dual role as both objects and
agents, but they did so with a critical difference: they appeared not as emblems of mass-market publicity but as spokeswomen for a counterpublic,
as products of a discursive arena that evolved in opposition to the dominant public sphere controlled by whites. Appreciating their role as press
icons allows us to better understand their position, as well as the occasional
vitriolic debates over such apparently trivial matters as their physical appearance. While such conflicts over representation arose in part from a
male-dominated system in which a woman's looks determined her value,
they also reflected the black press's symbolic investment in its female
journalists. By disrupting the conflation of whiteness and virtue, African
American women journalists undermined the symbolic system on which
stunt reporting depended. The figure of the black woman reporter thus
emerged from the repressed side of the same culture that had fostered the
intrepid image of the white "girl reporter."

The Rise of the Black Woman Reporter

African American women formed a significant subset of the group of women who took up journalism in the late nineteenth century. Recent studies have shown that, like their white counterparts, they embarked on journalism careers in unprecedented numbers in the 1880s and 1890s, particularly in the South. According to the historian Gloria Wade-Gayles, the "phenomenal percentage of Southern black women journalists" can be linked directly to the rapid expansion of the black press. Wade-Gayles has identified forty-six black newswomen whose work was published between 1883 and 1905.[25] In addition to Pauline Hopkins, Frances Harper, and Alice Dunbar-Nelson, this group included Mary E. Britton, Mary V. Cook, Victoria Earle Matthews, Lillian Parker Thomas, Meta E. Pelham, and Josephine Turpin Washington. Although these writers often covered "women's topics" for "women's departments," not all were restricted to etiquette advice, household hints, and fashion tips. Many, like Wells, wrote about government policies, political debates, and other issues of broad concern in the community. Many began writing for Christian publications designed expressly for African American readers, but most went on to contribute to more secular reformist journals as well. A few also freelanced for white newspapers. All of them faced widespread employment discrimination, since almost no mass-market white newspapers hired black writers for regular staff positions. Unlike white women, who could choose between mainstream and alternative venues, most had no choice but to write for black presses.[26] And they usually relied on other jobs, often as schoolteachers, to pay their bills.[27]

Despite daunting circumstances, black newswomen quickly attained enough status to merit attention even from white-dominated professional venues. In 1889, when *The Journalist,* a trade publication with a mostly white audience, devoted an issue to female news writers, ten of the fifty profiles featured African Americans. In 1890, Alice McEwen, associate editor of the *Baptist Leader,* the official organ of black Baptists in Alabama, delivered an enthusiastic paper, "Women in Journalism," at the National Press Convention. And in 1891, I. Garland Penn's groundbreaking historical survey *The Afro-American Press and Its Editors* profiled nineteen women journalists and named a half-dozen more. Penn concluded his sixty–page chapter on women by confessing that he knew he had not done justice to women's contributions.[28]

Within the black press, women journalists were celebrated as professional success stories. Articles reported that African American women faced *less* discrimination from their male colleagues than white newswomen and enjoyed more respect, a wider range of assignments, and broader public influence. This celebratory discourse suggested that being a journalist was easier for black women than white women. The welcoming, optimistic tone stands in striking contrast to the lukewarm-to-scornful responses white female reporters received in the mainstream popular press.[29] This commentary opposed white-dominated public discourse in at least three ways. It refuted racist stereotypes by circulating interpretations of black women as literate, creative professionals; it countered images of lynched black bodies with an appealing vision of ambitious, attractive writers; and it belied the assumption that long-established white institutions were necessarily superior to newer black ones. This counterdiscourse also positioned the African American newswoman as a figure of the alternative public forum. Produced by and through the black counterpublic, the newswoman represented the very possibility of making oneself heard.

Given the proliferation of violent attacks on African Americans in this era, the cheerful assessments of black women's professional prospects are somewhat jarring. The need for solidarity within the African American community probably discouraged women from airing grievances about sex discrimination. As Wade-Gayles acknowledges in her study of black women journalists, "there is no indication that black men were totally liberated males."[30] Moreover, rivalries simmered among both male and female journalists of the black press, occasionally resulting in acid exchanges in print. Wells, for instance, traded public barbs with sister newswoman Mary V. Cook, who published sharply worded fact-filled articles under the pen name "Grace Ermine."[31]

Yet evidence suggests that African American newswomen had reason to celebrate their professional opportunities. "Women and their interests had always been a significant part of the Afro-American periodical press," concludes press historian Penelope L. Bullock, who goes on to note that "the very first periodicals" published the work of women writers.[32] Women were more than passive supporters of black newspapers. Indeed, their interests were addressed directly and their achievements lauded enthusiastically. Many of the post-Reconstruction era's black newspapers quickly faltered, crippled by high rates of illiteracy, the lack of an advertising base, and the ongoing threat of retribution from resentful whites, but not before they gave women invaluable experience as writers, as editors, even as publishers. Promoting black newswomen as emblems of equality served the antiracist agenda of the black press, creating a potentially powerful platform from which female journalists could protest lynchings and pinpoint weaknesses in the white press's justifications of racial violence. T. Thomas Fortune, one of the most prominent editors of the black press and a key supporter of Wells, was generous in his public commentary about women journalists. "We have some very bright women contributors to the colored press," Fortune, the editor of the *New York Age*, declared in an 1888 interview. "I think our women are going to outstretch our men in the variety of their information, the purity of their expression and in having the courage of their convictions."[33] Such encouraging remarks fostered a cooperative atmosphere, placing the common goal of racial achievement over individual rivalries and sex-based resentments. While the black press did not offer women an equal opportunity utopia, it accorded them more respect than white mainstream newspapers and created a forum that made a public virtue of their private career ambitions.

"All who will do good work can get a hearing"

Gertrude Bustill Mossell, who served as both role model and advocate for black women who aspired to be journalists, offers a glimpse of the peculiar mix of professional audacity and caution that characterized the rise of the black woman reporter. A prolific columnist praised by the *Indianapolis Freeman* as "one of the most gifted, as well as versatile women writers of the country," Mossell wrote glowingly about the career prospects of black women reporters.[34] In 1886 she produced a series of articles in the *New York Freeman* that surveyed professional options for women writers and imagined female journalists as envoys of the black counterpublic. Calling women's attention to "a new opportunity for advancement for themselves and their sex," the first article in the series urges readers to seek employment at both black and white newspapers: "Let us prepare to occupy all we can both on our own and papers of the other race who are willing and anxious to hear what progress we are making."[35] Mossell's "occupation" strategy casts women as equal opportunity ambassadors within and without the black press, charging them to circulate news within the counterpublic while also transmitting oppositional messages to the white-dominated public sphere through the medium of sympathetic white papers.

Mossell identified the black press, however, as the best source of professional training and the most open field for new talent, and she was especially committed to promoting roles for women within that venue. In 1889 she proposed a plan to boost paper sales and syndicate writers, calling it "A Woman's Suggestion of Ways and Means." Her article praises the black press's openness to women, observing, "They do not even debar us from their Press Associations. For [that] we are truly thankful, and each editor will bear witness to the noble women who have strengthened his work."[36] Mossell's negative syntax—"they do not even debar us"—draws an implicit contrast with white press associations, which were less likely to accept newswomen into their ranks.[37] She strikes an accommodating pose, acknowledging men's acceptance and describing the "noble women" who strengthen male editors' work. But her womanly propriety does not preclude her writing a sharply argued proposal for major structural changes in the business practices of black newspapers. After making a graceful nod to the enlightened attitudes of African American newsmen, she advocates a business plan to improve the financial stability of the black press.

Mossell apparently steered clear of direct discussions of lynching, but she praised anti-lynching speeches by Wells and Bishop Henry McNeal Turner of the _Christian Recorder,_ and she worked to raise funds for social reform groups that sought to extend basic legal rights to African American men.[38] She struck a patient, reserved tone in an 1889 letter to the _New York Age,_ published under the title "Saved from Hanging: How a Philadelphia Protective League Secured the Commutation of a Death Sentence." Although she asserts that the accused man, Samuel Johnson, was unlawfully convicted, she dwells not on the outrage inspired by this injustice but on the success of a black organization in keeping Johnson from being put to death: "The case of Samuel Johnson, held for the murder of John Sharpless, a member of the Society of Friends, and unlawfully convicted, has been settled with the commutation of the prisoner to a life sentence in the State's Prison. The Board of Pardons, after the eighth respite, said that in view of the feeling in the minds of numerous citizens that the case of justice would be hindered instead of helped by the conferring of the death sentence, they had granted the commutation." Noting that this was the first case in which the Africa Protective League of Philadelphia had taken an interest, Mossell credits the League with inspiring sympathy for Johnson and achieving the commutation. She concludes by hoping that readers will recognize the utility of such organizations and support collective action to sway authorities.[39] She thus uses the case not to elicit renewed sympathy for the unfair treatment of Johnson but to foster support for organized social protest. In this case, the counterpublic's oppositional interpretation— "the feeling in the minds of numerous citizens" that Johnson's execution would be unjust—exerts such force that a white public institution, the Board of Pardons, bows to the collective will.

Mossell makes another nod to the power of popular opinion—and to the potential influence of the black press—when she promotes journalism as a particularly suitable profession for women. In an 1894 book on black women's professional work, she devotes a chapter to advocating careers in journalism. She contends that women have already attained near-equality with men, observing that "the corps of lady writers employed on most of our popular magazines and papers is quite as large as the male contingent and often more popular if not as scholarly." Arguing that their less "scholarly" approach enables women to reach a wider audience than men, Mossell touts women's ability to tap into popular tastes as a professional advantage, since women's "quickness of perception, tact, intuition guide us to the popular taste."[40] She notes, too, that because writing can often be done at home, journalism allows women to manage both domestic and professional tasks. She also articulates the black-women-have-it-easier position: "Our men are too much hampered by their contentions with their white brothers to afford to stop and fight their black sisters, so we slip in and glide along quietly. . . . All who will do good work can get a hearing in our best Afro-American journals." African American men are too busy fighting for basic rights, Mossell suggests, to spare time to restrict women's professional activities. Although Mossell does not characterize women as a revolutionary force—she imagines them in quiet roles, saying they "slip in and glide along quietly"—she installs them firmly in the black counterpublic's meritocracy, claiming that "all who do good work" can be heard.[41] Writing in careful, even excessively decorous language, Mossell sidesteps the question of whether African American men would (or should) object, were they less pressed by other concerns.

Such caution was typical of Mossell, the daughter of an affluent Philadelphia family who wrote as "Mrs. N. F. Mossell," using the initials of her husband, Dr. Nathan Francis Mossell. One critic reads this "strategy of public modesty" as a sign of Mossell's "intention to defend and celebrate black womanhood without disrupting the delicate balance of black male-female relations or challenging masculine authority."[42] Although I agree that Mossell cultivated a modest persona, her characterization of women news writers was so overwhelmingly upbeat that the overall effect may well have unsettled masculine authority. Even her most demure commentary hints at a steely edge that does not shrink from confrontation. In the 1886 *New York Freeman* series, Mossell advises hopeful female writers to follow a modest professional path, sending "short and lively communications" to editors without expecting payment. Then, once the editor has published the writer's pieces "a good number of times," "at length the gifted writer might modestly hint that if the able editor cared further for her contributions perhaps he would not mind putting a proper price on them."[43] This ladylike strategy may seem naïve at first; certainly readers familiar with the professional travails of the embattled writer-heroine of Fanny Fern's *Ruth Hall* (1855) may smile skeptically at the notion that an "able editor" would put "a proper price" on anything. Yet Mossell's genteel proposal is both realis-

tic and laced with irony. She recognizes the difficulty of earning money as
a journalist and she offers a plan that would allow aspiring writers to establish a market value and negotiate from a position of strength. In her
book chapter on women's journalism, Mossell instructs women to take
themselves seriously as professionals, seeking out information about all aspects of the newspaper business. As before, she is not content to restrict
women's journalistic ambitions to the black press; she encourages African
American women to prepare themselves to write for white papers as well.
"In the large cities especially of the North we have here and there found
openings on white journals," she reports. "More will come as more are prepared to fill them and when it will have become no novelty to be dreaded
by editor or fellow-reporters."[44] Although her predictions proved overly
hopeful, their buoyant optimism seems designed to act as a tonic for her
female readers, inspiring them to persevere in their career ambitions.[45] If
the counterpublic launches enough well-trained writers into the white-
dominated public sphere, she suggests, the woman journalist need no
longer be a dreaded novelty.

Mossell was not alone in her advocacy of journalism as a special province
of power and influence for black women. Some of her peers, less con-
cerned with projecting a genteel image, took an even stronger stand. Lucy
Wilmot Smith argued that the advantage enjoyed by black women journalists was rooted in the history of slavery, which had demanded equally
hard labor of both sexes.[46] Whereas Mossell asserted a middle-class professional identity, Smith, a Kentucky native who was probably born into
slavery, honored black men's and women's shared experience of manual
labor and drew a direct line from field work to journalism. In an 1889 article in *The Journalist,* Smith observed: "The educated negro woman occu-
pies vantage ground over the Caucasian woman of America, in that the
[latter] has had to contest with her brother every inch of the ground for
recognition; the negro man, having had his sister by his side on plantations
and in rice swamps, keeps her there, now that he moves in other spheres.
As she wins laurels, he accords her the royal crown. This is especially true
in journalism."[47] Smith casts black newswomen as beneficiaries of the
black community's commitment to fairness and honest work. Contrasting
the fair shake given the "educated negro woman" with the white woman's
bruising fight over "every inch of the ground," Smith turns the African
American woman reporter into a symbol of cooperation, living proof not
just of black women's writing ability but also of black men's generosity
and respect for women. Writing for *The Journalist*'s mostly white audience,
Smith characterizes the black press as a communal enterprise in which
women find chivalry and mutual understanding: "Doors opened before we

knock, and as well-equipped young women emerge from the class-room the brotherhood of the race, men whose own energies have been repressed and distorted . . . give them opportunities to prove themselves."[48] The experience of shared oppression, Smith suggests, has removed professional obstacles for black newspaperwomen. In the counterpublic she describes, sexism has been minimized, if not eradicated.

Press historians, citing accounts like Mossell's and Smith's, have echoed this vision of the African American newswoman's equality of place, agreeing that black men, accustomed to having women in the workplace, were less likely to object to women in the newsroom. While white women fought to escape the society pages, one historian observes, "black women have been welcomed onto the front page."[49] Black newswomen were also more likely to hold management positions. Wells, for instance, became one-third owner of the *Memphis Free Speech* in 1891. When the paper's offices were destroyed by a mob and Wells was unable to return to Memphis safely, T. Thomas Fortune gave her a one-fourth interest in the *New York Age*.[50] The contrast between this respectful treatment and the winking reception white female journalists so often received at mainstream newspapers gave the black press ample ground for presenting African American newswomen as icons of equality.

At times, the black counterpublic's celebration of women's equality took on a near-feverish tone. A fervent 1892 article by Carrie Langston, published on the front page of the *Atchison Blade*, a black newspaper, represents news writing as an expression of both patriotic duty and "true womanhood." Langston's report, "Women in Journalism," crafts a jingoistic narrative starring African American newswomen, imagining journalism as a field for the exercise of noble womanly ambition and suggesting that women are duty bound to pursue it because they are able to convey messages that men are "powerless to express." Langston argues, moreover, that American women are better prepared to be journalists than women in other countries because they "are admitted to all schools established and are in every respect treated as an equal of man."[51] Like Mossell, Langston writes with startling optimism. When she asserts, inaccurately, that American women are "admitted to all schools," she folds equal opportunity for women into a celebration of American exceptionalism. She also presents the achievements of the black counterpublic as an illustration of national virtue.

Langston's article integrates African American women into a history that celebrates American women's journalism as a victory of equal rights and a source of national pride. Journalistic work is portrayed as a democratic forum in which men and women meet as equals. Quoting a Cincin-

nati newspaper's report that "the number of women who figure on the metropolitan press can no longer be enumerated," Langston adds, "In the
sphere of journalism woman stands equal to her masculine contemporaries." Langston imagines the black newswoman as a hero to her race and
her nation, an emblem of equality and uplift. She concludes with a recruiting call, asking readers to pursue journalism with passion and determination, to commit themselves to seeking fame as writers:

> The time is not far distant when woman shall have no rival at her work in
> the field of letters. . . . Now is the time of achievements, now is the time of
> experiments—try your luck as a journalist on *The Atchison Blade,* climb
> higher, until you reach the editor's chair in one of the largest magazine of-
> fices of the world. Dare to brave each obstacle, dare to climb the steps of ad-
> versity, until your name shall have been written on the highest pinnacle of
> fame's temple, until you have created a name the storms of time can ne'er
> destroy, feel then and not till then that you will have a glorious sunset of your
> temples of fame.[52]

In her attempt to inspire dreams of personal glory in its readers, Langston
runs the risk of compromising the moral high ground she has staked out
for newswomen by appealing too directly to self-interest. Yet, given the female reporter's iconic status, the fame Langston urges her readers to chase
can be understood as double-sided, serving both individual and community. Her fanciful vision of women writers' names inscribed "on the highest pinnacle of fame's temple" suggests that by pursuing public writing
careers, African American women can not only attain professional success
but also help to ensure racial survival in an era when "the storms of
time" threatened to erase not just individual names but entire communities. This celebratory rhetoric was made possible by the counterpublic that
produced it. Even when white women reporters were receiving positive reviews in the trade press, they were not adjured to rise to editorial heights
or told to climb to their own personal temples of fame. African American
women reporters, however, were figured not as enterprising career women
but as icons of the counterpublic itself, collectively embodying the black
talent and promise that the mainstream press ignored or, worse, actively
denied. As women, they may have been, as Mossell argued, more in touch
with "popular taste" than their male colleagues, but the black press protected them from too close an association with the masses. The black newswoman's image, in other words, was carefully burnished. While their most
visible white counterparts—the stunt reporters and, later, the sob sisters—

became identified with the mass public and emblematic of sensational publicity, black newswomen became heroines in a national struggle.

Behind a Singular Achievement: Ida B. Wells as Press Icon

Carrie Langston's passionate appeal on behalf of women in journalism singles out one writer for special notice. Langston names Ida B. Wells as her star newswoman, enshrining Wells as the primary exemplar of women's triumph. Langston found an ideal newspaper heroine in Wells. In 1887 the National Afro-American Press Convention celebrated Wells as the most prominent black press correspondent, and in 1888 she became the first woman officer of the National Colored Press Association.[53] By 1889, Wells had been crowned "Princess of the Press" by her compatriots at black newspapers.[54] As I. Garland Penn wrote in his 1891 history of the black press, "No writer, the male fraternity excepted, has been more extensively quoted."[55] When Langston's article appeared in September 1892, less than four months had passed since Wells had published such a fierce anti-lynching editorial in the *Memphis Free Speech* that angry whites stormed the newspaper's offices and threatened to kill her if she set foot in Memphis again. The incident transformed an up-and-coming journalist into a nationally recognized crusader. Wells became not just one of the best-known writers in the black counterpublic but one of the few whose words also circulated in the white public sphere.

Wells's remarkable crusade against lynching has been well documented. After publishing the account of her railroad lawsuit in 1884, she began writing a column for the *Living Way* under the pen name "Iola."[56] Soon Iola's writings were syndicated in the black press in other states. In 1888, Wells left her position as a schoolteacher and became a full-time journalist. Charismatic and committed to bolstering black press readership, she was a popular and controversial figure well before the anti-lynching editorial that resulted in her exile from Memphis. Within months of fleeing northward, she used money raised by black club women in New York City to publish a compilation of her anti-lynching articles in a pamphlet, *Southern Horrors: Lynch Law in All Its Phases* (1892). She repeatedly sought the attention of white newspapers as well as black ones, but achieved little success until 1893, when she substituted for Frederick Douglass on a speaking tour of England, where *Southern Horrors* had been republished under the title *United States Atrocities: Lynch Law*.[57] The new title, by shifting the focus from region to nation, helped to position Wells as a national icon;

the atrocities she documented suddenly belonged to the nation as a whole, not only to the South. When American newspaper editors saw British news reports on Wells's lectures, they suddenly took notice of her crusade. In 1894, Wells was hired by a white newspaper, the *Chicago Inter-Ocean,* to make a second, extended tour of England, becoming the first African American foreign correspondent for a daily newspaper in the United States. She later published several more anti-lynching pamphlets, including *A Red Record* (1895), *Lynch Law in Georgia* (1899), and *Mob Rule in New Orleans* (1900).[58]

Although scholars have begun, in the last quarter-century, to give Wells the credit that is her due, she is often treated as an unusually successful writer and an individual aberration. In an introduction to an edition of Well's anti-lynching writings, for instance, Jacqueline Jones Royster characterizes the American public sphere as "fundamentally gender-restricted —that is, for males only," and describes Wells as "essentially a one-woman enterprise."[59] Royster rightly emphasizes the challenges Wells faced and the extraordinary nature of her accomplishments. But Wells is more accurately viewed as a standout in a constellation of writers, an icon whose stature was made possible, at least in part, by the worshipful attitude of the black press toward African American newswomen. She acted independently and resourcefully. She wrote brilliant social commentary. She defied social norms, braved censure in ways that her sister journalists did not, and suffered isolation that others avoided.[60] She was not, however, a one-woman enterprise. Her elevation to Princess of the Press required a court to award the title.

Wells's status as press icon emerged from a context in which black newswomen were already positioned as vehicles of counterpublicity, and a close look at her career reveals both the benefits and the drawbacks of being viewed as an embodiment of the black press. Her symbolic role gave Wells power and influence, but it also required her to suffer intense scrutiny. When the *Indianapolis Freeman* and the *Cleveland Gazette* published laudatory biographical sketches of Wells in 1889, both included drawings of the up-and-coming journalist. The likenesses were apparently not flattering, and although Wells acknowledged the kind attention from the other newspapers in the *Free Speech,* she also quoted "a young unmarried man" as saying, "Well, that woman certainly can write, but if she looks like that, good Lord deliver us!"[61] The rival editors rushed to defend their illustrations, accusing Wells of being excessively vain. The *Freeman* proclaimed, "Iola makes the mistake of trying to be pretty as well as smart."[62] Predictably, as Wells became more prominent, her colleagues in the black press criticized her more frequently.[63] Yet some lines were still not to be crossed; when

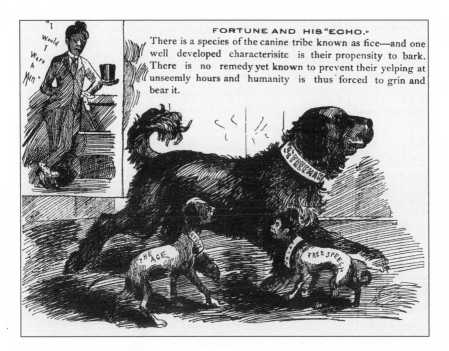

Figure 5. This cartoon, "Fortune and His 'Echo,'" inspired controversy for its offensive treatment of Wells. It suggested that she was no more than an echo of her editor, T. Thomas Fortune, and it attacked her womanhood, imagining her as both a simian-featured dog and a man. (*Indianapolis Freeman,* April 19, 1890. Collections of the Library of Congress.)

Wells was attacked too harshly and her womanhood questioned, editors rose to her defense. In 1890 the *Indianapolis Freeman* published a cartoon titled "Fortune and His 'Echo,'" satirizing Wells's working partnership with *New York Age* editor T. Thomas Fortune. It depicted Wells and Fortune as dogs, yapping at a bigger dog labeled "The Freeman" (see figure 5). The Wells dog is labeled "Free Speech," a reference that identifies Wells with her Memphis newspaper and also links her to the concept of free speech itself, a national ideal protected by the U.S. Constitution. In the upper-left corner of the cartoon, the text "I Would I Were a Man" accompanies an image of a woman, hair arranged in Wells's characteristic topknot, dressed as a male dandy.[64] The figure wears a cutaway suit and tie, holds a cane, with a top hat nearby, and leans on one elbow with a jaunty air.

The cartoon mocks Wells in several ways. Most obviously, it reduces her to a man's echo and represents her as a foolishly barking dog, and an especially ugly one at that. While the Fortune dog's face bears at least some passing resemblance to T. Thomas Fortune himself, the Wells dog has simian facial features and a curling tail that looks more likely to belong to a monkey than to a dog. The implication that Wells is a monstrous hybrid is echoed by the odd little "I Would I Were a Man" figure in the corner, which impugns Wells's femininity and imagines her as an effeminate man. It also associates her with the blackface minstrelsy popular in the late nineteenth century; the figure appears ready to step into a cakewalk.[65] This visual reference places Wells in a dynamic performance tradition in which scholars of African American culture have found a complex mix of resistance and accommodation to white domination. There is little question, however, that being cast as a minstrel would not add authority to Wells's voice as a journalist. Although she had a theatrical bent—she had organized a dramatic club as a young woman—Wells distanced herself from acting and professed "no knowledge of stage business."[66] Immediately, the cartoon was attacked as unfair, and editors assured her that she had "as protectors every gentleman journalist of color in the country."[67] Such incidents, even ones that ended in protective assurances, manifest the difficulties obscured by the equal opportunity rhetoric that surrounded black newswomen.

Wells's career also reminds us that the black women journalists and white women journalists of this era engaged in no cooperative effort of mutual advancement. Rather, in many ways, they worked at cross-purposes. As Hazel Carby observed in her classic study of black women novelists, "For the mass of black women, white women were not potential allies but formidable antagonists."[68] The assumption of white middle-class women's sexual purity was the bedrock on which white stunt reporters relied when they launched their carefully staged transgressions. But that same assumption subtended the myth of the black rapist, allowing white newspapers to recast acts of mob violence as expressions of moral outrage, necessary to protect white women's chastity. Charges of sex with white women became "the most emotional cause of lynching" black men, concludes the literary scholar Trudier Harris. After the Civil War, Harris notes, it was "the one 'crime' for which lynching became the only punishment."[69] As Wells sought ways to fight lynching and correct the distortions of the white press, she challenged the vision of white women as innocent victims. Without such a challenge, she realized, accusations of rape would continue to be used to deny the humanity of African Americans.[70] "Humanity abhors the assailant of womanhood," Wells acknowledges in *A Red Record,* "and this charge upon the Negro at once placed him beyond the pale of human sympathy."[71] She identified the belief in white womanhood's unassailable purity as a crucial flaw in the white community's pro-lynching propaganda, and she attacked it with a determination and fearlessness that set her apart from most of her male colleagues—and all of her female ones.

From the beginning, her assault on the rape myth brought her own image, attributes, and personal choices into play. The title page of *Southern Horrors* features a line drawing of Wells (see figure 6). In a high-necked gown, her hair neatly arranged, her head slightly tilted to one side, her expression calm and serious, she appears almost prim. She gazes not at the reader but off to the side. Only the slightest suggestion of a crease in her forehead hints at the "horrors" of her topic. But from the first page of the pamphlet, Wells dispenses with conventional womanly reserve. In the preface she writes: "This statement is not a shield for the despoiler of virtue, nor altogether a defense for the poor blind Afro-American Sampsons [sic] who suffer themselves to be betrayed by white Delilahs. It is a contribution to truth, an array of facts, the perusal of which it is hoped will stimulate this great American Republic to demand that justice be done though the heavens fall."[72] In a startling turnabout, Wells parallels black men to Samson, the Old Testament epic hero, and white women to Delilah, the Philistine woman who seduces Samson, learns the secret of his strength, renders him helpless, and turns him over to his enemies. This reversal positions white women as temptresses and disrupts the conflation of whiteness and chastity. Wells follows this contentious assertion by declaring her noble aim to pursue truth and justice by presenting "an array of facts"—facts that, she hopes, will inspire Americans to demand justice "though the heavens fall." The image of the heavens falling returns to the story of long-suffering Samson, whose strength eventually returns, allowing him to pull down the pillars of the Philistine temple where he is enchained, destroying himself and his captors. Wells's parallel thus aligns the citizens of "this great American Republic" with the Philistines, whose captive rises up against them when they least expect it.[73] This opening passage marks Wells's two primary strategies: first, her willingness to imagine a world in which white women are not simply passive victims; second, her emphasis on gathering facts—especially the kind that may bring the heavens down.

The preface also anticipates readers' discomfort with a direct discussion of interracial sex and violence, especially one conducted by a woman. "It is with no pleasure I have dipped my hands in the corruption here exposed," Wells writes. "Somebody must show that the Afro-American race is more sinned against than sinning, and it seems to have fallen upon me to do so."[74] She presents herself as dutiful protester, forced into action because no one else has spoken out, and she couches her work in terms of service to her race, designed to "arouse the conscience of the American people to a demand for justice to every citizen, and punishment by law for

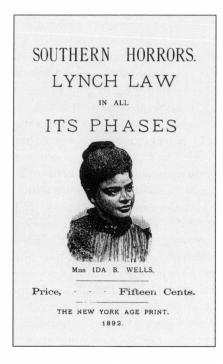

SOUTHERN HORRORS.
LYNCH LAW
IN ALL
ITS PHASES

Miss IDA B. WELLS,

Price, · · · Fifteen Cents.

THE NEW YORK AGE PRINT.
1892.

Figure 6. The cover of Ida B. Wells's first
pamphlet counters the "horror" of its violent topic with an attractive and respectable
image of its author. Wells appears both un-
ruffled and intent. (Ida B. Wells, *Southern
Horrors: Lynch Law in All Its Phases* [New
York, 1892]. Collections of the Library of
Congress.)

the lawless." Finally, Wells obliquely acknowledges the risks of dipping her
hands "in the corruption here exposed" with a brief concluding sentence
that seems purposefully vague: "other considerations," she writes, "are of
minor importance."[75] By mentioning "other considerations" but refusing
to name them, Wells encourages her readers to speculate about them. This
final line disavows any interest in the personal costs to the author yet calls
attention to those costs simply by disavowing them. The preface ends with
a recognition of Wells's own vulnerability, gently reminding readers that,
like Harriet Jacobs before her, she has risked public censure for a larger
cause.

Wells armed herself as thoroughly as possible against such censure, developing a style that was simultaneously aggressive and defensive. Graphic
detail proliferates in her anti-lynching writings, which contain excruciat-
ing descriptions of the torture and murder of lynching victims. She notes
the kinds of rope knots used to tie victims, the weapons used to beat, brand,
and mutilate them, the length of time they were hanged from trees, how
long it took for them to burn, and which body parts were removed as
souvenirs. She also points out occasions in which white women watched

killings with interest and enthusiasm. Although she did not flinch from controversy—as McMurry puts it, she "never hesitated to criticize *anyone* she thought deserved it"[76]—Wells modulated her tone carefully. Even when she was being bitingly sarcastic, she avoided intimate self-revelation, stressed accuracy, and cited white newspaper accounts to bolster her credibility. Her pamphlets feature long quoted passages from white-authored reports. Her journalistic voice emerges as she contextualizes and synthesizes the accounts, interweaving evidence from many sources—news dispatches, facts she gathered herself, sometimes even the reports of hired investigators. *A Red Record* cites the *Chicago Tribune* as its main source—"In order to be safe from the charge of exaggeration, the incidents hereinafter reported have been confined to those vouched for by the Tribune"[77]— but Wells also cites the *Arkansas Democrat*, the *New York Sun*, the *Chicago Record*, the *Memphis Commercial*, the *Chicago Inter-Ocean*, the *Memphis Appeal-Avalanche*, the *Cleveland Gazette*, the *Memphis Scimitar*, the *Cleveland Leader*, the *Times* of London, and the *Westminster Gazette*. Wells acts less as witness than interpreter. Although her arguments are impassioned, her method is fundamentally analytic, even metacritical. She opposes the pro-lynching discourse by quoting the voices of the white public in the context of the black counterpublic. By changing the context of those voices, she counters their racist rationales with her own tale of white hypocrisy and violence through what one critic has called a "montage of quarreling quotations."[78]

To illustrate the tendency to manufacture rape charges, Wells quotes a lengthy *Memphis Ledger* item about Lillie Bailey, a young white woman who had recently given birth to an interracial infant. Bailey had been taken in by a "Woman's Refuge," but when the charity home officials saw that the baby was not white, they sent Bailey to the city hospital. Bailey refused to name the baby's father. The article suggests that if Bailey "would be somewhat less reserved about her disgrace there would be some very nauseating details in the story of her life. She is the mother of a little coon. The truth might reveal fearful depravity or the evidence of a rank outrage."[79] Wells then glosses the passage, repeating the language to make her point:

> Note the wording: "The truth might reveal fearful depravity or rank outrage." If it had been a white child or if Lillie Bailey had told a pitiful story of Negro outrage, it would have been a case of white woman's weakness or assault and she could have remained at the Woman's Refuge. But a Negro child and to withhold its father's name and thus prevent the killing of another Negro "rapist" was a case of "fearful depravity." Had she revealed the father's name, he would have been lynched and his taking off charged to an assault upon a white woman.[80]

Wells acts as a textual critic, citing one source, then the next, sometimes pitting the sources against themselves, sometimes turning their own terms against them. She repeatedly quotes racist news reports in order to point out their inconsistencies and inaccuracies. As she writes in *A Red Record,* "Out of their own mouths shall the murderers be condemned."[81] While she responded emotionally to lynchings in her private diary writings,[82] her published reports stress logic and reason.

Wells follows her pattern of analyzing sources in *A Red Record* when she quotes from the well-known white activist Frances Willard's 1894 annual address to the Women's Christian Temperance Union. Willard professes sympathy for "all high-minded and legitimate efforts to banish the abomination of lynching" but protests Wells's "unjust" remarks about "white women having taken the initiative in nameless acts between the races."[83] Wells quotes a paragraph from Willard's speech, then offers her commentary, specifically objecting to Willard's euphemistic reference to interracial sex:

> This paragraph, brief as it is, contains two statements which have not the slightest foundation in fact. At no time, nor in any place, have I made statements "concerning white women having taken the initiative in nameless acts between the races." Furthermore, at no time, or place nor under any circumstance, have I directly or inferentially "put an imputation upon half the white race in this country." . . . Miss Willard protests against lynching in one paragraph and then, in the next, deliberately misrepresents my position.

Wells takes the opportunity to clarify her own position on interracial sex: "What I have said and what I now repeat . . . is, that colored men have been lynched for assault upon women, when the facts were plain that the relationship between the victim and the alleged victim of his assault was voluntary, clandestine and illicit."[84] Rejecting Willard's genteel circumlocution, Wells also rejects the white woman's role as moral beacon, pointing out that white women's social reform organizations had taken no action to protest lynchings.

Despite her impersonal method, Wells's anti-lynching work was imagined, and perceived, as deeply personal. Although she adopted the rhetoric of objectivity when she explained that she was using outside sources to avoid charges of bias or exaggeration, Wells did not seek to reproduce the "balanced" coverage of the disinterested reporter. Even if she had wanted to claim that sort of objectivity, her racial, sexual, and professional positions would have made it nearly impossible. One study of journalistic objectivity reminds us that Wells belonged in all three categories elite newspapers used "to define 'non-objectivity': she was an outsider, a woman, and a member of an 'uncivilized race.'"[85] The figure of Wells herself, as railroad litigant, exiled newspaper editor, touring lecturer, and of course writer, was always in play in her journalism. In each of these roles she was embodied in some direct way: sinking her teeth into a railroad conductor's hand, fleeing Memphis for her personal safety, performing before audiences, or detailing the terrible fate of lynched black bodies.

The opening exchange of *Southern Horrors*—probably the most personal of her pamphlets and the only one that featured a drawing of Wells on its cover—dramatizes just how fully the black body was implicated in anti-lynching journalism.[86] The pamphlet begins by quoting Wells's quickly infamous editorial from the May 21, 1892, *Memphis Free Speech,* which included an angry dismissal of white paranoia about black rapists: "Nobody in this section of the country believes the old thread bare lie that Negro men rape white women. If Southern white men are not careful, they will over-reach themselves and public sentiment will have a reaction; a conclusion will then be reached which will be very damaging to the moral reputation of their women."[87] Wells then documents the ferocious response of the white press to her editorial. The reactions of white newspapers indicate not only their investment in white women's chastity but also the flexibility of lynching as a means of social control and the disciplinary spectacle that racist discourse constructed from the mutilated black body. They offer such compelling illustrations of white brutality that Wells wisely quotes them first, allowing them to make her case before she makes it herself. Incorrectly assuming that the "atrocious paragraph" in the *Free Speech* had been written by a man, the commentators advocate violent means of silencing "him." "'The negroes may as well understand that there is no mercy for the negro rapist and little patience with his defenders," editorialized the *Memphis Daily Commercial.* It called attention to the "atrocious paragraph" in which Wells characterized rape charges as threadbare lies, then went on to issue a threat: "The fact that a black scoundrel is allowed to live and utter such loathsome and repulsive calumnies is a volume of evidence as to the wonderful patience of Southern whites. But we have had enough of it. There are some things that the Southern white man will not tolerate." The *Evening Scimitar* made the threat more specific: "If the negroes themselves do not apply the remedy without delay it will be the duty of those whom he has attacked to tie the wretch who utters these calumnies to a stake at the intersection of Main and Madison Sts., brand him in the forehead with a hot iron and perform upon him a surgical operation with a pair of *tailor's* shears."[88] The editorials, especially when quoted together, as Wells presents them, do much more for her cause than for their own.

They show how easily a pro-lynching mentality could be adapted to control not just rapists but any black person who protested the white status quo. Simply to utter "loathsome and repulsive calumnies" against white women was enough to warrant violent retribution. The second editorial details the nature of the retribution, suggesting that the writer be castrated. The journalist is imagined as the next lynching victim, and the brutalized black body, staked at a well-known Memphis intersection, is offered to readers as a symbol of white domination. The Wells scholar Sandra Gunning points out that the editorial's "unwitting merger of Wells's female body with that of the black beast" illustrates the black woman's invisibility in white supremacist ideology.[89]

Once Wells became known as the author of the anti-lynching editorial, she was no longer made the victim of textual castration; the angry white editors apparently did not revise their threatened attack to urge that a woman be tied to a stake rather than a man. But when Wells quoted their violent words, her readers—who knew she was a woman—could identify her as the intended target and thus substitute a female victim for the male "wretch" whose body was to be abused and displayed in public. Thus, in *her* text, Wells claims a victimization that pro-lynching propaganda reserved exclusively for men. By repeatedly referring to their figurative assault and identifying herself as its victim, Wells highlighted the brutality of the white newspapers and stressed the potential bodily harm she risked by protesting lynching so openly. The sadistic tone of the white newspapers' editorials illustrated the righteousness of her cause: their reaction was so savage that it undermined its own pretensions to civility.[90]

As a known woman writer, however, Wells was also subject to more subtle attacks that were less easily deflected. Her analytic brand of reporting did not keep the white press from labeling her sexually promiscuous and journalistically irresponsible. Attacks on her reputation began with her railroad lawsuit and never really ended, although they diminished after she married in 1895.[91] When Wells's speaking tour of Britain finally garnered her some long-sought attention from the white press, the *New York Times* called her "a slanderous and nasty-minded mulattress who does not scruple to represent the victims of black brutes in the South as willing victims."[92] Such attacks help us to understand why the "Fortune and His 'Echo'" cartoon, which depicted Wells as a barking dog and mocked her as wanting to be a man, inspired such controversy among black journalists. Although the black press's counterpublic did not—and, indeed, could not—insulate its writers from criticism, it had little to gain by condescending to its newswomen. By embracing women journalists and even

bragging about the respect accorded to aspiring women writers, the counterpublic refuted scurrilous rumors about "nasty-minded" black women
and promoted an alternative model, one that featured images of smart, dutiful, and morally upright women. In this oppositional sphere, female reporters represented the very possibility of a compassionate, rational public
exchange about the irrationality of racial violence and hatred.

⚜

The emergence of the African American newswoman, although initi-
ated and sustained by the black press, was not confined to that sphere.
Rather, it occurred simultaneously through and against the rise of the
white American woman reporter in mass-market newspapers—and through
and against white-authored coverage of lynchings. Black writers addressed
multiple reading publics, including those that denied their authority and
sought to silence them. As Houston A. Baker Jr. reminds us, "black Americans have always situated their unique forms of expressive publicity in a
complex set of relationships to other forms of American publicity (meaning here, paradoxically enough, the sense of publicity as authority)."[93] In
other words, African American journalists, even when writing solely for the
black press, responded to the method and content of the white newspapers that enjoyed wider circulations and stronger financial bases. Baker's
allusion to "the sense of publicity as authority" strikes at the core of African
Americans' historical struggle to be heard. Certainly, African Americans in
the 1880s knew that becoming objects of publicity did not necessarily
endow individuals with the authority to speak, write, or control their
destinies. Only by achieving the ability to control publicity could African
Americans lay claim to its authority. The black press, by creating a forum
that gave African American news writers just such authority, forged a counterpublic that ministered to the needs of a specific community and, at the
same time, contested the truth claims circulated by the white-dominated
press in the American public sphere. Black women played critical roles in
this oppositional arena. As vehicles of counterpublicity, they embodied not
just an ideal of equal opportunity but also the possibility of bodily whole-
ness in the face of a pro-lynching culture that circulated images of brutalized black bodies to illustrate the consequences of resistance. As Ida B.
Wells demonstrated so clearly, the myth of the black rapist allowed white
men to torture blacks with impunity while claiming that they were acting
in their "natural" role as protectors of white womanhood. In this racist discourse, the spectacle of the disciplined (mutilated and murdered) black
body acted as a necessary deterrent, both defending and policing white fe-

male sexuality. Black women reporters like Wells wrote against such spectacles rather than participating in them. The white women court reporters discussed in the next chapter played a very different role in a very different spectacle, although the theme was remarkably similar: a sexual threat to white womanhood. But this time, the perpetrator was a white man.

The Original Sob Sisters: Writers on Trial

For female journalists who sought to enter the male-dominated bureaucratic space of the courtroom, the 1907 trial of Harry Kendall Thaw for the murder of Stanford White resulted in both a breakthrough and a backlash. The sensational case gave white female reporters unprecedented visibility and new opportunities to cover serious news. For weeks, every major newspaper in New York City, where the trial was held, printed column after column of trial reports written by women. Female reporters had written about trials before this one, but never in such detail, at such length, with so much publicity, and in the company of so many other women.[1] Yet the case also spawned a dismissive label, "sob sister," that would dog the careers of female news writers for decades. Coined in the early days of the Thaw trial, the term referred to the four women who sat at their own special press table in the crowded courtroom: Winifred Black, Dorothy Dix, Nixola Greeley-Smith, and Ada Patterson.[2] As one early press historian tells it, the journalist Irvin S. Cobb, "looking a little wearily at the four fine-looking girls who spread their sympathy like jam, injected a scornful line into his copy about the 'sob sisters.' This was the origin of a phrase that in time became the hallmark of the girl reporter."[3] Denoting a female journalist who specialized in sentimental or human interest stories, or, more generally, a woman writer "who could wring tears," the term was in common usage by 1910, thanks in part to the voluminous newspaper coverage of the Thaw case between 1906 and 1908.[4] "For too long," one journalism historian remarks, "it was used to describe any woman reporter."[5] It also became a derogatory label for women novelists whose work was considered contrived and excessively emotional.[6]

In the space of three syllables, "sob sister" recast trailblazing professionals as gullible amateurs. Perhaps worse, the catchy alliteration implied that newswomen were inherently hypocritical, since they manufactured tears for profit.[7] It also linked female journalists to the emotionally charged sentimental fiction of the nineteenth century at a time when the American literary establishment was attacking the genre with renewed vigor and employing "sentimental" as a synonym for shallow and trite.[8] The hyper-expressive prose associated with the newswomen neatly extended the tradition of popular melodrama. Viewed through the standard framework of American literary history, however, these journalistic pioneers appear hopelessly behind the intellectual fashions of their times. Their work seems as distant from the era's unflinching realist and naturalist fiction as it does from the emerging experimental work of the modernists. Although recent scholarship on the interplay of sentimentalism, realism, and modernism has unsettled the once firm divisions between these expressive forms and challenged the literary periodization that rendered the sob sisters anachronistic,[9] the writings of these early newswomen have attracted attention only as a predictable enactment of pop culture pathos.[10]

Shrugging off the sob sisters has caused critics to miss a complex and far more compelling story of gendered assumptions overturned, sexual violence unmasked, and narrative authority in flux. The newswomen's role was more vexed—and less soothingly domestic—than the lightly told anecdote about "the four fine-looking girls who spread their sympathy like jam" suggests. The explicit sexual content of the trial testimony, combined with the commentary of women whose presence in the courtroom was itself deemed newsworthy, ignited a highly charged spectacle starring not just the trial participants but the women reporters as well. That spectacle gained force when a new professional visibility for women collided with the trial's conflicting narratives of female ambition and sexual vulnerability. Attending to the origins of sob-sisterhood reveals a dynamic of authorship and spectacle, publicity and power, that reverberated throughout early-twentieth-century journalism and fiction.

The sob sisters have much to tell us not only about the perils of being a woman writer but also about how the national imagination adapted the conventions of emotional expression to a new era of mass-market publicity. They wrote for the "yellow" press, not the more restrained, intellectually minded newspapers, in part because elite journals were much less likely to hire women.[11] Thus they were already embedded in a feminized phenomenon, since the brash popular newspapers that employed them were depicted as deviant, feminine, and uncivilized by rival newspapers such as the *New York Times*.[12] Sob-sisterhood, however, is best understood as a product of a print culture that included not only the yellow press but also elite newspapers such as the *Times*, whose trial coverage developed many of the same themes as the sensational journals.[13] Although the sob sisters were identified with the overdrawn emotional content of the most aggressive, self-promoting papers, their displays of feeling drew on conventions operating in both the highbrow and lowbrow press.

The newswomen's tears are metonymic, registering the emphatic embodiment of the woman writer. That embodiment shaped both their writing and its reception. Moreover, their assumed inability to transcend their tears, their bodies, their femaleness, confirmed their inability to act as disinterested citizens in the public sphere. Women, after all, could not be jurors in New York State in 1907. Yet the sob sisters, by interpreting the trial for their readers, anticipated future female jurors—a point that was not lost on the newswomen or their detractors. These reporters helped to set the stage for future debates not just about women writers but about all women who assumed public roles: Could women be admitted into a hierarchical, rule-bound space without damaging decorum beyond repair? Were women really more emotional than men? What place did emotion and sympathy have, if any, in rational deliberations? The news coverage addressed such questions day after day, as the trial attained the status of a national event.

Despite its modern venue, the sob sister phenomenon harks back to a nineteenth-century notion of sentimental reading that one influential literary critic has labeled "a bodily act," a physically intense experience in which "tears designate a border realm between the story and its reading." Thus these news narratives are indebted to the focus of literary sentimentalism on human connection and emotional suffering.[14] Yet the phrase "sob sister" and its contemporary, "sob story," inject a jarring note of self-interest and acknowledged artifice into the sentimental tradition. For the New Woman, crying became a career move. If, as one literary historian has argued, the sentimental always calls attention to the constructed nature of emotion, marking "a moment when the discursive processes that construct emotion become visible,"[15] then the newswomen became professional markers of just such processes. Newspapers marketed their stories as expressions of womanly sympathy, playing up a gender role that nineteenth-century sentimentalism had solidified. A close reading of the newspaper accounts, however, reveals not only that the accused murderer (a man) showed *more* emotion throughout the trial than the women in court, but also that male-authored and female-authored coverage of the case was equally overwrought.[16] Nevertheless, it was the sob sisters, not their male counterparts, whose public reception most clearly manifested anxieties about the content of the trial coverage, the wisdom of making the trial testimony so readily accessible to so many readers, and the publicity system that made it possible to do so.

The newswomen emerge as central to the Thaw case not because they write sentimentally about the trial but rather because they act as vehicles of publicity, dramatizing what the theorist Michael Warner has called the "impossible relation" between particular human bodies and the mass subject addressed and created by the mass media.[17] Playing the dual role of objects and agents within the tradition-bound, male-dominated structure of the court, the newswomen do more than transmit information to a mass reading public; they symbolize that public, representing its interests and manifesting its desires. The trial coverage—with its repeated professions of sympathy and its desperate need to imagine a universe where redemption is possible and evil can be recognized, contained, and adequately punished—also demonstrates American popular culture's refusal to relinquish the consolations of the sentimental. In the Thaw case, we see a newly secularized nation reimagining sentimentalism through a strikingly modern mass media spectacle. As agents of that reimagining, the sob sisters embody the contradictions on which it relies. In this chapter I turn to the news reports of the Thaw trial not simply to retell the story of this famous murder but rather to show that revisiting sob-sisterhood allows us a telling glimpse of women's place within the evolving, elusive, and endlessly influential mass public of America.

The Case

In June 1906, Harry Thaw shot and killed Stanford White in front of hundreds of witnesses in the rooftop garden of Madison Square. Because both the killer and his victim were well known, the crime became front-page news for months. A playboy with a bad temper, Thaw was born into one of Pittsburgh's richest families and was heir to a coal-mining fortune. White—who had designed New York City landmarks such as the Washington Square arch and the original Madison Square Garden (the site of his murder)—was as famous for his high living as for his brilliant architecture. A married man in his early fifties, White had cultivated a string of teenaged mistresses.

The central figure of the trial, however, was neither the volatile playboy nor the flamboyant architect but rather Harry Thaw's young wife, Evelyn

Nesbit Thaw. It was on her behalf, Harry insisted, that he had killed White. To support this claim, Evelyn, a former chorus girl and artist's model who had grown up poor in Pittsburgh, took the stand to testify, calmly and in compelling detail, about her sexual involvement with Stanford White. Her testimony, reprinted verbatim by every major newspaper in New York, explained exactly when (she was sixteen), where (in a mirrored bedroom), and how (he drugged her with champagne and possibly something else) she lost her virginity to White.[18] Harry's defense attorneys used the story to argue that his husbandly outrage at his wife's "ruin" caused him to go temporarily insane on that June night in Madison Square Garden. Thaw's was an oddly retrospective rage; his defense insisted that he went crazy over an incident that had occurred *before* he married Evelyn.

The prosecutor cross-examined Evelyn at length, questioning her about other men she had dated, forcing her to admit that her involvement with White lasted long after their initial sexual encounter, and confronting her with evidence that Harry was an abusive husband and a habitual drug user. It didn't work. Even faced with a four-year-old affidavit, signed in her own hand, describing a chilling incident that occurred while she was traveling with Harry in Europe—he rented an isolated castle in Austria, took her there, whipped her repeatedly, and kept her a virtual prisoner for three weeks—Evelyn did not waver. She so successfully cast Harry as a heroic avenger of besmirched innocence that the jury deadlocked and the state had to conduct another trial the following year.[19]

The *New York American*'s front-page coverage of Evelyn's testimony could serve as a classic example of sob sister trial coverage. The mournful article depicts Evelyn as a martyr who humiliated herself publicly to save her husband:

> Throwing aside all modesty and pride, sinking every feeling to woman dear, baring her bleeding heart to the world—Evelyn Nesbit Thaw flung wide open the book of her tragic life, that all might read.
>
> A tremendous sacrifice, and a soul-crushing story.
>
> But in the hour of deepest woe the girl wife of Harry Kendall Thaw has this consolation, which will be all sufficient balm to her broken heart,—she has probably saved the life of her husband.[20]

In its expression of moral outrage, its dramatic emphasis on emotional suffering, and its sympathetic identification with a wronged woman, this passage contains all the elements of the sob-sisterly story, save one: a sob sister. It was written by a man, William Hoster, who was responsible for most of the *American*'s front-page coverage of the Thaw trial. Hoster's reportage echoes the tone and content of many other accounts of Evelyn's testimony, authored by both men and women.[21] Assuredly, the sob sisters employed some bombastic rhetoric, occasionally trivializing not just themselves but all women, as when Greeley-Smith wrote of Harry Thaw's sister, "To the woman observer, quite the most peculiar thing about her is her fondness for pleats."[22] Yet the newswomen's prose was no more purple than that of their male colleagues, nor were their articles substantially more sympathetic to the accused murderer or his wife.

The sentimentality of the era's male-authored reportage has not escaped press historians. One study notes wryly, "The men who also covered the trials and did similar kinds of writing all escaped being called 'sob brothers,' 'weeping willies,' or any such appellative."[23] The "sob sister" label illustrates how easily misogynist stereotypes could be marshaled to restrict women's professional progress; the snappy phrase slipped newswomen into a well-articulated and easily dismissed category. Yet simply noting the injustice does not explain it. What allowed the label to stick so tenaciously to women even in an era of new opportunities for higher education and careers? Why could the "weeping willies" sink comfortably into obscurity, while the sob sisters' melodramatic excesses would haunt women writers for years to come?

Spectacle, not style, made the difference. It was the newswomen's role as vehicles of publicity, as both objects and agents of the news, that cemented their identity as sob sisters. This identity was forged by their contested physical presence in court, by the self-referentiality of the "woman's view" promoted in their articles, and by the always implied and sometimes overt reciprocity between Evelyn Nesbit Thaw's body and the bodies of the women reporters. Their womanhood, defined most vividly by their capacity for sympathy, was repeatedly emphasized. The genteel photographic portraits that accompanied the newswomen's articles made their gender explicit, as did headlines such as "Thaw in Court as Seen by a Woman" and "Actors in Thaw Tragedy Seen by Woman's Eyes."[24] In an era when bylines were still used sparingly, a sob sister's name often appeared in triplicate: in a headline, as a byline, and again as a caption for her own photograph.[25] Dorothy Dix and Winifred Black, the most established writers of the group, frequently received such attention, as in "Thaw Would Be Acquitted by Woman Jury, Says Dorothy Dix" and "Juror Voting to Convict Deserves Divorce, Declares Winifred Black."[26] While editors also published photographs and promoted name recognition of male columnists, they made women's pictures bigger and promoted their names more aggressively (see figure 7).

Newspapers also advertised women reporters' capacity for emotion.

Killing Through Jealousy Appeals to Female Heart

EMOTIONS WOULD ALMOST ENTIRELY GOVERN A DECISION BY FAIR SEX.

By DOROTHY DIX.

THE seventh session of the Thaw trial brought a blighting disappointment to Thaw himself, to the patient women of his house, sitting like statues of anxious love and watching behind his chair in the courtroom, and to all the lookers-on impatient to get to the real meat of the case.

For in their wisdom, and for a cause they declined to publicly state, the counsel on both sides agreed to excuse two jurors at the morning session, and in the afternoon these were followed by a third, with the result that when court adjourned the last empty chair in the jury box was still empty.

This makes six jurors in all that have been excused after having been acepted, and what with that and the difficulty of finding men who are willing to be locked up for two or three weeks, who have no family drawbacks and afflictions, whose business will not suffer, whose health is robust, who believe in capital punishment, have no views on insanity and no fixed opinions, it threatens to stretch the selection of a jury out to the crack of doom.

DOROTHY DIX.

into its depths. Only women know how many women's lives are ruined by men like that, and a jury of women would not deal as lightly with Thaw's sins and follies as a man jury will.

What the evidence presented will be we do not yet know. Assuming that the stories current are true, and that the main justification for the shooting of White will be Evelyn Nesbit's story of her friendship with him, a woman jury would want to know only two things. They would have to be shown first that after Evelyn married Thaw she was trying to live decently and honestly and that she had put the past behind her. Then they would want to know if White molested her in her

Figure 7. As was typical of the woman-authored reports on the Thaw trial, this article was illustrated by an image of its author, Dorothy Dix, whose name also appeared as a byline and in the story's bold primary headline, which is not visible here but which stretched all the way across the top of the page on which the article appeared. (Dorothy Dix, "Killing through Jealousy Appeals to Female Heart," *New York Evening Journal*, February 1, 1907. General Research Division, The New York Public Library, Astor, Lenox, and Tilden Foundations.)

Like male writers covering the trial, the sob sisters filed reports describing each day's main events. But unlike the newsmen, they were also expected to exhibit their "depth of womanly feeling."[27] Their niche well marked, the newswomen were assigned to take the courtroom's emotional temperature and to demonstrate the "depth" of their own feelings. At the same time, they were on display from the moment they stepped into the courtroom. In the spectacle of sympathy they enacted, the white female body—as source of tears, as object of desire—became both fetish and filter, anchoring their narratives. As tears became their trademark, their bodies mediated the trial's most explosive content, delivered through the testimony of the accused murderer's wife.

Evelyn's witness-stand story of sexual victimization, recounted to an overwhelmingly male audience, placed extraordinary demands on the small cadre of newswomen in the courtroom. As the designated providers of "the woman's view," they were called upon to identify with the long-suffering wife while also maintaining enough distance to protect their respectability. Confronted with their vulnerability as women, they found it both necessary and dangerous to flaunt the link—the bodily reciprocity—between themselves and the seductive star witness. As a group, the sob sisters embodied the contradictions of the publicity that surrounded the case. How were they to legitimize their journalism? If they wrote with "great depth of womanly feeling," they performed as advertised but risked being dismissed as irrational. If they wrote like the men, they destroyed the most frequently cited rationale for their presence in court, their ability to offer a woman's point of view. The newswomen did, in fact, write much like the men. But the spectacle required them to appear, in the words of one woman columnist, as "women first, writers after."[28]

Subjected to near-constant surveillance, literally set apart from the rest of the courtroom, the newswomen came to embody not just the special concerns of the female sex but also the sexual vulnerability of white women. The sob sisters' whiteness, though unmarked textually, was made explicit through their photographs. So was Evelyn's, whose whiteness was repeatedly stressed in descriptions of her courtroom appearances. "Her skin was like an Easter lily, white and transparent, with only the slightest trace of color in spots upon the cheeks," observed Viola Rodgers.[29] Greeley-Smith called her a "fragile, white-faced child"; Black called her "slight, waxen-pale, big-eyed, a human camellia"; Samuel Hopkins Adams called her "a pale slip of a girl."[30] These references to whiteness do not purport to categorize Evelyn racially; rather, they appear to use skin color to suggest innocence and youth. Nonetheless, the descriptions gain force from racialized notions that intertwined whiteness, beauty, and virtue.[31] A fierce preoccupation with the vulnerability of white women, as we saw in chapter 2, figured prominently in white supremacist discourse and especially in public justifications of lynchings, which claimed that mob murder was the only way to keep black men from raping white women.[32] Evelyn's whiteness was not incidental to the horror expressed about her violation. As Ida B. Wells pointed out in her reports on lynching, violence against African American women did not inspire similar outrage.[33]

The fact that *none* of the trial reports interpreted Harry Thaw's obsession with his wife's loss of virginity as abnormal is a trenchant reminder of the privileged place that white women's sexual purity held in the national imagination. It was the horror of Evelyn's "ruin," not the act of murder, that constituted the trial's emotional core. The sob sisters mediated that emotion, but it was the murderer himself whose horror was portrayed as most authentic. According to all news accounts, the first and loudest sobs in the courtroom came from Harry, not from his wife, mother, or sister, or from the women reporters. When Evelyn testified about the first time she had sex with Stanford White, Harry burst into tears. The *New York American's* front-page headline announced, "Prisoner in Tears during Wife's Ordeal."[34] "Harry Thaw sobbed unrestrainedly," reported the *New York Evening World*.[35] The same man who had donned a long black raincoat on a warm June night to hide his gun could not listen dry-eyed to the story of his wife's champagne-soaked encounter with White. According to the *New York Times*, "his agony had no hint of theatrical effect about it. He drew a handkerchief from his pocket, when he could stand the story no longer, and his heavy shoulders bent over the table. His face was hidden, but the broad shoulders twitched. Those near him could hear great gulping sounds as he fought to master his emotion."[36] Harry's agony appears both reassuringly masculine and deeply authentic. His sobs, we are told, betray no evidence of theatricality. Unlike Evelyn, whose performance on the stand was reviewed like a play, and unlike the sob sisters, who were accused of manufacturing tears to advance their careers, Harry escaped the charge of playacting. This is all the more startling because his loss of composure so clearly reinforced his defense against the murder charge. Evelyn testified that Harry had asked her to repeat the details of her initial sexual encounter with White over and over, both before and after they were married. During these retellings, he would grow agitated, pace the room, and sob aloud, Evelyn said. Harry's attorneys, in turn, argued that Evelyn's story drove Harry to commit murder. The tears Harry shed in court bolstered his defense by illustrating the story's continued effect on him. Somehow, however, Harry's sobs were transferred to the women who wrote about them. Tracing that transference requires a closer look at the newswomen's physical presence in court, their bodily reciprocity with Evelyn, and their interpretations of the case against Harry.

"Excluded as far as possible": The Spectacle of Women in Court

The courtroom was packed on opening day, according to the *New York Times,* which reported that "there was a collection of reporters and newspaper artists such as has never come together before, even in New York." When Evelyn tried to leave court at the end of the first day, "down swooped the mob," and the police had to battle "a wild stampede" to create an escape route.[37] From the beginning, female spectators were singled out as particularly disruptive. "Foremost among those clamoring for admission were women, attired in gorgeous raiment, and to whom 'No' had no significance," claimed another first-day report.[38] Before the trial even began, at least one editorial cartoonist mocked women's interest in attending it: the *New York Evening World* published a drawing titled "The Eternal Enigma—Woman's Curiosity," depicting a flock of women rushing headlong through a door labeled "The Thaw Case" (see figure 8).[39] Blank-eyed but determined, moving en masse, the women bend forward eagerly, yet they are almost indistinguishable from one another in a crush of skirts, coats, muffs, and plumed hats. To a person, they appear unthinking, aggressive, careless of others. That women's curiosity about the case would be labeled an "enigma" is itself mysterious. Given that the testimony centered on a woman's experience, why *wouldn't* women be interested? The implication is that the women's curiosity was necessarily idle; they were assumed to have nothing but a prurient interest in the case. The cartoonist thus channels general anxieties about the mass public's access to the courtroom into his treatment of women's interest. The court echoed this strategy. Most of the people hurtling toward the courtroom door were men, yet it was primarily the women whose presence was regulated, reported, and debated.

Excluding women swiftly became the primary strategy for controlling the crowd.[40] Citing "the necessity of absolute decorum," the presiding judge, James Fitzgerald, imposed strict rules to keep order. Journalists, perhaps eager to curry favor, reported these measures approvingly, as in the *New York Times* article that noted: "Women especially will be excluded as far as possible. There really is not too much room for those with legitimate business."[41] Only women who could prove they were on official reporting assignments would be welcomed inside.

By banning all women from the courtroom except the newswomen and the defendant's family and friends, the judge created a professional pressure cooker for the female reporters. While his order, by allowing the newswomen to stay, recognized their "legitimate business," it also ensured their visibility and made their presence worthy of comment. Since the reporters were the only women allowed to remain other than Harry's wife, mother, sister, and two family friends, they were inevitably linked to that small group, the nexus of trial publicity. Moreover, the newswomen acted as a lightning rod for the most troubling questions raised by the testimony. They took notes while witnesses documented the privileges of wealthy men and the limited options of poor women. They listened to detailed descriptions of Stanford White's parties, where provocatively dressed adolescent girls were made available to gratify rich, powerful men. They watched

Figure 8. Before the Thaw trial even began, editorial cartoons like this one mocked women's intense interest in the sensational case. (Maurice Ketten, "The Eternal Enigma—Woman's Curiosity," *New York Evening World,* January 23, 1907. General Research Division, The New York Public Library, Astor, Lenox, and Tilden Foundations.)

the prosecutor try to rattle Evelyn by implying that an operation to remove her appendix had actually been an abortion. In short, they observed a frontal assault on middle-class norms, and their response to the testimony indexed its disorienting effects. After the first day of Evelyn's sexually explicit testimony, the front-page report in the *New York Times* called attention to the female spectators to heighten the story's shock value. The article begins sedately: "Dressed as a schoolgirl might have been dressed by her mother, Mrs. Evelyn Nesbit Thaw yesterday told the jury . . . the whole story of her life, and her relations with White." The article then pauses to observe: "There were women in the courtroom. The story caused them to bow their heads and hide their faces."[42] The news was not just the revelation of White's coerced sex with a teenaged Evelyn. Rather, it was the combination of Evelyn's testimony and the presence of the women who were in court to hear it.

Even without a female audience, the trial's content was likely to inspire public fascination. In addition to front-page coverage—including multiple articles each day, drawings of participants, and diagrams of the studio to which Stanford White had taken Evelyn—the newspapers filled pages with full stenographic reports of the proceedings. The publicity blizzard dismayed some readers. Church groups from as far away as Chattanooga, Tennessee, debated its wisdom, and some asked the government to censor the news coverage.[43] President Theodore Roosevelt took such umbrage at the newspapers' willingness to print "the full disgusting particulars" of Evelyn's testimony that he asked the Postmaster General to refuse to mail the offending journals. Although the threatened censorship never occurred, it inspired yet more front-page news.[44]

Once the testimony veered into the territory of dog whips, drug syringes, and the sexual initiation of adolescent girls, reports suggest that even more unauthorized women tried to gain entry to court.[45] The sob sisters had to tread carefully to avoid antagonizing the court, while articulating women's legitimate interests in the trial and separating themselves from the unauthorized observers. Several mentioned approvingly the judge's ban on female spectators. None complained in print. Some did argue, however, that female readers, particularly young girls, *needed* to know the details about sexual predators. "Girls, are you reading all about the Thaw trial?" asked Beatrice Fairfax. "If you are, I want you to take it to heart and profit by it. There is a lesson for every one of you in it. No doubt at one time in her career you all envied Evelyn Nesbit Thaw. . . . But now, girls, see where that 'luck' has landed her. Every one of you, no matter how poor or hard-worked you may be, is a thousand times better off."[46] Fairfax, like many of her colleagues, recognized that fascination with Evelyn's wealth, beauty, and celebrity could mitigate the morally bracing effects of her downfall. Thus Fairfax reminds her (presumed) virginal readers that in the economy of virtue, Evelyn was poor indeed.

Despite their willingness to defend female readers, the sob sisters expressed no solidarity with the women who attended court without "legitimate business."[47] They vigorously denied any sisterhood with the interlopers, sometimes even joining in the game of mocking the spectators. Adopting a brisk tone of professional condescension, they sought to divert their readers' attention from the humiliating implications of their own embodiment and to resist their role as symbols of the mass public's prurient interest. Winifred Black's commentary shows that the newsmen held no monopoly on condescending descriptions of women:

> The ladies were out in pairs at the Thaw case yesterday. They came into the courtroom two by two, as the animals are said to have gone into the ark, and oh! the gorgeous plumage that they wore!
>
> One woman was so bedecked in strawberry pink and brilliant blue that she looked like one of the little paroquets that come from Mexico and cry "Stop thief!" if you try to pass the cage without giving them a cracker. The storm was at its height when the court opened, but through the snow they came, plunging to the shoe tops in the slush and jostling with the men to get into the courtroom.
>
> I think it was rather a disappointing day for the ladies.[48]

Black characterizes the women's interest in the trial as shallow; they come only to display themselves and to be titillated. Like trained birds in cages, the members of her "gayly plumed brigade" demand attention without understanding why.[49] Black's portrayal, in short, is no less demeaning than those written by her male counterparts. The sob sisters may have had even more reason to scoff at the female spectators than did the newsmen, who ran little risk of being identified with the curious crowd in strawberry pink dresses. Because their professional place in court was so tenuous, they repeatedly set themselves apart from those whose attendance could be dismissed as frivolous and unseemly.

At least one writer went beyond condescension to outright scorn. Annette Bradshaw's trial commentary takes a common misogynist tack by insisting that the courtroom transgressors had unsexed themselves. "It is almost impossible to imagine them filling a woman's place in any sphere of life," she declared. "All trace of femininity seems wiped completely off their faces, and especially out of their eyes, as soon as they set foot within the courtroom."[50] Displacing an accusation that could be leveled against the newswomen as easily as against the gatecrashers, Bradshaw illuminates the fragility of her own professional authority. Femininity was not a negotiable asset for writers whose work was marketed on the basis of their ability to provide "the woman's point of view." Here we arrive at an essential conundrum of the female court reporter's situation. Her womanhood *was* her angle. But her womanhood was also the primary obstacle to her getting the story.

If, as one reporter put it, "no woman was allowed to pass the door save those who represented newspapers,"[51] the newswomen earned special notoriety simply by being the only *authorized* female observers. Their comings and goings were reported with equal interest. During the district attorney's aggressive cross-examination of Evelyn, for instance, several of them left the room. William Hoster used the departure to punctuate his description of Evelyn's performance on the stand. The passage reads almost like a rehearsal of a sexual assault, crowned by the newswomen's exodus:

> She who had passed through the terrible ordeal of direct examination without tears or faltering, finally broke down under the strain. The tears came, great waves of emotion swept over her, and then, like an avalanche, came her confessions—a vast outpouring of hidden secrets, rapidly, eloquently, with entire abandonment. . . .
>
> [The prosecutor] took her in detail through every meeting she had with White following the incident of the studio [where they first had sex], pinned her down to the most damning facts, extorted admissions, drew forth explanations, descriptions, sentiments, thoughts, motives. The only women present—newspaper writers, in a measure hardened to the facts of the underworld—rose and hurried from the courtroom.[52]

By noting that "the only women present" fled from the spectacle of Evelyn's distress, Hoster caps his portrayal with the suggestion that even newswomen "hardened to the facts of the underworld" could not bear to witness this pseudo-rape. In doing so, he correlates Evelyn's sobs, her sexual victimization, and her forced confessions with the women reporters and their abrupt departure from court. The passage links the witness to the newswomen, but, even more remarkably, it connects tears and sex, linking one physical expression to another. Hoster's narration of Evelyn's breakdown in sexualized terms is not particularly unusual; much of the news coverage highlighted Evelyn's sexuality. But in shifting directly from the witness's tears to the newswomen's rush for the door, he suggests that the newswomen responded to Evelyn's loss of bodily control by losing control of themselves. Rather than being riveted to their seats, scribbling down

Evelyn's "vast outpouring of secrets," they ran away. Their embodiment—registered through Evelyn's tears—impaired their reporting. Their flight indicates not only their genteel femininity and their emotional bond with Evelyn but also a professional conflict of interest: How can a reporter cover a trial when she can't stand to hear the testimony?

Obviously, if the newswomen had to prove their femininity by leaving every time a witness broke down or a spicy detail was introduced, their trial coverage would not cover much. To succeed, the women had to answer this challenge or at least deflect attention from the question. They needed another way to reassert their womanhood, one that would protect their special angle while legitimizing their continued presence in court. They found it in the figure who dominated the news reports: Evelyn Nesbit Thaw.

The "Enigma Wife": Interpreting Evelyn

"Mother's Younger Brother was in love with Evelyn Nesbit. He had closely followed the scandal surrounding her name and had begun to reason that the death of her lover Stanford White and the imprisonment of her husband Harry K. Thaw left her in need of the attentions of a genteel middle-class young man with no money. He thought about her all the time. He was desperate to have her."[53] In E. L. Doctorow's novel *Ragtime,* based in part on the Thaw case, the fictional Younger Brother cultivates an obsession that was probably not unusual among real-life younger brothers in early 1907. Not if they were old enough to read newspapers, at least. Evelyn was the pivot around which the trial coverage revolved. "So far as the outsider can see, Harry Thaw's case looks doubtful," Clara Morris wrote as the trial began. "Yet it is impossible to consider him without including his enigma wife. Nowhere can you open a door in this case without finding Evelyn Nesbit Thaw behind it."[54] Dix made a similar point after the trial was well under way: "As the Thaw trial goes on, interest does not wane, but rather increases, in the personality of the little butterfly woman who was the cause of the tragedy, and to whom every thread of the tangled evidence goes back."[55] Behind every door, at the end of every thread of evidence, Evelyn was imagined as the key that would unlock the case. No wonder everyone was desperate to "have" her.

Newspapers reported minutely on Evelyn's dress, hair, complexion, voice, and demeanor. The coverage featured sultry photographs from her modeling days: Evelyn adorned in jewels, curled up in a kimono, sprawled on a tiger skin, draped in gauzy fabric. These images were supplemented by drawings depicting her demure appearance in court, veiled and girlish (see figure 9). Often the sketches took up more space on the front page than the text of the trial reports.[56] The sob sisters shared the general fascination with the chorus girl who married a millionaire. Yet they also produced some notably dry-eyed evaluations of her. "I have no illusions about Evelyn Thaw," wrote Greeley-Smith in a cool analysis of the star witness's sexual history. "I think merely that she was sold to one man and later sold herself to another."[57] Greeley-Smith interprets Evelyn's sex life through an economic, not moral, framework, and characterizes her marriage as a form of legal prostitution, displaying more keen awareness of the consequences of socioeconomic oppression than "depth of womanly feeling."

Such remarks, however, grow increasingly rare as the trial progresses. Their rational tone threatened the newswomen's niche as emotional chroniclers of the proceedings. Moreover, the newswomen's critical distance from Evelyn narrowed as they became increasingly pulled into the trial as participant-observers. Their visibility echoed Evelyn's, both in court and in newsprint. The photographs that accompanied their articles often ran side by side with images of Evelyn. Drawn into the spectacle they wanted to write about, the newswomen managed their visibility by rearranging the lines of sisterhood in strategic ways. Already vulnerable to charges of unwomanly conduct, they authorized their role as courtroom interpreters by claiming special insight into Evelyn's plight.

By identifying with Evelyn, the sob sisters turned their assumed womanly weakness, particularly emotional vulnerability, into an asset. In a report on a day of especially harsh cross-examination of Evelyn, Ada Patterson makes this strategy explicit. Recalling the judge's "eminently proper order that no women should be admitted to the courtroom as spectators," Patterson describes Evelyn's glances toward the newswomen as appeals for sisterly sympathy: "'You are women,' she seemed to say. . . . 'Being women won't you understand?'"[58] Patterson emphasizes the special rapport the women journalists enjoyed with Evelyn. To the question she plants in Evelyn's mind—"Being women won't you understand?"—Patterson implicitly answers yes. Her article rings with assurances that the newswomen did, indeed, understand. Such claims of intimacy gave the sob sisters' reports an insider's edge.

Yet that intimacy came with a price. A hypersexualized figure in the eye of a publicity hurricane, Evelyn posed special challenges to the writers who staked a professional claim on their sympathy for her. Those challenges— and the bodily reciprocity that was both imperative and dangerous for the newswomen—are vividly apparent in Greeley-Smith's report on Evelyn's cross-examination. The headline, "The Vivisection of a Woman's Soul," fig-

REMARKABLE INTERVIEW WITH
MRS. EVELYN THAW IN COURT

"I Wont Break Down—Not a Bit of It—Harry Needs Me," She Declares.

BY VIOLA RODGERS.

Day by day and hour by hour through the week that has seen seven of the jurors chosen who will decide the fate of Harry Thaw, little Evelyn Nesbit Thaw has sat behind her husband and listened with intentness to every word uttered by the lawyers for the defence and the prosecution, and with eager, searching eyes the little veiled figure has anxiously watched each juror as he walked into the box—the men who will decide whether the young prisoner shall walk out of that courtroom a free man, or whether he shall be found guilty.

The situation is one of the most awful

Figure 9. Viola Rodgers's interview with Evelyn Nesbit Thaw, like almost every other news story on the Thaw case, was accompanied by a sketch of the former chorus girl. Evelyn's image took up more space on the page than the text of the article about her. ("Remarkable Interview with Mrs. Evelyn Thaw in Court," *New York American,* January 26, 1907. General Research Division, The New York Public Library, Astor, Lenox, and Tilden Foundations.)

ures the soul as a material body and suggests a display of bodily dismem-
berment. The metaphor anticipates the article's portrayal of an intensely
physical threat, not just to Evelyn but to the women reporters as well.

Greeley-Smith begins by establishing the image of a young woman
forced to make sexual confessions to a male crowd: "Before an audience
of many hundred men young Mrs. Thaw was compelled to reveal in all its
hideousness every detail of her association with Stanford White after his
crime against her." Greeley-Smith then describes the reaction of the female
reporters: "The newspaper women, perhaps half a dozen in number, whose
duty it is to report the trial, writhed under the sting of the prosecutor's
questions, bowed their heads before the hideousness from which Mr.
Jerome [the prosecutor] ruthlessly tore the veil. Some of them fled before
it. I honor those who remained, though I was not of them."[59] Here the sob
sisters' identification with Evelyn is graphically physical: they writhe over
questions directed at her. Their response to the testimony is more than visceral; they are said to feel as if they were on the stand themselves. The
boundary that separates the witness from the writers—"the railed space"
where, as Patterson noted, the newswomen were ensconced—collapses.
This passage illustrates the bodily reciprocity between Evelyn and the
women writers, then uses that reciprocity to confront the writers' conundrum: How can they write about testimony they can't bear to hear? In Greeley-Smith's report, her flight from court asserts her femininity while also
dramatizing her deep identification with Evelyn. In the logic of bodily reciprocity, even the gaps in her reports—the moments when she had to look
away, the times when she left the room—intensify her connection to
Evelyn.

Having confessed to fleeing from Evelyn's distress, Greeley-Smith
launches into a commentary on "duty" which highlights the tensions that
structured the women's reportage. Definitions of womanhood clash with
models of professionalism, while the desire to identify with Evelyn com-
petes with the fear of being swept into the category of sexual victim:

> There is no duty to a newspaper—and none that any newspaper would
> wish to enforce—that should not have succumbed to the horrors spoken in
> that courtroom. But there was a duty of giving to the trembling, weeping
> woman on the witness-stand any support that the presence of members of
> her own sex might afford. I think all the women present felt it, and only a
> sense of utter mental and physical nausea made any of them forget it and fly
> from the flaunted shames, the dark horrors of that court-room.
>
> Moreover, they fled from it in vain. For these horrors followed them into
> the sunlit street, into their offices, back to their homes, and kept relentless

vigil at their pillows, making them wonder if the iniquity through which Evelyn Thaw had passed was to leave a permanent polluting stamp on all who heard it.[60]

Articulating a position in which gender solidarity comes first, Greeley-Smith argues that even professional duty would not require the newswomen to sit through Evelyn's testimony. Rather, it was the duty of sisterhood, of providing Evelyn with the support that "members of her own sex might afford." Moreover, only personal weakness—"a sense of utter mental and physical nausea"—excused the newswomen from fulfilling this higher duty. Watching Evelyn's cross-examination apparently made them sick. Yet even running away does not allow them to escape the specter of sexual victimization. Greeley-Smith imagines them haunted, at work, at home, in their bedrooms, by their new insight into sexual predators. With bodily reciprocity came a fear of contamination reminiscent of Nellie Bly's horror in the bathtub scene at the Blackwell's Island asylum. If the physical link between Evelyn and the writers gave the women's news writing a special edge, it also made them vulnerable. Would they carry "a permanent polluting stamp"?

Managing the Blush of Authorship

As Greeley-Smith's haunted report intimates, identifying with Evelyn Nesbit Thaw was both profitable and dangerous. It was a tricky business to be linked so intimately with a figure who inspired so much ambivalence. Was she victim or vixen? Noble truth-teller or accomplished liar? Reporters of both sexes searched for clues. Nearly every writer noted the contrast between Evelyn's sordid story and her girlishly innocent appearance. Her youth, her diminutive size, and her childish clothes were cited repeatedly. Patterson called her "the slim girl whose wan face is waxen as the petals of a calla lily, the wife whose strength is frailness."[61] The *New York Times* struck a similar note, calling Evelyn "a little bit of a thing who seemed as if she could never be the cause of all this trouble."[62] Evelyn was, in fact, petite: Viola Rodgers reported that she was under five feet tall and weighed ninety-two pounds.[63] But in these accounts, and many others like it, Evelyn appears not just as small but as a child, a passive victim who cannot be held responsible for what happened. Later, Dix expressed this view more baldly: "Whatever her faults, she has never had a chance, poor little plaything of fate."[64] This sexless vision positioned the child-woman as object of desire, perversely made more desirable by her own *lack* of desire.

But Evelyn's commanding performance in court belied this innocent image. The reporters' fascination went beyond the incongruity of her schoolgirl demeanor and sleazy past. It was not just her story but the way she told the story: articulately, precisely, calmly. How could this small person—a "plaything of fate" blown about by a bad world—remain so tough on the witness stand? Her self-control inspired almost as much comment as her appearance. Reporters contrasted Harry's display of feeling with Evelyn's self-possession. The same article that noted the "great gulping sounds" Harry made while Evelyn described her first sexual encounter also observed that she "never once lost control of herself."[65] Although William Hoster, in a passage already noted, made much of an apparent breakdown during an early phase of cross-examination, most reporters marveled at Evelyn's lack of emotion. After days of testifying, even while answering hostile questions from the prosecutor, she showed few visible signs of distress.

The sob sisters found Evelyn's stoicism as remarkable as their male colleagues did. "She held her self-control wonderfully for a time," noted Black. "Clenching her little fists, she had herself go on and on to the very depths of horror."[66] The paucity of Evelyn's tears contradicted the repeated assertions of her childlike nature. Her self-possession also stood in ironic contrast to the bodily control she had lost to the men in her life. Moreover, her ability to suppress her tears during painful self-disclosure contradicted the feminine stereotype used to brand the newswomen as sob sisters. To some, then, her self-control was itself suspicious. At least one writer faulted Evelyn for her composure. Calling her "extraordinarily shallow," Emma H. deZouche condemned her: "Evelyn Thaw is not shameless; she is deficient in sensibility."[67] That Evelyn could face all those men without visible embarrassment proved her moral failings. DeZouche's review of Evelyn's testimony, vicious as it was, accurately observed that Evelyn defied standards of middle-class femininity. Objectified by every newspaper in the city, alternately presented as the consummate sex kitten and the virgin wronged, Evelyn confounded the categories. No matter how often they called her little and flowerlike, she presented a hard-edged publicity problem for the sob sisters. Somehow, the newswomen had to acknowledge that, girlishness aside, Evelyn was not passive; this object of desire had her own desires as well. The sob sisters' male counterparts faced this same problem, of course, but with much less at stake: the newsmen were not identified with Evelyn in the same visceral way.

This struggle to represent Evelyn is especially clear in the accounts of the moment on the witness stand when, according to most reports, Evelyn's poise utterly deserted her. In a last-ditch attempt to unsettle the star witness during cross-examination, the prosecutor read aloud from her diary. The diary had been obtained from Evelyn's mother, who was cooperating with the prosecution. (Evelyn was estranged from her mother, in part because Harry's lawyers had insinuated that her mother had prostituted her to White.) The prosecutor selected a diary passage—reprinted the next day by every newspaper in the city—drawn from Evelyn's observations of her classmates at a school she attended briefly when she was in her teens. It suggests that young Evelyn harbored ambitions that went beyond the domestic sphere:

> A girl who has always been good and never had a word of scandal breathed about her is fortunate in more ways than one.
>
> These girls are all just that kind. They have been kept from the world all their lives and know very little of the mean side of it. And then, on the other hand, there is not one of them who will ever be "anything." And by "anything" I mean just that. They will perhaps be good wives and mothers and die good wives and mothers. Most people would say, What could be better? But whether it is ambition or foolishness, I want to be a good actress first.[68]

Hoping to embarrass Evelyn, the prosecutor had chosen a passage that struck at the heart of her witness-stand persona as a dutiful wife who would sacrifice her reputation for her husband. The diary documented the teenaged Evelyn's critique of the societal expectations for women that the witness-stand Evelyn was striving to fulfill. It proved not just her awareness that "most people" believed nothing could be better than for a woman to die a good wife and mother, but that she knowingly resisted the prescription. When she writes of her classmates, "There is not one of them who will ever be 'anything,'" she means that they will not be anything *except* wives and mothers, equating traditional womanhood with achieving nothing. By invading Evelyn's privacy, the prosecutor exposed her as a woman who cared more about having a career than being a wife and mother. It was that much better that the career Evelyn had chosen was acting, since this ambition could be used to discredit her testimony as a nice bit of stage work. *Had* she become "a good actress first"?

The tactic worked. After days of trying, the prosecutor succeeded in forcing Evelyn into an involuntary revelation. Under the front-page headline "Witness Blushes for First Time in Her Six Days of Testimony," the *New York Times* coverage opened by reprinting the quoted diary passage. Then the reporter gleefully described Evelyn's reaction, repeating that the witness "blushed for the first time during the six days she has been on the witness stand. The soft, ivory tint of Evelyn Nesbit Thaw's face became suffused with a delicate pink, which gradually deepened on the cheeks to a blush. She had not expected a disclosure of the secrets of her own mind and heart as a schoolgirl."[69] Building on Evelyn's confessed acting ambition, the reporter describes her courtroom appearance as if she were in costume, "still garbed as a schoolgirl and affecting a childish lisp." He juxtaposes the outfit and voice to her blush, a physical response over which Evelyn apparently has no control. The blush, then, becomes a visible corollary to "the secrets of her own mind and heart"; it authenticates the diary's sentiments and belies the innocence suggested by Evelyn's dress and manner.[70] More important, the blush authenticates Evelyn's desire, disavowing her child-woman role: she is no longer the sexual object made more enticing by the absence of her own desires. The blush reveals not just her personal ambitions but that she is self-aware enough to be ashamed of them.

Samuel Hopkins Adams, writing for the *World,* also noted that Evelyn responded to the diary "with a distinct reddening of the cheeks." Like the *Times* reporter, he interpreted this uncharacteristic lapse as deeply telling. "It was the blush of authorship," Adams wrote, "and it was, I believe, the first weakness of the sort that the witness had evinced at all. The most distressing parts of her testimony had brought no blood to her face—only given her a waxy pallor."[71] Evelyn's blush—an uncontrollable sign of physical discomfort, a bodily betrayal of sorts—appeared not when she described waking up disoriented in White's bedroom, not when she rejected the prosecutor's insinuation that she had had an abortion, and not when she denied that Harry had stripped her naked and whipped her in an Austrian castle. Rather, she blushed over her own written words, over her professed desire to be something other than a wife and mother. When Adams calls it "the blush of authorship," he imagines Evelyn not as a bashful writer but as a woman whose own body has betrayed her duplicity. Stressing her surprise at the diary's appearance in court and assuming that Evelyn could not blush on purpose, Adams juxtaposes the crimson truth of her worldly ambitions with her lily-white performance of innocence.

Male- and female-authored articles diverge more distinctly in their coverage of Evelyn's blush than in any other part of the trial. The sob sisters refused to gush over this testimony as their male colleagues had. Less eager to crow over a young girl's privately documented career ambitions, more sensitive to the blush of authorship that might appear on their own faces, they downplayed the diary's significance. Dix wrote that Evelyn's cross-examination "was brought to a dramatic and pathetic close by the foolish introduction of her schoolgirl diary" and called it "a quaint and rather piteous human document."[72] Here, youthful ambition appears natural, not pathological. "Though Mr. Jerome [the district attorney] read the slangy passages of this interesting human document with as insinuating an emphasis as his varied voice could summon," Greeley-Smith reported, "the worst interpretation that Mrs. Thaw's worst enemy could place upon it is that at sixteen her view of life was, as the New York vernacular phrases it, 'hip.'"[73] The newswomen defended Evelyn's right to express herself without restraint in her own diary and scoffed at the portentous tone of the newsmen's coverage. Their response, calibrated to sidestep debate over the propriety of Evelyn's ambitions, was indulgent, understanding, sisterly. In deflecting attention from the revelation of Evelyn's desires, they deflected attention from their own.

The blush of authorship resonates along racial as well as gender boundaries, marking Evelyn's place in a racial and moral hierarchy at least as directly as the countless references to the pallor of her skin.[74] Thus, even at her most potentially transgressive moment, Evelyn's blush articulates her racial whiteness and links her to a cultural tradition that intertwined female beauty, purity, and whiteness.[75] The sob sisters, tied to Evelyn's whiteness through their own photographs and through the logic of bodily reciprocity, also benefit from the implicit bond between whiteness and morality. The trial testimony itself contradicted that link, of course. For weeks on end, a white man was presented as a sexual predator of the worst order. And this transgressor was not just any white man but Stanford White, a native-born European American whose family had been established in America for more than two hundred years.[76] Indeed, the suggestion that white women had *no* adequate protectors may have fueled the intense national interest in the case. But the Thaw trial reports, preoccupied with evaluating Evelyn's enigmatic performance and Harry's role as defender of female virtue, acknowledged no such contradiction. Certainly the newswomen, whose whiteness allowed them some much-needed room to maneuver in the male-dominated courtroom, did not seek to dismantle their own racial privilege. They let it stand.

Called for Jury Duty: On the Judgment of Women

By bringing the blush of authorship into the courtroom, the sob sisters inevitably engaged fundamental questions about how the public sphere was constituted and who should be allowed to operate within it. Barred from being jurors, the sob sisters nevertheless judged the evidence.[77] Thus the question "What if women *were* jurors?" demanded to be asked and answered. Early in the trial, Clara Morris confesses that she is grateful the defendant is a man. Ever sensitive to the male gaze, Morris asks, "When was a female defendant ever tried by twelve of her equals?"[78] Certainly the En-

lightenment ideal of the civil public—where individual interests are es-
chewed in favor of interests that can claim universality—sought to exclude
the emotional baggage that women, whether burdened by natural inclination or societal expectation, brought into court. But if women were already interpreting the trial for the public, why couldn't they interpret it for
the law?

The few times when the newswomen defend their presence in court and
acknowledge the controversy surrounding their trial coverage, they take
on just such concerns. Some argue for women's judgment as an alternative mode of justice, while others minimize the threat women pose to the
disinterested ideal championed by male-dominated courts of law. Beatrice
Fairfax employs a conventional line of defense, arguing that the newswomen's excessive sympathy was a badge of honor: "The little handful of
women journalists who sit together in one corner of the courtroom have
been dubbed the 'pity platoon' by some scoffer who wrote better than he
knew. The 'pity platoon' they may be, and all honor to them that they are
women first and writers after."[79] Fairfax reassures her readers that the
newswomen have not abandoned traditional sex roles. Her blithe formula
supports the logic of the "sob sister" label by representing the newswomen's sex roles as necessarily prior to and more important than their
professional roles. Equating a capacity for pity with honorable womanhood, Fairfax imagines the female writers as release valves for human emotion in court. Shunted into one corner of the courtroom, Fairfax's pity
platoon feels a great deal but takes up little space. Thus the sob sisters
promise to humanize the law without disrupting the male hierarchy that
governs the public sphere.

Not all of the newswomen take such a safe route, however. Despite the
myriad ways in which they were aligned with Evelyn, several journalists invoked a model of public service that proved more soldier-like than sisterly.
In one of the most illuminating defenses, Patterson argues for the value of
the women reporters' emotional contributions as writers *and* potential jurors. Her article, "Women Juries in Future Foreseen as Real Necessity," performs an extraordinary balancing act of advocating women's public roles
while apologizing for them (see figure 10). By disavowing her role as an
embodiment of the mass public's interest, Patterson also writes *against* the
spectacle that was defining sob-sisterhood. She begins by acknowledging
the controversy in general terms, suggesting that her male colleagues resented the presence of newswomen: "Perhaps by reason of their presence
the certain male representatives were relegated to less comfortable seats.
Perhaps that presence suppressed a tendency to too candid comment. Perhaps it represented to the caviliers [sic] a lessening of their revenue." Im-

WOMEN JURIES IN FUTURE FORESEEN AS REAL NECESSITY

By ADA PATTERSON.

Copyright, 1907, by American-Journal-Examiner.

Soon after the Thaw trial began it became clear that certain newspapers, or certain male representatives of those newspapers, or both, resented the presence of women in that portion of the courtroom reserved for the writers of special articles on the case.

Perhaps by reason of their presence the certain male representatives were relegated to less comfortable seats. Perhaps that presence suppressed a tendency to candid comment. Perhaps it represented to the cavilers a lessening of their own revenue.

When Judge Fitzgerald issued his order that because of the nature of the evidence no women except those employed on the newspapers should be admitted to the courtroom there were some queries as to why even these women should be admitted.

By his act in admitting them Judge Fitzgerald reflected the spirit of his time. That spirit is that woman must shoulder her burden and march on uncomplainingly on all the forced marches of life. If woman has ever been a mere kitten of humanity that time has passed. She is a soldier in the army of life.

Of the handful of women in the so-called royal box of the yellow walled courtroom there is not one who, if asked whether she wanted to attend the Thaw trial, would not have answered 'No.' Of course, they would rather have gone shopping or to a matinee or for a drive in the park. Or, if thoughts of impending rent and grocer and dressmaker bills required the active pen, they would have preferred to write of the latest lace bodice or to construct a tea table dialogue.

ADA PATTERSON.

Figure 10. In this carefully argued article, Ada Patterson suggests that it is women's duty—as journalists and, someday, she hopes, as jurors —to meet the public demand for the "feminine angle of vision." (Ada Patterson, "Women Juries in Future Foreseen as Real Necessity," *New York Evening Journal*, February 16, 1907. General Research Division, The New York Public Library, Astor, Lenox, and Tilden Foundations.)

plying that the objections to women's presence are inherently selfish, she suggests that the male reporters wanted only more space for themselves, more freedom to make inappropriate remarks, and more money. Patterson also acknowledges the strength of the public disapproval, however. She notes that some people disagreed with the judge's decision to allow any women into court, including those employed by newspapers, and she delicately defends the judge's ruling: "By his act in admitting [newswomen] Judge Fitzgerald reflected the spirit of his time. That spirit is that woman must shoulder her burden and march on uncomplainingly on all the forced marches of life. If woman has ever been a mere kitten of humanity that time has passed. She is a soldier in the army of life." By linking women's public roles to the "spirit of time," Patterson recognizes women's rise in power as a critical feature of modernity itself.[80] At the same time, her martial metaphors contradict the assumption that the newswomen's curiosity was idle and their writing trivial.

Adopting a self-consciously masculine model, Patterson insists that the newswomen are performing an unpleasant public duty. Stressing its disagreeable nature, she distinguishes the reporters from the casual female spectators who were accused of frivolity and voyeurism. She even insists that the newswomen would prefer to avoid the trial altogether: "Of the

handful of women in the so-called royal box of the yellow-walled courtroom there is not one who, if asked whether she wanted to attend the Thaw
trial, would not have answered 'No.' Of course, they would rather have
gone shopping or to a matinee or for a drive in the park." Reminding her
readers that the newswomen enjoy typical feminine pastimes, Patterson
feminizes her colleagues while turning the charge of frivolity on its head.
In her formulation, the sob sisters have proved their seriousness by forcing themselves to attend the trial, by *not* going shopping or to a matinee.
She elaborates on the military analogy: "Good soldiers they, when ordered
to serve in the Thaw trial they obeyed. The managing editors who, in planning the handling of the big trial as generals plan their campaigns, assigned women to the field, took no arbitrary step, obeyed no erratic
impulse, made no experiment. They supplied what the public demands,
and the public demands that women shall supplement men in the world's
work." Patterson characterizes the newswomen as patriots serving the interests of the republic, not the morbid curiosity of the masses. The sob sisters are "good soldiers" who—she is careful here—are "*supplementing* men
in the world's work." She then offers a broad vision of women's influence
on the public sphere, prophesying that women will help to transform the
American justice system. Refusing to duck the thorny questions raised by
the sob sisters' presence in court, she casts them as the logical forerunners
of women jurors. "The judgment of women writers is the nearest present
day approach to that actuality of the future, the women's jury," she writes.
"The public wants the individual feminine angle of vision on the Thaw
case. The world has plenty of cumbersome masculine logic in the admin-
istration of its affairs. What it needs . . . is the logic plus a woman's insight."[81] Patterson has taken Fairfax's formula to the next step. "Woman's
insight" is so valuable, she argues, that it should be fully integrated into the
public sphere. It is emphatically women's duty, she insists, to meet the public's need for the "feminine angle of vision."

   Greeley-Smith took a slightly different approach when she defended the
sob sisters' reputation for sympathy. In a tart response to the critics, she reminds her readers that the American justice system requires defendants to
be presumed innocent. "Yet," she wrote, "women who have ventured to do
this, who have given young Thaw the benefit of this provision which the
sternest juryman has to observe, and written about him as a presumably
innocent and very unfortunate young man, have been termed contemp-
tuously the 'sympathy squad' by persons who seem to consider that the
whole duty of newspaper writing consists in securing a talesman's [poten-
tial juror's] middle initial."[82] Here Greeley-Smith mocks the obsessive attention to detail and the worship of objectivity that helped give rise to the

realist aesthetic. Moreover, she insists that the newswomen were doing what "the sternest juryman" had to do: giving Harry the benefit of the doubt. She aligns the sob sisters' sympathy for Harry with the traditions of the American justice system and even suggests that male reporters' pursuit of the disinterested ideal has kept them from recognizing the complex emotional reality of the trial. She also cites Harry, not Evelyn, as the primary object of the newswomen's sympathy.

Because it was Harry, after all, who was officially on trial, the newswomen's judgment of *him* offered the best glimpse of how women, given the chance, might perform on a jury. And the sob sisters judged Harry very gently indeed. Despite—in part because of—their bodily reciprocity with Evelyn, the women writers ultimately professed more sympathy for her violent husband than for her. They made him into the hero of the trial, refracting their identification with Evelyn into sympathy for Harry. The newswomen thus reinstated the white man as the legitimate protector of white women and of the nation as a whole. They demonized Stanford White, while holding up Harry as a good man whose murderous act was best interpreted as rightful vengeance, even a necessary purification of a corrupt society.[83] They embraced Harry's cause with disturbing enthusiasm, presenting him as a hero for marrying Evelyn despite her promiscuous past and glossing over Harry's own promiscuity and his class privilege. They obfuscated his abuse of Evelyn, suppressing evidence of his violent behavior and drug addiction in their reports. Worse, they normalized his obsession with Evelyn's "ruin." They let pass unremarked the disturbing evidence that Harry had forced Evelyn to retell her story of coerced sex again and again. Indeed, the newspapers, by repeatedly retelling Evelyn's story, encouraged readers to identify not with Evelyn but with Harry; they assumed that readers wanted to hear the story as frequently, and as fully, as Harry did.

Treated to a courtroom drama that vividly documented the systematic exploitation of (white) women by (white) men, the sob sisters blinked. Rather than negotiate the complex terrain of early-twentieth-century sexual politics, they cast Harry as the heroic avenger in a seduction plot. Granted *most* news reports, not just the women's, cast Harry as the heroic avenger. But given the newswomen's demonstrated willingness to challenge norms of female behavior, their interpretations of Harry's actions are strikingly conventional. Black wrote that if she had a husband on the jury, she would sue him for divorce if, after hearing Evelyn's story, he voted to send Harry to the electric chair.[84] Other newswomen embraced Harry's cause with similar enthusiasm.

Positioned on the front lines of women's journalism, Patterson's "good soldiers" picked their battles carefully. They were not about to challenge men's role as protectors of women. Nor did they shy away from generalizing about women's essentially emotional nature and consequently impaired ability to reason. In their judgments of Harry, the sob sisters often reinforced damaging stereotypes. In a story headlined "Thaw Would Be Acquitted by Woman Jury, Says Dorothy Dix," the subheadings say it all: "Killing through Jealousy Appeals to Female Heart" and "Emotions Would Almost Entirely Govern a Decision by Fair Sex." Women, according to Dix, were incapable of achieving a disinterested stance: "If a woman jury acquitted Thaw—and I think it would—it would do more so on its emotions. Whether it would be more emotional than a man jury we cannot tell until we hear the verdict of the man jury."[85] Here we find some skepticism, perhaps even an incipient critique, of the legal system's claims to disinterestedness. Having categorized women's reasoning as emotional, Dix concludes by suggesting that men's reasoning may not be so different. Interestingly enough, in both of Thaw's trials, "the verdict of the man jury" supported her suggestion. Thirty years before a woman would be allowed to serve on a jury in New York, the male jurors in the Thaw case followed the sob sisters' lead. Thaw was never convicted.

⁂

Although the original sob sisters, like most of their fellow reporters, did not go on to write successful fiction, they helped to forge an emotion-bound template that shaped perceptions of literary labor long after the Thaw trial ended. By accepting the sentimental call to sympathize, the newswomen undertook a necessary but largely thankless task. In a study of nineteenth-century adultery cases, Laura Hanft Korobkin argues that although sentimental conventions often shape legal discourse, trial transcripts, with their contradictory assertions and moral complexity, can never create wholly sentimental narratives.[86] Korobkin's point is particularly relevant to the Thaw trial because so many newspapers printed complete trial transcripts in addition to the standard coverage. Readers had access to a broad range of information about the case, including competing interpretations of Harry's (and Evelyn's) behavior. This profusion of information made the newswomen's roles as sentimental advocates both more crucial and more vexed. Presiding over an overwhelming amount of information, they promised to guide readers through the morass of data.

Women reporters were called upon to mediate a violent, contradictory narrative, and their bodies, along with their words, helped to serve their ends. When the trial narrative threatened to veer out of control, disrupting too many cherished assumptions about gender, race, or national identity, the sob sisters offered a soothing vision based not just on their reports but on the visible combination of their whiteness and femaleness. By managing "the blush of authorship" so successfully, the newswomen achieved status as proponents of sentimentalism in an increasingly heterogeneous and fragmented modern world. As many scholars have noted, nineteenth-century sentimental narratives tended to encourage readers to identify with the sufferings of the disempowered, often enslaved persons, women, even children. With chilling success, the Thaw trial coverage adapted sentimental conventions to inspire compassion for the sufferings of Harry Thaw, a rich white man whose own father had so little confidence in him that he changed his will so Harry's entire inheritance would go into a trust fund controlled by his mother.[87] The sob sisters were not the only—or even the primary—architects of this spectacle of sentiment. Nevertheless, they became its standard-bearers. In the process, they wrote themselves into national prominence even as they wrote themselves out of literary history.

A Reporter-Heroine's Evolution

enry James created one of American fiction's most vivid images
of the female reporter in the character of Henrietta Stackpole,
Isabel Archer's intrepid friend in *The Portrait of a Lady* (1881).
An American journalist whose letters for the *New York Interviewer* are "uni-
versally quoted," Henrietta has come to Europe to write a series of letters
from abroad. Single and without family money, Henrietta uses her earn-
ings to pay the school bills for three of her widowed sister's children.[1]
Acting at various points as Isabel's foil, moral touchstone, and comic relief, Henrietta appears especially brash among the contemplative parlor-
dwellers of James's novel. She writes to Isabel immediately upon her arrival
in England:

> "Here I am, my lovely friend," Miss Stackpole wrote; "I managed to get off
> at last. I decided only the night before I left New York—the *Interviewer* hav-
> ing come round to my figure. I put a few things into a bag, like a veteran jour-
> nalist, and came down to the steamer in a street-car. Where are you and
> where can we meet? I suppose you're visiting some castle or other and have
> already acquired the correct accent. . . . Do appoint a meeting as quickly as
> you can. . . . [Y]ou know everything interests me and I wish to see as much
> as possible of the inner life." (78)

The letter expresses frankness, easy mobility, and professional confidence,
as well as Henrietta's cavalier assumption that the "inner life" will yield
readily to her inquiring gaze. By giving her the feminine version of his own

94

name and having this "literary lady," as Ralph Touchett calls her, profess a desire to see "the inner life," James invites a wry comparison between author and character (78–79).

Scholars have long noted the self-referential potential of James's literary lady, but they have rarely taken her seriously as a figure for the author. A bit player who ends up taking up a surprising amount of space, Henrietta is often discussed in terms that echo James's own dismissive commentary on her, as a character who somehow got away from him—particularly when he revised *Portrait* for the New York edition, some twenty-seven years after its original publication.[2] In this chapter I consider precisely how and why Henrietta Stackpole got away from her author. In the process, I argue that the reporter-heroine in American fiction has gotten away from literary history as well—and that James's fascination and frustration with Henrietta evoke literary culture's vexed relationship with newspaperwomen in general. The complexity and significance of that relationship becomes evident when we place Henrietta in the context of other representations of female reporters and read them against the historical backdrop of real-life newswomen. The history of James's reporter-heroine spans the critical years in the rise of the Girl Reporter: he finished the first edition of *Portrait* at a time when women were just beginning to enter newsrooms in significant numbers, only a few years before Nellie Bly staged her first stunt, and he revised it at the same time the sob sisters were reporting on Harry Thaw's murder trial.

In this chapter I show not only that the evolution of Henrietta's character registers the changing position of newspaperwomen in American culture, but also that her status as an authorial figure, as a mocking reflection of James himself, demands more attention. In this, Henrietta's case mirrors that of other newspaperwomen in fiction, who have rarely been taken seriously as figures of authorship, whether imagined by male or by female writers. This New Woman figure updated the nineteenth-century model of the popular female author, assuming both the burden and the power of writing for the masses. But the reporter-heroine's mad dash into public consciousness has attracted little interest from literary scholars, in part because, at least from the standpoint of literary history, she had bad timing. She fell on the wrong side of a growing cultural divide in an era marked by anxious attempts to distinguish high art from mass culture, at a moment when women writers were seeking recognition as artists more aggressively than ever before.[3]

The reporter-heroine's male counterparts have not suffered similar neglect. A rich critical tradition has analyzed depictions of male journalists in order to gain insight into authorial identity, the modern phenomenon of publicity, and the evolving relationship between literature and mass culture.[4] Henry James's responses to mass culture, particularly his antipathy toward the popular press, have received intense scholarly scrutiny.[5] Although James frequently condemned the press as vulgar and superficial, he did not simply reject new forms of publicity, critics such as Richard Salmon, Ian F. A. Bell, and Thomas Strychacz have argued. Rather, James drew upon those forms in his fiction, representing the complex dynamics of publicity and seeking new possibilities for making meaning in a publicity-driven world.[6] Readings of James's fictional newsmen—Matthias Pardon in *The Bostonians* (1886), George Flack in *The Reverberator* (1888), and Howard Bight in "The Papers" (1903)—dominate these studies.[7]

Yet critics have long noted that the inspiration for *The Reverberator,* James's most extended fictional treatment of newspaper publicity, came from a young woman who wrote for a newspaper. Mary Marcy McClellan, daughter of the Civil War general George B. McClellan, caused a scandal when she published a gossipy letter in the *New York World* (November 14, 1886) about a family with whom she was staying in Venice. James wrote that he was "struck" not just by the letter itself but by "the strange *typicality* of the whole thing." He went on to note, "One can't say a pretty and 'nice' American girl wouldn't do such a thing, simply because there was a Miss McC. who did it." In the frequently quoted passage that immediately follows this claim, James suggests that a novelist must find a way to depict "the invasion, the impudence and shamelessness, of the newspaper and the interviewer, the devouring *publicity* of life, the extinction of all sense between public and private."[8] Although many scholars cite the second part of the passage, in which James calls upon novelists to respond to "the invasion" of journalism, few acknowledge its proximity to the claim about American girls. Yet James identified "the devouring *publicity* of life" with the "typicality" of the nice American girl writing for a newspaper. Attending to women's journalism helps to explain why, when James revised *Portrait,* he made a point of making Henrietta less likeable and her career more offensive.[9] Although he did have real-life models for his original lady-correspondent—Kate Field and Constance Fenimore Woolson, among others[10]—opportunities for women in journalism grew substantially in the years after *Portrait* was first published.[11] By the time James revised *Portrait,* the Girl Reporter had arrived.

It wasn't simply the Girl Reporter's arrival that bothered James, however. It was what she had to do to get there. By 1908, as we have already seen, women reporters were no longer easily dismissed in the culture at large; far from being quaint anomalies, they had become a national spectacle in their own right. Anchored in their physicality and expected to express emotion on cue, they were deeply implicated in the mass media's attempts to court new readers. Their strategies, as we have seen, required them to manage their self-representations very carefully. Because the publicity that surrounded newspaperwomen was so often sexually charged, they sought to project an image of sexual inviolability, even while placing themselves in situations that posed possible sexual threats. Even reform-minded African American newspaperwomen, who spurned the masquerades and emotionalism of stunt reporters and sob sisters, found it difficult to avoid being represented in sexualized terms.[12] Meanwhile, a good proportion of the articles written by white women for mainstream newspapers had become, more or less explicitly, a commentary on themselves and how they managed their own reporting.[13] Although their topics ranged from accused murderers to the plight of the urban poor, their primary object of inquiry remained themselves. Thus they promoted intensely personal reporting of the news through a medium that was growing more and more impersonal. And, in their boldest move, they cast themselves as intimates of their mass readership, placing an extraordinary—indeed, an impossible—burden on their own claims of representativeness.

To be intimate with the masses was to manufacture a kind of mass-produced promiscuity that endlessly circled back on itself. As the white newspaperwoman's body became increasingly implicated in her own stories, her intimacy with her readers demanded more and more of her own physical experience: her body had to serve as a catchall receptacle of public feeling, public interest, and public passion. Her reported self, in other words, promised to embody the public, to manifest its needs and desires in visible form through her own corporeality. But how could she achieve such a thing when the American public was so vast, so heterogeneous, so fractured? She could not, of course. Instead, the newspaperwoman came to embody that "devouring publicity" itself. She personified not the disparate individuals who made up the mass public, but rather a system of mass-produced spectacle, the very dynamic that made her career possible.

This dynamic, a subtext in the narratives of real-life newspaperwomen, inevitably influenced fictional portrayals of them. James originally cast Henrietta Stackpole as a fair-minded investigator, an agent of what Jürgen Habermas would call critical publicity.[14] Her invasions of privacy are as disinterested as they are indelicate. By the time James revisited Henrietta's characterization for the 1908 edition, however, mainstream newspaperwomen had become so visibly identified with manipulative publicity that James recoiled from his own lady correspondent with a combination of horror and fascination. That he had presented a newspaperwoman, even noncommittally, as a reflection of his own professional identity only intensified that recoil.

Henrietta and Her Evil Twin

Given the rapid changes in newswomen's status—their rising number, their spectacle-based reporting, and their special appeal to the mass public—it is hardly surprising that there are really *two* Henrietta Stackpoles. When James substantially revised *Portrait* for the 1908 edition, he altered her character significantly. The changes, scholars have long noted, make Henrietta less sympathetic; Nina Baym aptly calls it "the systematic vulgarization of Henrietta Stackpole."[15] In both versions, Isabel views Henrietta as "an example of useful activity," a "model," and "proof that a woman might suffice to herself and be happy" (55). In the revised edition, however, Henrietta is so belittled that her status as role model becomes ridiculous, her friendship with Isabel almost inexplicable. Ultimately, James remakes Henrietta as inhuman, as more of a publicity engine than a person.

Changes in American journalism had made untenable the terms through which Henrietta had originally been conceived, as a bossy but essentially genteel character, a woman who barges in on others' private lives but who blushes and nearly cries when Isabel accuses her of not respecting people's privacy. In the 1881 version, when Isabel tells Henrietta that she has "no sense of privacy," Henrietta responds, with dignity, "You do me a great injustice. . . . I have never written a word about myself!" (82). This funny and sweetly un-self-conscious Henrietta had grown irrelevant by 1908, and James apparently knew it. When Henrietta makes this remark in the earlier version, Isabel "marvelled more than ever at her inconsistency"; when Henrietta says the same thing in the later edition, Isabel "found her more than ever inconsequent" (82). The new Henrietta is inconsequential rather than provocatively inconsistent. Such revisions ring with defensiveness, almost as if the older James resented the character he had created and felt compelled to denigrate her, even at the expense of his own narrative.

Henrietta's larger role as a symbol of America in *The Portrait of a Lady* makes her devolution even more striking. A national cheerleader, she preaches the superiority of American men, American customs, American hotels. When Ralph criticizes Henrietta as "too personal," as the kind of person who "walks in without knocking at the door" (87), Isabel defends her friend by imagining Henrietta as the embodiment of the American nation. This often quoted passage suggests that James recognized that the struggle to define the "reporter in petticoats" had broad implications for national identity. In the 1881 version Isabel says of Henrietta, "There's something of the 'people' in her. . . . . [S]he's a kind of emanation of the great democracy—of the continent, the country, the nation. I don't say that she sums it all up, that would be too much to ask of her. But she suggests it, she reminds me of it" (87, 504). In the later version, this passage stands untouched except for the last line, which says that Henrietta "vividly figures" the great democracy instead of reminding Isabel of it (87), a slight change that bolsters Henrietta's status as national icon. Although there is no doubt that the figure of the spectacle-seeking newspaperwoman that James identified with "the devouring publicity of life" was racially white, it is worth noting that Isabel's description of Henrietta as a national icon endows her with a status similar to the one the black press accorded to African American newspaperwomen such as Ida B. Wells. A critical difference, however, is the nature of the public with which they were identified. The black press celebrated women journalists as representatives of an embattled counterpublic. But in the mainstream press to which James was responding, female reporters often appeared as vehicles of mass-market publicity, called to serve no higher cause than that of attracting attention from as many readers as possible.

James's revisions suggest that he recognized how the American woman journalist's symbolic power intensified in the decades between the two editions of *Portrait*. He emphasized Henrietta's iconic status even more when he revised Isabel's appreciation of "what stands behind" Henrietta. In 1881 Isabel declares, "I am immensely struck with her; not so much for herself as what stands behind her." In 1908 Isabel says instead, "I'm straightway convinced by *her;* not so much in respect to herself as in respect to what masses behind her" (88). In the revision, Isabel stresses both Henrietta's person (*her*) and "what masses behind her," a pun on the "masses" she represents. Isabel goes on to link her fondness for Henrietta and the "masses" to the American landscape itself in a striking passage that remains virtually the same in both editions: "I like the great country stretching away beyond the rivers and across the prairies, blooming and smiling and spreading till it stops at the green Pacific! A strong, sweet, fresh odour seems to rise from it, and Henrietta—pardon my simile—has something of that odour in her garments" (88). Isabel's enthusiasm for Henrietta, as Ralph immediately points out, expresses more about her own imagination than Henrietta herself. Yet this grand vision also acknowledges the reporter-heroine's escalating power. In 1881, after Isabel's speech, Ralph remarks that Henrietta is "decidedly fragrant." In 1908 he responds instead with "Henrietta . . . does smell of the Future—it almost knocks one down!" (88). The original Henrietta may have made Ralph's nose wrinkle, but the revised Henrietta threatens to knock him off his feet.

James's distaste for journalism is well known—after all, in a 1905 speech he characterized newspapers as a threat to American civilization. His revisions of Henrietta, however, constitute more than simply another instance of what one scholar refers to as James's "fear and loathing of journalism."[16] Baym concludes that the new Henrietta is most likely a casualty of James's "growing absorption with the inner life," which "made a character who was engrossed in the world of work and action appear inconsequential."[17] Some recent interpreters disagree, arguing for Henrietta's significance as an alternative model of womanhood and even marriage. These newer readings, however, are so committed to advancing Henrietta as a positive force that they tend to downplay the pejorative effect of the 1908 revisions on her character.[18] They cannot account adequately for James's striking hostility toward Henrietta. She is called a "monster" twice in both editions—first by Ralph in jest, later by Gilbert Osmond in earnest.[19] But only in the 1908 edition does she come close to living up to the label.

Despite the revised novel's insistence on Henrietta's inconsequence, she continues to turn up at critical moments in the life of Isabel, James's beloved heroine. Gilbert's failure to find Henrietta amusing gives Isabel her first glimpse of why she should not have married him. His judgment of Henrietta makes Isabel "secretly disappointed," and she wonders if her husband's sense of humor is "defective" (328). It's also worth recalling that Henrietta literally walks away with the novel's final lines, after James has left Isabel standing with her hand on the latch of Gardencourt's door. While the ever-insistent Henrietta gets the last word in both editions, she becomes truly insufferable in 1908. In the earlier edition, after Henrietta delivers the news to the desolate Caspar Goodwood that Isabel has left for Rome, the novel closes with a suggestive exchange:

> "Look here, Mr. Goodwood," she said; "just you wait!"
> On which he looked up at her.

In the revision, James elaborates on the final sentence fragment at Henrietta's expense:

> "Look here, Mr. Goodwood," she said; "just you wait!"
> On which he looked up at her—but only to guess, from her face, with a revulsion, that she simply meant he was young. She stood shining at him with

that cheap comfort, and it added, on the spot, thirty years to his life. She
walked him away with her, however, as if she had given him now the key to
patience.

This revised ending is often read as a sign that James was trying to quash
Goodwood's hopes more thoroughly. However the revisions may change
readers' perception of Goodwood's chances for a reunion with Isabel, one
thing seems clear: this baggy ending sacrifices an elegant conclusion for
the sake of another set of jabs at Henrietta. It is she, not Goodwood, who
is quashed, and the narrator's insults are not subtle. Evidence from James's
notebooks suggests that he always intended to end with an expression of
Henrietta's optimism. In the last scene, James wrote, Goodwood would see
"Henrietta who has the last word—utters the last line of the story: a characteristic characterization of Isabel."[20] But recognizing James's original intention does not resolve the questions raised by this scene, which stresses
not Henrietta's optimism but her incompetence and obnoxiousness. The
Henrietta who gets the last word in 1908, of course, is not the same character who gets the last word in 1881. In the revised novel, she has become
a woman who can add thirty years to a man's life with a single look. A survey of the newspaperwoman in fiction at the turn of the century, followed
by a closer examination of the revised Henrietta's "look"—both her appearance and her gaze—will help us to understand why.

Newspaper Fictions

Writers with more humble literary aspirations than James shared his
conviction that "the devouring *publicity* of life" was a compelling subject for
fiction. As newspapers gained readers and reporters gained professional
status in American newsrooms, fictional journalists of both sexes appeared
more frequently. Celebrity reporter Richard Harding Davis has been credited with inventing the genre of the newsroom adventure tale in 1890 with
the popular "Gallegher: A Newspaper Story," which starred a fatherless
newsboy with a nose for news. Displaying quick wit, physical courage, and
perseverance, Davis's newsboy navigates an all-male fraternity of police of-
ficers, journalists, sportsmen, and cabbies in order to get his newspaper an
exclusive story and, at the same time, apprehend a notorious criminal in
the middle of a boxing match. At the end, the newsboy is rewarded with
the paternal affection of the managing editor.[21] "Gallegher" and similar
stories represent masculinity so self-consciously that literary historians
have interpreted the newspaper reporter as almost exclusively male.[22]

But at the turn of the century, female journalists appeared in many guises, from starring roles to sidekicks, in a range of texts, from self-consciously literary novels such as *Portrait* to serialized narratives designed for mass consumption.[23] In the opening scene of Jack London's "Amateur Night" (1901), an editor responds with exasperation to a young woman's pleas for advice on how to become a reporter: "I must inform you, my dear young lady, that there have been at least eighteen other aspiring young ladies here this week, and that I have not had the time to tell each and every one of them how."[24] In this depiction of a city editor besieged by female applicants, London acknowledges women's growing presence in newsrooms.

By the early 1900s, fictional newspaperwomen were common enough to inspire a backlash from media critics, who grumbled that the portrayals glamorized a brutal profession and gave young women unrealistic, even dangerous ambitions. "These newspaper women of fiction," complained Eleanor Hoyt in 1903, "are likely to put false notions into the head of the young person who comes up from Podunk to try newspaper work in a great city. If she has taken the careers of these heroines as her standard of measurement, she is doomed."[25] Doomsaying aside, a cursory survey of the era's women journalists suggests that Hoyt was right to suspect that fictional newspaperwomen were igniting the career ambitions of young readers. Journalist-turned-novelist Edna Ferber recalled her youthful dream of emulating the heroine of Miriam Michelson's novel *A Yellow Journalist*.[26] Reporter Lorena Hickok—who went on to cover national stories including the Lindbergh kidnapping—imitated the newswoman from Ferber's own early novel, *Dawn O'Hara* (1911), when she was starting out.[27] Elizabeth Jordan's *Tales of the City Room* (1898), a story collection chronicling the professional lives of a half-dozen newspaperwomen, was the favorite girlhood book of Mary Elizabeth Prim, a star *Boston Transcript* reporter of the 1930s.[28]

The phenomenon was not restricted to women, of course. Fictional depictions of newsmen inspired young men to try news writing, too, including H. L. Mencken, Jack London, Frank Norris, and Ernest Hemingway. Richard Harding Davis, famous not only as the author of "Gallegher" but also as a dashing war correspondent, made journalism appear both manly and glamorous. In his own experience and in his fiction, Davis's version of reporting required equal parts physical courage and dramatic flair. His charismatic model, however, has helped to obscure the reporter-heroines who existed alongside the reporter-heroes. The masculine reporter model was powerful, but in fiction, as in real life, courage and flair were not the exclusive property of male reporters. Mencken, after all, cited both "Gallegher" *and* Jordan's woman-centered *Tales of the City Room* as part of his journalistic education.[29]

Newspaper fiction included female characters such as Rhoda Massey, the irrepressible heroine of Miriam Michelson's gleefully over-the-top popular serial *A Yellow Journalist* (1905). Rhoda will do almost anything for a scoop: she masquerades as a prostitute to expose police corruption in Chinatown, poses as a nurse in the home of a wealthy family to solve a murder mystery, and persuades a sheriff to let her accompany a prisoner in danger of being lynched. When Ted, her journalistic rival and love interest, tells Rhoda that her aggressive reporting is unwomanly, she interrupts him to declare, "Oh, I'll be womanly to beat the band . . . after the paper's gone to press" (15–16). Later, after Ted has asked her to marry him, Rhoda becomes so involved in a developing story that she forgets a date with him. He responds angrily, and Rhoda concludes that she just doesn't have time to be engaged. As she begins to explain, however, she hears the newspaper's presses start to roll. Appalled, she turns her back on Ted. "Oh, stop them, stop them!" she sobs.[30] By having Rhoda sob to stop the presses, not to mourn a lover's loss, Michelson merges the image of the careerist New Woman with conventional characterizations of women's emotionality. This sprawling tale celebrates Rhoda's verve even while it suggests that her tactics are morally suspect. Although the narrative concludes with a chastened Rhoda walking home under the stars with Ted, Michelson requires only that Rhoda adjust—not sacrifice—her professional aspirations. Despite her occasional excesses, Rhoda comes across as an ideal New Woman, plucky, smart, introspective, and compassionate.

A peculiar balance of vulnerability and courage is characteristic of the newspaperwoman in fiction. If the reporter-heroine is often laughed at, she is also memorable and powerful. Self-sufficient and fun-loving, she proffers an appealing blend of sentimental realism; she is modern without being *too* modern. In Booth Tarkington's 1899 bestseller *Gentleman from Indiana*, the idealized heroine takes charge of her lover's newspaper when he is in the hospital. She starts by dusting the office, but goes on to improve the paper's content, expand its readership, and launch her lover's candidacy for public office.[31]

Most characterizations of newspaperwomen have more of an edge than Tarkington's, however, and reporter-heroines often become public spectacles themselves. In London's "Amateur Night," the young protagonist is so determined to get a newspaper job that she signs up for amateur night at a vaudeville theater, dons a wig, and takes a turn on the stage. Afterward, she writes a Sunday feature, earning the respect of a veteran newsman and an edge over her many female rivals. But not all stunts are so benign; fic-

tional newswomen are more likely than fictional newsmen to manipulate
sources emotionally. After tricking a sweet old lady into betraying her family secrets, for instance, Michelson's Rhoda Massey articulates self-hatred,
speaking of herself in the third person: "Such poor little fake pretenses,
these were of saucy, dashing Miss Massey, and black with deceit! Her smart
little lies were cheap, detestable. Her courage was brazen."[32] Rhoda eventually rallies and is even allowed to make up for her deception, but not
before Michelson has dramatized some of the damage caused by her
scheming female reporter, who does not hesitate to strike a pose to get a
scoop.

Gertrude Atherton's *Patience Sparhawk and Her Times* (1897) similarly
celebrates and denigrates the spectacular bent of women's newspaper reporting. When Patience, the brilliant heroine, resolves to become a reporter to escape a bad marriage, she performs so well that she is awarded
her own column in a matter of weeks.[33] By the end of the novel, however,
she is no longer writing sensational stories; she is starring in them. Accused
of poisoning her husband, Patience is tried for murder and sentenced to
death in the electric chair. Her name, face, fashion choices, and romantic
mistakes become the stuff of headlines, and she loses control over the publicity she once managed so effectively. Enmeshed in a public nightmare,
Atherton's heroine is victimized by the sensationalism that helped to establish her career.[34]

Writing Professions: The Journalist as Author

Whether real or imagined, both male and female journalists held an uncertain status in fin-de-siècle literary culture. Some scholars would insist
that this popular model of authorship, sprung from a profession in which
writing can have only ephemeral value, could never be *literary* at all. In
some sense, they would be right. Many authors and critics continued to
sneer at the commercial impulses and deadline demands of newspaper
work, even as they professed to value newspaper reporters' access to "the
real." Depictions of newswomen, like those of newsmen, were invested with
their authors' ambivalence about journalism as a writing profession. Often
written by former or active reporters, newspaper novels depict journalists
alternately thrilled by the adrenaline rush of writing on deadline and alien-
ated by the job's relentless demands.[35] A lingering wish to recapture the
reporter's easy access to a large readership often haunts fiction authored
by former journalists, who have given up a guaranteed audience of readers to pursue self-directed creative work. Even when authors recognize re-

porting as a legitimate profession, they cling to the model of the newsroom as a place of literary apprenticeship, a school from which writers must graduate or be doomed to mediocrity.

The most admiring characterizations of journalists, whether male or female, show them leaving the business, while the most damning show them committed to newspapers for life. In a typical portrayal, *A Modern Instance* (1881) by William Dean Howells follows the successful career of newsman Bartley Hubbard with unmistakable distaste. A telling exchange between Bartley and his naïve wife, Marcia, acknowledges Bartley's professional degradation directly. When Marcia tells him, "I want to believe in everything you do,—I want to be proud of it—," Bartley responds with cynicism "That will be difficult," suggested Bartley, with an air of thoughtful impartiality, "for the wife of a newspaper man."[36] Howells stresses Bartley's essential weakness and corruption; the ease with which he accepts moral compromise allows him to thrive as a journalist.

In a predictable split, most men who abandon journalism become fiction writers at the end of newspaper novels, while most female reporters marry.[37] Rarely are reporter-heroines invested with literary aspirations. In Michelson's *Yellow Journalist*, it is Rhoda's boyfriend, not Rhoda herself, who expresses a desire to write something other than news. In the final scene of "Miss Van Dyke's Best Story," the last story in Jordan's *Tales of the City Room* (1898), a newsman asks the reporter-heroine to "drop this" and marry him. As she ponders the proposal, she thinks to herself, "After all, a woman's place is in a home!" then responds, "I—I think I'll take the assignment."[38] The comment reframes marriage as a professional occupation, but the story's ending affirms unpaid domestic work as women's true business.

To discover what the reporter-heroine can tell us about American women and authorship in the late nineteenth and early twentieth centuries, then, we have to look at something more than whether female reporters in fiction are imagined as having literary potential. Generally, they were not—an unsurprising finding, since real-life newswomen were more tightly linked than newsmen to perceived threats to literary art: mass readership, sentimentality, sensationalism. Instead, we must consider how fictional treatments of newswomen depict the special representative burden of embodying publicity—the burden, that is, of being both distinctively female and distinctively emblematic of mass production. How can a newspaperwoman be simultaneously particular *and* generic, intimate yet impersonal, irreducible yet easily reproduced? The paradoxical demands that bedevil the girl reporter, of course, echo the conditions encountered by novelists in the early-twentieth-century literary marketplace. The problem was not easily resolved, as the case of Henry James's lady correspondent makes abundantly clear.

Back to James: Caging the Newspaperwoman

The changes in Henrietta's characterization in the 1908 edition of *Portrait* suggest that James wanted both to implicate her in and protect her from the sensational phenomenon of newspaperwomen. He adds comments that link Henrietta to journalistic spectacle and sensational crime, although she is writing travel reports, not covering tearful trials or lynchings, and certainly not performing any stunts. At the same time, he alters Henrietta's physical description, depicting her as machinelike and even as a newspaper itself. These changes deflect attention from her sexual attributes and isolate her from the sexualized publicity associated with stunt reporters, anti-lynching crusaders, and sob sisters. But they also treat her as a vehicle of publicity, equating her body with her text, representing her as a distressingly mechanical person who acts as both agent and object of the news.

In the revised novel, it is not just the narrator who likes Henrietta less. Everyone else does, too. Even Isabel cools.[39] Most often, the characters' dislike of Henrietta is expressed as an aversion to her penchant for self-exhibition—a penchant that did not even exist in the original edition. When Ralph ponders Henrietta in the 1881 version, he notes that "she was brave: there is always something fine about that." But in the 1908 revision, nothing "fine" about Henrietta stands unqualified. Ralph's comment is changed to read, "She was brave: she went into cages, she flourished lashes, like a spangled lion-tamer" (86). Henrietta's fine courage becomes a circus spectacle; she is now more foolish than brave. Ralph's simile puts Henrietta in a cage with Meg Merrilies, the *New York World*'s pseudonym for the girl stunt reporter who entered a lion's den for the sake of a story.[40] In this cage, newspaperwomen appear as objects of publicity; as their bodies become agents of news, their writing slips into narcissistic parading.

Mrs. Touchett disapproves of Henrietta in both versions, but only in the 1908 version does she attack Henrietta for turning herself into a spectacle. Speaking of Henrietta in 1881, Mrs. Touchett "defined her to Isabel as 'a newspaperwoman'" and expressed surprise that Isabel would choose such a friend. In 1908 James substitutes a more precise and damning label, apparently having decided that calling Henrietta a "newspaperwoman" was too vague. Instead, Mrs. Touchett describes her as "both an adventuress and a bore—adventuresses usually giving one more of a thrill"

(88). This dismissal puts Henrietta back in the cage with Meg Merrilies, only this time she fails to deliver even the thrill of sensationalism. Her self-display, Mrs. Touchett implies, falls flat. In 1881 Mrs. Touchett declares: "I don't like Miss Stackpole—I don't like her tone. She talks too loud, and she looks at me too hard" (505). She objects to Henrietta's professional qualities: her tone, her loud voice, her powers of observation. In the 1908 revision, Mrs. Touchett's objections become more personal and more encompassing: "I don't like Miss Stackpole—everything about her displeases me; she talks so much too loud and looks as if one wanted to look at *her*—which one doesn't" (89). Now Mrs. Touchett objects to literally *everything* about Henrietta. But her more specific criticism has also altered significantly: instead of accusing Henrietta of looking too hard at others, Mrs. Touchett complains that Henrietta expects others to look at *her.* James italicizes *her* as if to stress the point: Henrietta is represented as someone who puts herself forward to be gazed at.

Always defined by her career, the new Henrietta suffers because her career appears more and more repellent, particularly in its dependence on spectacle and violence. The changes in her professional identity are especially striking in James's revisions to the scene in which Henrietta first appears. In the 1881 version, Isabel and Ralph anticipate her arrival with light banter:

> "Shall I love her, or shall I hate her?" asked Ralph, while they stood on the platform, before the advent of the train.
>
> "Whichever you do will matter very little to her," said Isabel. "She doesn't care a straw what men think of her."
>
> "As a man I am bound to dislike her, then. She must be a kind of monster. Is she very ugly?"
>
> "No, she is decidedly pretty."
>
> "A female interviewer—a reporter in petticoats? I am very curious to see her," Ralph declared.
>
> "It is very easy to laugh at her, but it is not as easy to be as brave as she."
>
> "I should think not; interviewing requires bravery. Do you suppose she will interview me?"
>
> "Never in the world. She will not think you of enough importance." (79, 503)[41]

In this exchange, Isabel puts the flirtatious Ralph in his place and loyally defends her friend. Henrietta is represented as admirably brave and independent, a model of American individualism. She may be funny, but she is principled. In 1908 the tone changes; Henrietta is associated not simply with interviewing but with sensationalism. In the revised scene, after Isabel tells Ralph that it is easy to laugh at Henrietta but not easy to be as brave, Ralph says: "I should think not; crimes of violence and attacks on the person require more or less pluck. Do you suppose she'll interview *me*?" (79). Linking Henrietta's interviewing with a vaguely defined sensational attack journalism, Ralph appears no longer as curious friend or potential suitor but as a potential victim of publicity. In the original version, Ralph appears as a jesting sexual adventurer. In the revision, he is under threat from the feminized masses, which seem more likely to victimize than to titillate him. Moreover, Ralph's remark elides the difference between Henrietta and the content of the stories she might write. The nature of her connection to "crimes of violence and attacks on the person" is left unexplained. Does Henrietta require "pluck" because she is consorting with criminals? Does she publish personal attacks, commit violence herself, or risk becoming a victim of violence? Either way, the revision casts new light on James's woman journalist. Although Henrietta's career as police reporter exists only in Ralph's imagination, comments like this one create an almost lurid glow around her character, associating her with a sensational mode of female reporting that came into its own only after *Portrait* appeared in 1881.

Fiction over Fact: The Newspaperwoman Who "Saved" Lizzie Borden

At times, the spectacle of the reporter-heroine threatens to overwhelm any individual act of reportage or literary invention, blurring the line between reporter and subject so thoroughly that writing and self-promotion become one and the same. One telling instance of this dynamic, involving a notorious murder trial in 1893 and the real-life newswoman who covered it, warrants special attention. It features a woman with whom James was acquainted, a reporter-turned-author who knew him socially and even helped to schedule his U.S. lecture tours in 1904 and 1905. It is the story of Elizabeth Jordan, Boston reporter Mary Prim's girlhood favorite, the newspaperwoman who earned a reputation for having saved Lizzie Borden from the electric chair.[42]

Jordan, a reporter for the *New York World*, was one of the few women who covered the widely publicized 1893 trial of Lizzie Borden, a demure young woman from Fall River, Massachusetts, who was accused of killing her elderly father and stepmother with an axe. The bloody crime was immortalized in the children's rhyme "Lizzie Borden took an axe, gave her mother forty whacks. When she saw what she had done, she gave her father forty-one."[43] Despite circumstantial evidence and a potential motive (a substantial inheritance), Borden was found not guilty. No one else was ever charged with the murders. Released from jail, Borden sold her family's home, bought a bigger house in a more expensive neighborhood, and began attending the theater in Boston. She never got around to resuming her work for the Christian Endeavor Society, where she had served as secretary-treasurer before the murders. The small town of Fall River never forgave her; many remained convinced of her guilt.

Elizabeth Jordan's trial reports, published in the *New York World*, were, like most of the news coverage, sympathetic to Lizzie Borden and skeptical of her guilt.[44] Although the intense media interest in the accused murderer anticipated the publicity storm that swirled around Evelyn Nesbit during Harry Thaw's murder trial, Jordan's work on the Borden trial differed in significant ways from that of the Thaw trial reporters fourteen years later. The newspapers' marketing of the woman's angle had not yet reached the fever pitch that helped to create sob-sisterhood in 1907. Although Jordan stood out because of her sex in the Fall River courtroom, she sat with her male colleagues, not at a table by herself. Her reports, unlike the Thaw trial reports authored by women, were published without bylines. And Jordan herself seemed tailor-made to deflect attempts to turn her presence into a news sensation. A committed Roman Catholic who once planned to enter a convent, the socially privileged Jordan was known for her self-possession and "immaculate shirt-waists."[45] Her career plan did not include elaborate stunts or public displays of emotion. According to her autobiography, Jordan was "thrilled" to meet Nellie Bly during a Milwaukee stop on Bly's much-publicized around-the-world tour, but she and Bly did not hit it off, particularly after Jordan told Bly "that I was not to attempt the wonderful things she and Nell Nelson [another stunt reporter] were doing, but was to confine myself to news reporting."[46] Jordan's breakthrough scoop for the *New York World* involved no daring pretense of insanity or poverty. It was a story on President Benjamin Harrison's grandson, obtained by charming the first lady into an interview on the family's private beach on the Jersey shore.[47] Never a celebrity like Nellie Bly, the dignified Jordan nonetheless achieved considerable success as a journalist. The Borden trial was only one of many significant news stories she covered, and she enjoyed a long career as a news reporter, editor, and fiction writer.[48] One study of early-twentieth-century American literary culture singles Jordan out as "an exponent and exemplar" of her era's changing model of womanhood.[49] Her polish was not armor against publicity, however, and her reserved demeanor did not keep her from becoming part of the Lizzie Borden story.

The buzz caused by Jordan's presence at the trial shows just how easy it was for newswomen to become objects, not just agents, of publicity. More-over, the trial's impact on Jordan's professional reputation illuminates the complex relationship between reporter-heroines, sensational journalism, and models of authorship. Shortly after Borden was acquitted, Jordan published her first short story, "Ruth Herrick's Assignment," in *Cosmopolitan* magazine.[50] The story tracks a newspaperwoman—the Ruth Herrick of the title—when she reluctantly accepts an assignment to interview a woman on trial for murdering her husband. In a moment of nervous collapse during the jail cell interview, the accused woman confesses her guilt. The woman, an abused wife named Helen Brandow, tells Herrick that her husband brought her to "the depths of human misery and degradation," and that she was moved to kill him after a particularly brutal night in which he struck her elderly mother. "It didn't seem to me that he was a human being," Brandow tells Herrick, "and I killed him as I would have killed a poisonous thing that attacked me."[51] Unwilling to tell Brandow's story and essentially guarantee her conviction, Herrick keeps the secret and sacrifices the story. In sentimental fashion, her sympathy, signaled by tears in her eyes and a lump in her throat, triumphs over her professional ambition. She struggles inwardly for a good two pages, however, before she decides to deny herself and her newspaper the exclusive. And before she leaves the jail, she makes Brandow promise not to talk to any other reporters. Brandow keeps her word, and a jury acquits her. In the story's final scene, the editor who had assigned Herrick to the jailhouse interview muses to his secretary about the outcome of the case: "'I believe she's guilty; but a pretty woman who can hold her tongue will escape the consequences of almost any crime. Strange how Miss Herrick failed on that case; she felt it, too. Has been working day and night ever since, and all that sort of thing. But, after all, you can't depend on a woman in this business.' The managing editor was more nearly right than he knew."[52] When the narrator steps in to validate the editor's lack of confidence in women, Jordan wraps up her story at the expense of female professionalism. In its tale of protective sisterhood triumphing over public truth, "Ruth Herrick's Assignment" anticipates Susan Glaspell's "Jury of Her Peers" and *Trifles,* in which women conspire to conceal evidence that implicates an abused wife in her husband's murder.[53]

But Jordan's story dramatizes an authorial conflict of interest, not a feminist intervention, and her reporter-heroine remains ambivalent about her choice to suppress the confession. When Herrick leaves the jail and hears the cell door lock behind her, she comments to herself ironically: "'That's good,' she murmured, in grim self-abasement. 'In another moment I should probably have been helping her through the window.' "[54] By choosing *not* to tell the abused wife's story, Herrick protects her from publicity. Yet she also veils the horror of domestic violence and perpetuates the managing editor's ignorance, virtually ensuring that he, and everyone else, will never understand the cause and nature of the murder. Jordan thus imagines a world in which reporters betray their editors, husbands and wives betray each other, and the path to justice remains uncertain. Her vision opposes the unambiguous moral universe of Davis's "Gallegher" (1890), where justice and loyalty never conflict. Whereas Davis celebrates the newsroom fraternity as a substitute family for a fatherless boy, Jordan reveals the family itself as a potentially dehumanizing unit, in which a wife may kill her husband as if he were a snake or a scorpion.

Given the proximity of Lizzie Borden's acquittal to the publication of "Ruth Herrick's Assignment," it is easy to see why readers would have interpreted the fictional managing editor's conclusion about Helen Brandow—"I believe she's guilty; but a pretty woman who can hold her tongue will escape the consequences of almost any crime"—as a commentary on Borden's fate. Despite substantial differences in the cases, the Borden trial shadowed the reception of Jordan's story and the book in which it later appeared. As Jordan observed: "With my reports of the trial fresh in the public mind, it was immediately suggested and then generally assumed that Lizzie Borden had confessed her guilt to me, and that I had let her off. Even the managing editor of the *World*, then James Farrelly, sent me this note: 'So, Ruth Herrick, *that's* the kind of reporter you are, is it?' "[55] Jordan insisted that the story had been written before the Borden trial, but to no avail. In a complex interlacing of fiction and fact, she was transformed from skeptical observer to emotional participant, from reporter to object of publicity.

Rumors about Jordan's special connection to Lizzie Borden proved so resilient that the reporter-author addressed them at length in her autobiography, published more than forty years after the trial. She recalls being the only woman reporter in court on the tense day when Borden's father's skull was put into evidence. "The reporters around me were for Miss Borden as one man—convinced of her innocence, showing the conviction between the lines of their reports, and burning with sympathy for her. I was as sure of her innocence as they were, but at first I refused to give them my opinions."[56] The defense exhibited the old man's skull, Jordan explained, to illustrate the "terrific force" of the death blow, which split the victim's head diagonally through his jawbone. The gruesome exhibit startled Jordan into making a revelation to her male colleagues.

No woman, the defense held, had enough strength to deliver that blow. The skull was resting on a small oblong board, and the split jaw had been fastened in place with a piece of wire. Miss Borden's leading lawyer . . . held the skull high, that the jury and the spectators in the court-room might see it. Then the very walls of the room seemed to lean forward to look and listen. For the wire slipped, and the old man's jaw sagged back and forth in a grisly suggestion of speech. Spectators caught their breath and then exhaled in a gasp that swept the courtroom. . . .

"The old man is trying to testify," I murmured to my friend Julian Ralph, who sat next to me.

"What's he saying? What's he saying?" Julian gulped. I was so shaken that I gave myself away.

"He's saying that she's innocent," I answered, and Julian looked his relief. All the newspaper men had been afraid that being a woman, and therefore without a man's great natural sympathy, I would show a bias in my reports that might divert some of the current of popular feeling which was sweeping toward Miss Borden.[57]

In a startling reversal, the male reporters worry that Jordan will not be sympathetic enough; the story positions *men* as natural sympathizers, not women. Jordan's account contradicts popular assumptions in multiple ways. Indeed, given the dynamic she describes, "Ruth Herrick's Assignment" seems to pander to gender stereotypes that were belied by Jordan's own experience.

Perhaps Jordan was guilty of twisting gendered assumptions to her advantage; the rumors of her secret knowledge of Lizzie Borden's guilt probably bolstered sales of her first collection of short stories, *Tales of the City Room* (1898).[58] Perhaps the story's link to the Borden trial was just an unintended echo, as coincidental as the odd similarity in the two women's names. Either way, the assumed power of womanly sympathy proved so strong that it trumped the evidence, which suggests that women had no monopoly on melodrama, and that male reporters wrote just as emotionally and as sympathetically about their subjects as female reporters. Jordan's story illustrates the opportunities—and consequences—of the newspaperwoman's affinity for spectacle. Although Jordan apparently had more in common with nuns than with stunt reporters, she could not avoid being implicated in the sensational content of her news articles. She, too, became an emblem of gender and publicity, an icon of womanly sympathy and an agent of the mass media for which she wrote. No wonder James resisted being identified with Henrietta, his namesake newspaperwoman. By

1908, she had far too many disturbing counterparts, both in real life and in fiction.

Going Mechanical: How a Lady Correspondent Loses Her Vision

Given the revised Henrietta's association with exhibitionism, it is not surprising that James's other revisions to her character repeatedly blur the distinction between Henrietta's writing and her body. Her womanhood becomes more and more implicated in her profession. In the 1881 version she is simply a "newspaper-correspondent," but in 1908 James marks the gendered nature of her professional identity by calling her a "newspaper-lady" instead (82). As her femininity becomes more marked, however, she becomes, paradoxically, *less* feminine. The more Henrietta's profession depends on her access to the woman's angle—the more she has to perform femininity to be a journalist—the less she appears to be an actual woman. James remakes the descriptions of Henrietta's person so that she appears not merely less feminine but less human. Likened to a series of inanimate objects, the revised Henrietta is so thoroughly a product of her profession that her body becomes a thing, all surfaces and hard edges.[59]

In the 1881 version Henrietta is brave and unlikely to be interested in Ralph, but she is also potentially sexually desirable. When she gets off the train, she lives up to Isabel's assertion that she is "decidedly pretty": "She was very well dressed, in fresh, dove-coloured draperies, and Ralph saw at a glance that she was scrupulously, fastidiously neat. From top to toe she carried not an ink-stain" (80, 503). Her distinctly feminine primness is stain-proof; she bears no markers of her profession. In the revision, Henrietta is not so much tidy as frighteningly mass-produced. She becomes mechanized, her body subordinated to the mechanics of her profession. When she gets off the train in the 1908 version, she is not pretty but only "delicately . . . fair," and she is no longer "well dressed": "She rustled, she shimmered, in fresh, dove-colored draperies, and Ralph saw at a glance that she was as crisp and new and comprehensive as a first issue before the folding. From top to toe she had probably no misprint. . . . [S]he struck him as not all in the large type, the type of horrid 'headings,' that he expected" (80). This Henrietta's attributes are not feminine, not sexual, and not individual, but rather the surface-oriented technologies of mass production.[60] She is less a writer than a newspaper. No longer resistant to ink stains, her physical person now embodies her profession. Even the good qualities that surprise Ralph—"no misprint," "not all in the large type"—

are defined in negatives that call attention to the "horrid" products of her profession, with its threat of mindless replication and personal exposure.

Henrietta's gaze is a critical index of her character, the window to her soul as well as the key to her ability "to see as much as possible of the inner life." James's revisions to that gaze are the most chilling of all. Indeed, they help to set up that last look of Henrietta's, the one that ages Caspar Goodwood by thirty years. Her eyes, originally described as "polished buttons," become in the revised version "buttons that might have fixed the elastic loops of some tense receptacle" (80). The new Henrietta is hard, glaring, tense, almost explosive. Later, when Ralph wrongly assumes that Henrietta is trying to entrap him into a marriage proposal, she fixes him with a serious gaze. In the 1881 edition, her "brilliant eyes expanded still further," but in the 1908 revision, Henrietta scarcely seems to have eyes at all. Instead, James writes, her "ocular surfaces unwinkingly caught the sun" (86). This weird image is more mechanical than human, nearly robotic. The original Henrietta's bright gaze indicates her lively powers of observation and her personal honesty. The revised Henrietta's gaze, in contrast, reflects nothing from within. Recast as a shiny surface that catches the glare of the sun, it is no longer a gaze but rather an interaction of light and surface, nothing more than a glinting effect. Originally, when Henrietta sees Isabel in Rome after her marriage, the narrator observes that Henrietta's "eye had lost none of its serenity" (406, 565). In the revision we are told instead that "her remarkably open eyes, lighted like great glazed railway-stations, had put up no shutters" (406). This industrialized description links Henrietta to rapid transit and artificial illumination, casting her as a brightly lit station, a building through which travelers move, not as a person with reliable or even idiosyncratic, vision. She is no longer human enough to express serenity. She is no longer human enough to *see* at all. James has effectively blinded her. The revised Henrietta is so aggressively inhuman that Gilbert Osmond—who can be counted on to make cruel observations—no longer sounds so far off when he tells Isabel that Henrietta reminds him of "a new steel pen" (409). Gilbert imagines Henrietta as a mass-produced writing instrument.[61]

Echoing the dynamic being played out by actual women reporters of his era, James imagines Henrietta, quite literally, as a publicity machine. He acknowledges the embodiment that had become a hallmark of newspaperwomen by turning Henrietta's body into a mechanism of mass production. Despite Ralph's remark about crimes of violence, the revised Henrietta has little in common with the emotional and sexual excesses associated with sensational journalism. James negates the sexual subtext of women's sensational journalism by turning Henrietta's body into a desexualized machine. Paradoxically, the revisions make her both more explicitly female and more mechanical. James insulates her from sexualized publicity by recasting her as an industrial product of a person.

Through Henriettta, James suggests that the more newspaperwomen relied on their womanhood to justify their profession, the more mechanical, mass-produced, and inhuman they would become. We can see this logic at work in reverse in his characterization of another newspaperwoman, the aspiring journalist Maud Blandy in "The Papers" (1903).[62] Only a lack of visible femininity can keep a Jamesian newswoman from being reduced to a set of reproducible surfaces. (Remember that even in the revised *Portrait*, Isabel continues to insist that Henrietta is pretty.) To save Maud from Henrietta's mechanical fate, James makes her into a pseudoman, and thus denies her the woman's angle that would ensure her journalistic success. Maud is introduced to readers as "a shocker . . . in petticoats" who has "about her naturally so much of the young bachelor" (543–44). The narrator observes that Maud "might as easily have been christened John" (545) and comments frequently on her lack of femininity. "I ain't a woman," Maud sighs at one point. "I wish I were" (562). Yet Maud's androgyny is her salvation: she escapes being a publicity machine. Unlike Henrietta Stackpole, Maud becomes no mechanical monster. Her inability to make that transition spells her failure as a reporter—and her success as a James heroine. "I'm a fatal influence," Maud tells Howard Bight, her reporter friend and love interest. "I'm a nonconductor" (565). James rewards Maud's nonconductivity with a marriage proposal and an escape from a scurrilous profession.[63] At the end of the story, Howard and Maud quit the business and walk away, arm in arm, planning their future together.

In another story about a female reporter published a year before "The Papers," the Jamesian newswoman fares far worse. In "Flickerbridge," a short story that first appeared in *Scribner's Magazine* in February 1902, James charts a young man's realization that he cannot marry the newspaperwoman to whom he is engaged. This newspaperwoman, named Addie, never actually appears, but her potentially venomous presence haunts the story, and in the end, Frank, her fiancé, resolves to flee from her permanently. Frank rejects Addie not because of any personal failing of hers but because of the publicity machine she embodies; as he notes at one point, "She's intelligent, remarkably pretty, remarkably good" (435). In trying to explain his somewhat hysterical need to avoid seeing Addie again, Frank launches into a speech that indicts her as a vehicle of publicity. Although he uses a masculine pronoun in this passage, the context makes it clear that he is actually describing the woman to whom he is engaged:

"We live in an age of prodigious machinery, all organised to a single end. That end is publicity—a publicity as ferocious as the appetite of a cannibal. The thing therefore is not to have any illusions—fondly to flatter yourself, in a muddled moment, that the cannibal will spare you. He spares nobody. He spares nothing. It will be all right. You'll have a lovely time. You'll be only just a public character—blown about the world for all you are and proclaimed for all you are on the housetops."[64]

The narrator's sympathies are with Frank. The horror is not simply that the cannibal (the press) will eat you for lunch, but that you won't even mind. In fact, "you'll have a lovely time." In Frank's formula, having one's worth proclaimed from the housetops is an intimate violation, a consumption of one's person by others. Although Frank refers to the publicity machine with the masculine pronoun "he," the story makes sense only if we recognize that Frank has acquired a new and more accurate perception of Addie. Now that he sees her as a cannibalizing, impersonal force, he has no choice but to run away. James, in revising *Portrait,* could not follow his own character's lead; with Henrietta Stackpole, flight was not an option.

Superabundance: Not in the Plan

The more unattractive James tried to make Henrietta, the more space she occupied in his *Portrait.* He knew that she was a problem. In the preface to the 1908 edition, he apologizes at length for allowing such a minor character to "pervade" his novel. When he describes his imaginative link to the novel's characters, he admits to feeling some connection "even with so broken a reed (from her slightness of cohesion) as Henrietta Stackpole" (12). Even in the preface he vacillates between fascination and condescension in his treatment of her character. He goes out of his way to explain that she does not "belong" to his primary subject, and he cites her as one of those characters who "is but wheels to the coach; neither belongs to the body of that vehicle, or is for a moment accommodated with a seat inside. There the subject alone is ensconced" (13). Unlike Isabel Archer, the heroine who rides in the carriage, characters like Henrietta are "of the light *ficelle,* not of the true agent; they may run beside the coach 'for all they are worth,' they may cling to it till they are out of breath (as poor Miss Stackpole all so visibly does), but neither, all the while, so much as gets her foot on the step, neither ceases for a moment to tread the dusty road." Having denied Henrietta's status as "true agent" and left her breathless on a dusty road, James then compares her to the "fishwives who helped to bring back to Paris from Versailles, on that most ominous day of the first half of the French Revolution, the carriage of the royal family" (13). Through this comparison, James imagines Henrietta as part of the mob of women that delivered the royal family to prison and ultimately to their death. As Carolyn Mathews has argued, James's comparison is indebted to the description of this riot, the so-called Insurrection of Women, in Thomas Carlyle's history *The French Revolution*.[65] Since James's analogy has placed Isabel, the heroine of *Portrait*, in the royal carriage, the image is ominous: Henrietta, the embodiment of the American masses, threatens the novel's queen. It also aligns her, of course, with the people who revolutionized France.

James acknowledges the question posed by the revised Henrietta in a tone of exasperation which suggests that he lost control of his own character: "I may well be asked, I acknowledge, why then, in the present fiction, I have suffered Henrietta (of whom we have indubitably too much) so officiously, so strangely, so almost inexplicably to pervade" (13). But he has no answer for his own question. Why *did* he allow Henrietta to pervade the novel? If she is officious, strange, and inexplicable, obviously he has made her that way. If the American masses, in the person of a newspaperwoman, have invaded his novel and threatened his Queen Isabel, it is because he allowed it to happen.

James drops this problem entirely until the final paragraph of his preface—which, like the ending of the novel, belongs to Henrietta. But it is as unsatisfying as the revised ending of *Portrait*. He continues to express regret about his newspaperwoman: "As for Henrietta, my apology for whom I just left incomplete, she exemplifies, I fear, in her superabundance, not an element of my plan, but only an excess of my zeal." He then suggests that Henrietta was intended to be amusing, a "lively" addition to the book. Finally, he notes his interest in "the 'international' light in London," without bothering to explain how Henrietta's character—she is, after all, a transatlantic journalist—might have allowed him to represent such international light. With an abrupt "But that *is* another matter. There is really too much to say" (15), the preface ends. Instead of trying to explain Henrietta, James avers that she is too large a subject to tackle. This move is typical not just for James but for American literary history, which has been so busy apologizing for the crass publicity associated with newspaperwomen that it has rarely bothered to try to explain them. Like Henrietta, their "superabundance" does not fit into the plan; when there is too much to say, as James implies, sometimes there is nothing to say at all.

※

When Ralph dies at the end of *Portrait* and leaves Henrietta his library "in recognition of her services to literature," we are told that she plans to auction it off and set up a newspaper (482). This scene remains unchanged in the 1908 edition. We can dismiss Ralph's gesture, as does his mother, as a practical joke. Or we can read his will as an ironic commentary on the gloomy future of literature and assume that Henrietta's "services to literature" go unnamed because she does not perform any. But is this necessarily so? For aspiring women writers, popular reporter-heroines may have smoothed the way by making it easier for readers to imagine women writing in the public sphere. Yet newspaperwomen in fiction suggest a version of authorship that does not fit easily into the established categories of late-nineteenth- and early-twentieth-century American literature. Even when granted access to the gritty reality so prized by practitioners of realism and naturalism, reporter-heroines are often compromised. Their viewpoint is not objective enough to be linked to realism, not experimental or self-consciously artistic enough to be linked to modernism. In their failure to be literary, however, they may have provided the most critical service of all. By embodying the manipulative publicity that threatened serious literature, they gave authors such as James a clear target to attack, a visible force against which to define themselves. Women journalists who became authors, of course, were faced with a more complicated task, since they were already identified with the supposed enemy. How they managed is the topic of the next chapter.

From News to Novels

It's astonishing what women will do when they take to newspaper work.
—W. D. Howells, *Fennel and Rue*

In William Dean Howells's 1908 novel *Fennel and Rue,* an author of serialized fiction receives a letter from a young woman who says she's dying and begs him to tell her the end of his story before it comes out in the magazine. The author's editor suggests that he ask someone to certify the woman's identity before responding, concluding that "if she isn't the real thing, but merely a woman journalist trying to work us for a 'story' in her Sunday edition, we shall hear no more from her."[1] The editor's offhand reference suggests how fully newspaperwomen had penetrated the consciousness of the literary world by 1908. Common enough that Howells's editor immediately suspected an unknown female correspondent of being a scheming reporter, newspaperwomen shaped turn-of-the-century attitudes about readership, authorship, and publicity in ways we have yet to appreciate fully.

In this chapter I restore newswomen's place in the American reporter-novelist tradition by examining how three prominent women writers— Edna Ferber, Willa Cather, and Djuna Barnes— negotiated the roles of author and reporter. Newspaperwomen were often expected to dramatize themselves in ways that men were not, and Ferber, Cather, and Barnes wrote from different points on what we might call the self-dramatization spectrum. This unlikely threesome registers the depth and complexity of newswomen's impact on American fiction, which influenced not only Ferber's middlebrow realism but also the more artistically ambitious fiction of Cather and Barnes, whose aesthetic tastes were profoundly different but equally uncompromising. Each of these writers owed a debt to journalism, and each developed a literary vision that took up the newspaperwoman's legacy of public embodiment. Ferber embraced that legacy as a resource, albeit with irony and skepticism; Cather repudiated it but nonetheless put it to use in her fictional treatment of sexuality and creativity; and Barnes exploited it by seeking out its farthest possible extremes. Not coincidentally, all three engaged in various degrees of gender-bending themselves, as they maneuvered in male-dominated newsrooms and crafted authorial personas of influence and power. Considered together, Ferber, Cather, and Barnes make visible a distinctly different reporter-novelist tradition, one that evolved not from masculine performances of neutral observation but from the spectacle associated with the female journalist. Recognizing the female body as a source of both the real and the unreal, authenticity and artifice, these writers invested meaning and value in women's bodies, even as they acknowledged the disturbing ways in which mass-market consumerism and media technologies were redefining those bodies. Their strategies created, in effect, an alternative reporter-novelist, less a single entity than a vibrant, multilayered response to the all too visible figure of the newspaperwoman in turn-of-the-century American culture.

Skepticism about the value of women's journalism shaped women fiction writers' responses to their reportorial origins in multiple ways. The demands of directing and attracting publicity, as well as the special costs and vulnerabilities of embodiment, are more likely to inform the work of female reporters-turned-novelists than the work of their male colleagues. As we have seen, newspaperwomen reported on themselves as much as they reported on the news. Fiction writers who stepped into the legacy of women's journalism, then, could not simply pursue "the real." They had to confront the circular process of publicity and the intense body-consciousness that often stood in for "the real" in the reports of mainstream newspaperwomen. More likely to appear in the text of their own reports, more likely to be depicted visually along with their stories, female reporters displayed their bodies, their emotions, and their essential femininity, whether they were performing stunts or expressing sympathy for the subjects of their stories. Thus they often appeared less involved with documenting a reality that existed outside themselves than with transmitting their own experiences, inventing and circulating stories that became "news" simply because they were being made public.

These conditions made it difficult for women writers to lay claim to the supposed literary benefits of journalism. Their open avowal of personal subjectivity and vulnerability, coupled with their dependence on a system of mass-market publicity, distanced them from the assets accorded journalists in the reporter-novelist tradition defined by writers such as Mark

Twain, Stephen Crane, Theodore Dreiser, and Ernest Hemingway. No matter how many hours women spent in spittoon-lined city rooms, how closely they observed real life, or how many gritty experiences they endured, they were not credited with the heightened sense of reality that was imagined to be a special gift of a reportorial background. Nor could they claim to be cultivating a fresh, objective approach to representing the real, as did the realist writers who denied readers the reassuring interventions of kindly narrators and sought to remove themselves from their own fiction. Newspaperwomen's visibility could be dismissed as a product of a decidedly nonliterary enterprise, their journalism as little more than a predictable commentary on their essential womanhood.

To recover the context in which turn-of-the-century newspaperwomen launched their literary careers, I revisit the history of journalism's impact on fiction and the familiar tradition of the male reporter-novelist. I then turn to Ferber, a best-selling novelist of the early twentieth century who liked to tell her fans that she had learned to write in a newspaper office. Although Ferber emulates the male reporter-novelist model in her use of realistic detail and close observation of everyday life, a careful reading of her work reveals a keen awareness of the ironies of the Girl Reporter's performative role. That awareness drove some of Ferber's best work, especially her sharply drawn portraits of women who act with an awareness of an audience even in the most intimate moments of their lives. Ferber's willingness to tout her newspaper background was not necessarily typical, as becomes apparent when the discussion moves on to Cather, whose vision of herself as a literary artist led her to dismiss her journalistic past and to avoid any association with the sensational practices of women's journalism. Cather worked primarily as a drama critic and an editor, not as a daily news reporter, and her fiction rarely draws directly on her city room experiences. But reading her authorial persona in the larger context of women's reporting illuminates new dimensions of her authorial choices, particularly her rejection of the realism associated with male reporter-novelists and her incorporation of female embodiment into her own artistic ideal. I conclude with Barnes, whose avant-garde approach enabled her to transform the same journalistic traditions Cather scorned, thus remaking stunt reporting as a modernist experiment. Barnes's early journalism, when viewed as a revision of the woman-identified tradition of stunt reporters and sob sisters, suggests that sensational reportage served as an essential backdrop for her later, more radical explorations of desire and trauma.

Reporter to Artist: Paths and Counterpaths

The path from news to novels has never been particularly direct. Crane's experiences as a war correspondent in the 1890s, for instance, came *after* he wrote his famous war novel, not before.[2] But in the late nineteenth century, reporting became a more recognizably literary activity, and scores of aspiring writers sought apprenticeships in newspaper offices. Scholars have convincingly demonstrated that newspapers helped shape the imaginative literature of the late-nineteenth- and early-twentieth-century United States.[3] When the genteel literary amateur went out of fashion at the turn of the century, claiming kinship with professional journalists gave authors a new kind of legitimacy. As the ideal of journalistic objectivity gained currency, using a detached narrative style allowed novelists to strike their own pose of professional neutrality. Literary historians have long acknowledged this shift. They have called the American novel's affinity with journalism one of its most striking qualities, identifying the interweaving of fiction and nonfiction as a significant characteristic of most of the era's major literary movements, including the documentary impulse of realism and the montage techniques of modernism. Even the esoteric language of the High Modernists did not escape the influence of newspapers, since its very inaccessibility can be read as a reaction against journalism's ability to reach masses of readers through easily consumed narratives.

Yet the assumed masculinity of newspaper writing has been left unquestioned, even by those who have challenged other commonplaces of the reporter-novelist tradition. Scholars have agreed not simply that news reporting energized the American novel at the turn of the century but that all the key players in the reporter-novelist tradition were men. From this assumption grew the misleading view, which persists even in recent studies of Progressive Era journalism and literature, that daily journalism promoted a singularly masculine prose style in an exclusively male domain.[4] Thus the primary influence of newspapers on the American novel has been construed as a masculinizing one. According to this model, seeking out the rough edges of the news business allowed novelists to reassert the masculine nature of a genre that some feared had been taken over by women. By depicting the stark realities of urban life and scorning sentimental conventions, reporter-novelists promised to rescue fiction from irrelevant escapism, trivial domesticity, and other ills that the American literary establishment associated with women's novels.

The popular figure of the cigar-chomping newsman who reported the news with resigned detachment, however, always had a counterpart in the madcap girl reporter who could cry on cue to manipulate a source but who still couldn't help getting emotionally involved in her stories. As designated provider of the woman's angle, the girl reporter offered a version of the news that was necessarily partial, circumscribed by her own body and her own performance. But even as this kind of newspaperwoman was being written out of literary history, dismissed as trivial, lowbrow, and overly emotional, women with literary ambitions were finding ways to bridge the gap between newspaper work and literature.

Women, like men, followed no single trajectory from journalist to novelist. And most female reporters, like most male reporters, did not become novelists. But attending to the women who did reveals female-authored reportage as a significant force in American letters. Newspaper offices provided a jumping-off point, steady work, a source of material, and an alternative publishing venue for some of the nation's most compelling women writers. An impressive set of female authors, including best-selling novelists and Pulitzer Prize winners, launched their careers by writing for mainstream newspapers in the late nineteenth and early twentieth centuries. The group includes celebrated figures such as Cather and Barnes, as well as popular but now forgotten writers. *New York World* reporter Elizabeth Jordan published her first book of fiction in 1898 and enjoyed a long career as a novelist and editor. Zona Gale, whose adaptation of her best-selling novel *Miss Lulu Bett* made her, in 1921, the first woman to win the Pulitzer Prize in drama, started out as a newspaper reporter in Milwaukee in 1895.[5] Susan Glaspell's two best-known works, the one-act play *Trifles* (1916) and the short story "A Jury of Her Peers" (1917), were inspired by her own newspaper coverage of a 1901 murder trial in Iowa.[6] Sophie Treadwell, author of the expressionist drama *Machinal* (1928), began writing for the *San Francisco Bulletin* in 1908 and served as a foreign correspondent in World War I. Rose Wilder Lane, a *San Francisco Bulletin* features writer in the 1910s and 1920s, wrote popular short stories and collaborated with her mother, Laura Ingalls Wilder, on the "Little House" series of children's books.[7] Short story author and novelist Katherine Anne Porter began her long apprenticeship in journalism writing for the *Fort Worth Critic* in 1917 and quickly moved on to the *Rocky Mountain News*.[8] Josephine Lawrence, who began publishing adult fiction in the 1930s, started her career as children's page editor and advice columnist for the *Newark Sunday Call* in 1915. Martha Gellhorn, accomplished novelist and foreign correspondent, launched her journalism career at *The Albany Times Union* in 1929. Tess Slesinger, author of the trenchant feminist novel *The Unpossessed* (1934), graduated from the Columbia School of Journalism in 1927 and wrote for several New York newspapers before she began publishing magazine fiction in the 1930s.[9] This cursory list does not include the many women who wrote for literary newspapers, ethnic presses, and alternative journals run by suffragists, socialists, anarchists, and advocates of equal rights for racial and ethnic minorities.[10] Nor does it include women who entered journalism *after* gaining fame as novelists, such as the popular mystery writer Mary Roberts Rinehart, who became a war correspondent for the *Saturday Evening Post,* and beloved novelist Fannie Hurst, who covered several national news events (trials, natural disasters, strikes) as a freelancer.[11] Yet this catalog, incomplete as it is, suggests the vital role that women's journalism has played in American literature.

The singularity of newspaperwomen—who were always in the minority even when they were making headlines—guaranteed that their path from journalism to literature would take a different course from that of most newspapermen. "Everyone on the city desk was writing a play or a book," recalled Dorothy Day, who worked as a reporter in the 1910s.[12] Notwithstanding the visible increase in the number of female reporters, almost "everyone" on the city desk was a man. And as we have seen, newspaperwomen, more regularly than men, were called upon to dramatize their experiences. Images of newspaperwomen—circulated through fictional narratives about reporter-heroines and through news narratives written by actual female reporters—often drew on women's bodily experience as a primary source of news, emphasizing the reporters' femaleness, emotional expressiveness, and physical, often sexual vulnerability. At the same time, newswomen were identified with attempts to appeal to a broadly defined mass reading public, held up as emblems of the mass-market publicity system that reproduced their images along with their stories. When Joseph Pulitzer's *New York World* pioneered pictorial journalism, printing an unprecedented number of photographs, sketches, cartoons, and banner headlines, competitors across the nation followed suit. New technology such as the photoengraving process allowed visuals and text to support each other, and newspapers could experiment more freely with representing the tellers of the news along with the news itself. The explosion of illustrations in the popular press coincided with the rise of women journalists, and although female journalists were always outnumbered by men, they were more often pictured along with their articles. Women were also more often employed by the sensational dailies rather than the more sedate, less heavily illustrated papers.[13] The demands of managing this spectacle inevitably affected how aspiring women writers treated their reporting backgrounds. As we saw in chapter 4, fictional characterizations of both male and female reporters registered the often antagonistic relationship between journalists and writers of literature. For women, however, the roles of serious author and mainstream reporter were even more thoroughly opposed than for men.

Both male and female writers, of course, could aspire to the standard literary realism that is usually considered the province of the reporter, by cultivating an ability to survey the world with detachment and to discern the salient details in the swirling chaos of modern urban life. But these were not the skills sought after in female reporters. The newspaperwomen discussed in chapters 1, 2, and 3 were not celebrated for their objectivity; even anti-lynching crusader Ida B. Wells, who spurned the sensational tactics of the stunt reporters and sob sisters, represented herself as passionately, even bodily engaged in her news writing. Women's journalism thus updated and reinforced the custom of viewing women's texts through the bodies of the writers who produced them. At the same time, it made female reporters emblematic of a mass-market system of publicity, through which words and images were circulating more quickly and reaching a broader audience than ever before. Women's journalism, yoked to attempts to cultivate a mass reading public, operated less as a source of literary authenticity than as a reminder of the power of the feminized masses. A newspaperwoman, almost by definition, was a public spectacle, designed to appeal to a mass audience. Women writers who made the shift from journalism to fiction, then, had to contend not only with the familiar tendency to align women with corporeality and men with intellect, but also with a more specific, more modern manifestation of female embodiment, which recast the bodies of newspaperwomen as products of a media-driven spectacle. Given the newspaperwoman's thoroughgoing identification with mass-market consumerism, perhaps it is not surprising that in the early twentieth century, the woman writer who staked the loudest claim to her place in the reporter-novelist tradition was Edna Ferber, whose breakthrough fiction starred not a journalist but a traveling saleswoman.

She Used to Be a Newspaperman: Edna Ferber

Ferber's memoir shows how she aligned herself with the male-dominated reporter-novelist tradition, confronting its self-conscious manliness even as she acknowledged her own participation in the sensational tradition of girl stunt reporting. While carefully maintaining an ironic distance from her own experience, Ferber claimed the standard literary benefits of a newspaper background that were usually denied to women: breadth of experience, training in observation, economy of language. Fond of saying

"I was once a newspaper man myself," she struck an uneasy balance between mocking the assumed masculinity of reporters and claiming it for herself.[14] At the same time, she conceded her own participation in the spectacle of being a newspaperwoman, noting both the pleasure she took in her public role as Girl Reporter and the limits it imposed on her authorship. Ferber's reportorial origins paved the way not only for her stubbornly practical vision of writing but also for her subtle depictions of the performative qualities of women's most intimate lives.

Ferber achieved extraordinary success as a novelist in the early years of the twentieth century. Popular and well paid, she was praised as a writer who celebrated the ordinary workers of America's Main Streets. She published her first novel in 1911, soon earned wide recognition for her short stories starring businesswoman Emma McChesney, and went on to write intergenerational sagas about American families, including the Pulitzer Prize–winning *So Big* (1924), *Showboat* (1926), and *Giant* (1952). Several of her novels became best-sellers; thirteen were made into movies. The jacket copy of *Half Portions,* an edition of her short stories published by the University of Illinois Press, identifies Ferber as "a journalist and author."[15] Ferber would have approved. She traced many of her early plots and characters to stories she covered and people she met as a reporter.[16] Although Emma McChesney, her first popular heroine, was not a reporter, Emma's bold forays into the male-dominated world of traveling salesmen had much in common with the popular model of the girl reporter that Ferber emulated as a young woman. (A divorced mother, Emma supports herself and her son with her wages.) Ferber used her reportorial skills throughout her career, especially in her historical fiction, where she excelled at playing the outsider who could recognize and capture the human drama unfolding in the diverse regional cultures of the United States. Factual detail accumulates rapidly in the Milwaukee reporting exploits of *Dawn O'Hara,* the midwestern truck-farming saga of *So Big,* the Mississippi River trips of *Showboat,* the Oklahoma pioneer vistas of *Cimarron,* the daunting Texas landscapes of *Giant.*

Ferber affectionately documented her journalism career in her bestselling 1939 autobiography, *A Peculiar Treasure.* She calls herself the first woman reporter in Appleton, Wisconsin, and she names newspaper reporting as *the* catalyst for her vocation as a novelist. Her writing career "accidentally began," she writes, when she went to work for the *Appleton Daily Crescent* for three dollars a week immediately after graduating from high school. It was 1902, and she was seventeen years old: "Well, there I was, a girl reporter. I didn't want to be a writer. I never had wanted to be a writer. I couldn't even use a typewriter, never having tried." Like former reporters such as H. L. Mencken and Richard Harding Davis, Ferber recalls her early newspaper work with enthusiasm and wistfulness. She confesses that the smell of wet ink, hot lead, and tobacco still gives her "a pang of nostalgia for the old reporting days," and she vividly recollects the thrill of being a newspaper insider.[17] Journalism gave Ferber an education (her family could not afford to send her to college), a set of role models, even the plot of her first novel. In her memoir she claims that the job taught her more than a university could have and credits reporting with giving her habits of "trained observation and memory," not to mention a "storehouse of practical and psychological knowledge, and a ghastly gift of telling the sham from the real."[18] After eighteen months on the *Crescent,* she moved to the *Milwaukee Journal,* where she wrote for the city desk for nearly four years. There she met Zona Gale, a former reporter whose success as a fiction writer was legendary in the Milwaukee newsroom.[19] When Ferber collapsed from overwork and was forced to return to Appleton to convalesce, she wrote her first novel, *Dawn O'Hara* (1911), and sent it to a literary agent she had once heard Gale recommend. The novel's protagonist was a woman reporter whose story, with a few significant changes, echoed Ferber's own.

Ferber's celebration of her cub reporting days attests to her labor-oriented notion of authorship, her commitment to appealing to ordinary readers, and her interest in documenting the lives of average Americans. Asserting her place in the reporter-novelist tradition did not go far toward earning her a place in the literary canon, however. A novelist with a broad popular readership, she was never much lauded by critics.[20] Ferber used her reporting background to bolster her reputation as a worker, as someone who wrote for a living rather than someone who worshiped in the church of the highbrow.[21] She took steps to avoid becoming a "hack reporter,"[22] but she nonetheless presented herself as a shrewd observer of common people, not a producer of high art. Although her novels celebrate female workers, criticize social conventions, and occasionally dramatize the injustices of class and racial oppression, their plots tend to move characters inexorably up the social ladder, rewarding hard work and perseverance with moralistic regularity. In some ways, in tone and content, despite their attention to realistic detail, they have more in common with the popular sentimental novel of the nineteenth century than with realist or modernist fiction—a tie that did not bode well for Ferber's critical reputation.[23] Her *New York Times* obituary noted her extraordinary popularity but also called her books "not profound."[24]

Yet journalism points the way to what may be Ferber's most striking achievement and deepest concern: her ability to register the demands—

and the inescapability—of publicity, particularly for women. Whether they are farmers or society wives, saleswomen or newspaper editors, women find no shelter from public demands in the private spheres of Ferber's fiction. Ferber returns repeatedly to the public dimensions of women's bodies, particularly in the context of a male-dominated business world where commercial interests are paramount. She depicts even the home as a place where women perform and are scrutinized, where women's performances result not just in emotional transactions but in economic ones as well. Emma McChesney, the traveling businesswoman who lives on the road in full view of her customers and business rivals, is followed in Ferber's fiction by a long line of other public performers. In *Showboat*, the heroine grows up on a touring stage; in *Cimarron,* she takes on the role of municipal housekeeper for an entire pioneer town; in *Giant,* she presides over a Texas ranch that houses a never-ending stream of curious guests. Ferber's novels center on home and family even as they track the expansive career ambitions of their heroines, showing again and again the imbrication of domestic and business concerns.

Introduced to writing via the newspaperwoman's public role, Ferber remained both fascinated and repelled by the ways in which the public sphere conscripted women's bodies and behavior in the service of profit motives and hierarchies of race and class. Even when Ferber acknowledged her place in a woman-identified journalistic tradition, implicitly accepting the rhetoric and the readership associated with the newspaperwoman, she voiced deep suspicion of the nature of the "work" required of female reporters. Given the centrality of *work* to Ferber's authorial persona, it is telling that she adopts an exclusively male idiom when she notes the strenuous nature of newspaper reporting. She stresses the demands of journalism by calling attention to its purported masculinity. "I found myself covering a regular news beat like any man reporter," she writes; she describes her newspaper work as "doing a man-sized job" and recalls that she "worked like a man."[25] Yet Ferber's cross-gender identification goes only so far. Her memoir makes it clear that having been a newspaper*woman* was at least as significant to her as having been a newspaper*man.*

Ferber evinces a fine sense of irony about the excesses of the newspaperwoman's public image, an image she mocks and revises from within. She frequently calls herself "a self–dramatizing Girl Reporter," ironically capitalizing the phrase as if she had been cast in a play. Ferber says that she modeled herself after the title character of Miriam Michelson's popular serial *A Yellow Journalist* (1905), which Ferber describes as "fresh and racy newspaper stories all about a woman reporter and her dashing adventures on a big-town newspaper. There was the kind of newspaper woman I wanted to be. Immediately I dramatized myself as the Girl Reporter. . . . I used to pray for a murder."[26] Ferber's breezy tone expresses considerable fondness for her youthful, ambitious self. Her newsroom nostalgia, however, does not deter her from observing that her editors exploited her "self-dramatizing" in sometimes disturbing ways. Looking back, she is critical of the *Journal* for taking advantage of her "unadult posturing."[27] Her investigation of a poorly run girls' home sounds like a classic stunt in the Nellie Bly tradition, but Ferber largely declines to celebrate the exploit: "I spent a couple of uncomfortable nights in a Refuge for Girls because I had heard of unfairness and cruelty in practice there. To get out of the place I had to escape down a precarious fire escape, with a long drop to the sidewalk. I made it, skedaddled for home, had a bath, turned in my story and the place was cleaned out as a result, but I didn't really care about that. I merely had wanted to get a sensational exposure story."[28] Ferber recounts the adventure with muted pride, adopting an it-was-really-nothing air even as she reports that she spent two "uncomfortable" nights in the institution and that she was forced to execute a physically daring exit from a place with a reputation for cruelty. In the passage's conclusion, however, Ferber strips stunt reporting of its sentimental gloss and foregrounds her own career interest, not her sympathy for the inmates of the refuge. She also deflects attention from her own physical and possibly sexual vulnerability, suppressing any details about why she had to slip down the fire escape, noting only that she came home and took a bath right away. Even without particulars, however, it is easy to see that her reporting gained impact from the contrast between the degradation associated with her topic and the innocence associated with her youth and femininity. Ferber's role as self-dramatizing Girl Reporter is emphatically embodied. In this and other stories, she acts not as a neutral witness but as an intimate participant, getting physically close enough to require a bath afterward. Once, she recalls, she closed a peepshow by attending it and then describing its "pornographic filth." This sort of tactic required the reporter to act not simply as a mediator but as a cleansing agent, impervious to the appeal of the "filth" she was describing.

Ferber's memoir recalls such tactics without the nostalgia that bathes her descriptions of the newsroom's ink-and-tobacco camaraderie. "I was pleased with myself for this and various other sensational exposé stories," she confesses, but she adds that her salary of fifteen dollars a week never went up. "I didn't know I was being exploited by a wealthy little paper. The Girl Reporter was still dramatizing herself twelve hours a day."[29] Ferber aptly characterizes the stunt reporters, who generated stories by exposing themselves to areas of the urban landscape that were off-limits to respectable women—group homes, sex shows—and then sharing their personal reactions to what they saw. She also equates her performances with economic exploitation, imagining her young self as a sort of sweatshop stunt girl. Throughout, Ferber documents the newspaper's exploitation of her ambition and acknowledges her own complicity.

Even as Ferber criticizes the self-dramatizing Girl Reporter, she recognizes the role's utility: being willing to make a spectacle of herself allowed her to avoid women's page assignments and to gain access to stories otherwise reserved for male reporters.[30] But the potential costs of self-dramatizing were considerable, and the peepshows were not always easy to close down. Ferber recounts a chilling incident of sexual harassment, a reminder that newswomen's sexual vulnerability was not simply a fiction manufactured for dramatic effect in sensational stories. She was in a fashionable doctor's office conducting an interview for a story when the doctor locked his office door and forced her to look at pornographic pictures. He allowed her to leave only after she threatened to tell her city editor.[31] This kind of encounter suggests some of the physical and psychological stresses that would eventually lead to her breakdown and departure from the *Journal*.[32]

Those stresses cause fractures in her fictional newswomen, too. Ferber imagined reporter-heroines as models of public career women, investing them with courage and creativity. But she also suggests that their rebellion against conventional womanhood could produce gender-based exploitation and oppression rather than protecting them from it. Ferber's newspaper fictions revolve less around the job's standard difficulties, such as long hours and sustained contact with emotionally draining events, than the challenges of managing public expectations about newspaperwomen. The reporter-heroine of Ferber's first novel, *Dawn O'Hara* (1911), suffers a breakdown and consults a "nerve specialist," who cures her in part by falling in love with her.[33] Ferber's portrayal of journalism is predictably ambivalent, and she gets her reporter-heroine out of the business by the novel's end, rewarding Dawn with both a book contract and a husband. Romance and retirement notwithstanding, the heroine expresses more passion in her nostalgia for the news business than she does for the specialist she marries:

> I want to be there when the telephone bells are zinging, and the typewriters are snapping . . . and the big city editor, collar off, sleeves rolled up from his great arms, hair bristling wildly above his green eye-shade, is swearing gently and smoking cigarette after cigarette, lighting each fresh one at the dying glow of the last. I would give a year of my life to hear him say:
> "I don't mind tellin' you, Beatrice Fairfax, that that was a darn good story

you got on the Millhaupt divorce. The other fellows haven't a word that isn't re-hash."

All of which is most unwomanly; for is not marriage woman's highest aim, and home her sphere?[34]

Ferber invests her title character with both a love of newsroom culture and a tendency to question whether, as a woman, she has a right to be there. Dawn O'Hara embraces gritty realism—the smoke, the noise, the chaos, the professional rivalry—and then catches herself, interrupting her own ecstatic vision with a cold splash of doubt about the appropriateness of her desires. But the male reporter-novelist tradition of urban realism is also undermined here. In Dawn's fantasy, the scoop for which she is praised is about a divorce; her big-city editor is excited about publicizing details of a marital breakup, not documenting poverty or crime.

Ferber's novel is more explicit in its challenge to the popular dismissal of female reporters as sob sisters. Dawn is especially eloquent when she protests the common assumption that newspaperwomen are manipulative and emotionally corrupt. She argues not only that newspaperwomen don't have time to cry but also that when they exercise the emotional restraint necessary to do their jobs, they are unfairly stereotyped:

> "If a woman reporter were to burst into tears every time she saw something to weep over she'd be going about with a red nose and puffy eyelids half the time. Scarcely a day passes that does not bring her face to face with human suffering in some form. Not only must she see these things, but she must write of them so that those who read can also see them. And just because she does not wail and tear her hair and faint she popularly is supposed to be a flinty, cigarette-smoking creature who rampages up and down the land, seeking whom she may rend with her pen and gazing, dry-eyed, upon scenes of horrid bloodshed."[35]

Dawn voices her frustration that female reporters who do not display conventional signs of hysteria in the face of disaster are classified as predators, practically unsexed by their self-control. This vision of the newspaperwoman as hard-boiled harpy suggests that, despite her defiant assertion of her right to a place in the reporter-novelist tradition, Ferber realized that the spectatorial politics of women's journalism were unavoidable. Dawn's complaint illustrates just how difficult it was for female reporters to lay claim to the objective observer model of the realist novelist. In her formulation, newspaperwomen who claim the power to gaze dry-eyed at the world become rampaging "creatures," not aspiring artists.

As Ferber's authorial vision matured, so did her portrayals of the power
and danger of being a public woman. Ferber again draws on her newsroom
experiences, and again imagines a newspaperwoman with ambivalence, in
Cimarron (1930), a story of Oklahoma pioneers who start a frontier newspaper.[36] *Cimarron*—which became the best-selling novel of 1930 and was
made into an Academy Award–winning movie in 1931—documents the
transformative power of publicity in a pioneer town. But Ferber depicts
that transformation, wrought by a heroine who combines a deeply conventional view of womanhood with a drive for power and a keen news
sense, as more of a tragedy than a victory. Ferber herself rejected the common view that *Cimarron* was a romance of the frontier; she insisted that it
was a satire, intended to present "a malevolent picture of what is known as
American womanhood and American sentimentality."[37] The swaggering,
big-hearted hero, Yancey Cravat, opens a newspaper office, but his wan-
derlust soon takes over. He leaves the newspaper in the hands of his wife,
Sabra, who was already doing most of the work anyway. Sabra then supports
herself and their two children by running the *Oklahoma Wigwam*, which becomes the most powerful newspaper in the Southwest. By the novel's conclusion, Sabra has become a congresswoman, a person of wealth and
influence. Although the plot traces the rise of a pioneering newswoman,
the novel does not celebrate Sabra's achievement. Instead, the narrator
holds up Sabra's delinquent husband, Yancey, as the true hero, a defender
of Native American rights whose inability to live in civilized society signals
his imagination and his virtue.

Ferber's characterization of Sabra bears out her claim that she intended
to create a "malevolent picture" of American womanhood. Sabra's ad-
mirable courage is offset by her disturbingly conventional racism, and her
political success is hypocritical, based on her parroting of her husband's
heartfelt respect for Native Americans. The novel's final two chapters deal
a double blow to Sabra's triumph. First, an artist commissioned to make a
statue of the Spirit of the Oklahoma Pioneer asks to interview Sabra, but
rather than using her likeness, as everyone expected, the artist crafts a
statue in Yancey's honor, enshrining Sabra's vanished husband instead of
her.[38] Second, Yancey dies a hero, sacrificing his own life to save others in
an oil field accident. So, after effacing the image of her pioneer newspaperwoman with the glamorous figure of a swashbuckling husband, Ferber
wraps up her story by making him a martyr. Yancey remains a transcendent
figure, embodying a frontier spirit that had been conquered by "the sun-
bonnets" (as the narrator calls female pioneers) who domesticated the
West.[39] The novel portrays the sculptor's erasure of Sabra as both ironic
and prescient. Ultimately, Ferber indicts her newspaperwoman as the cre-

ator and beneficiary of a publicity machine that prioritizes profits and brutalizes Native Americans. Sabra, conventional woman and public figure, poses a more substantial threat to Ferber's hopeful vision of America than does the stereotype of the predatory newspaperwoman conjured by *Dawn O'Hara*'s title character. Driven by desire for power and profit, Sabra's public performances constitute a rampage in their own right.

Ferber was both skeptical and self-aware about women's performative journalism; she mocked it as demeaning, hypocritical, and even, as in Sabra's case, morally reprehensible, while at the same time she acknowledged its centrality to her own reporting career as a young woman. Her ability to see herself as a full participant in the reporter-novelist tradition can be attributed, at least in part, to her facility for imagining herself on the far side of the gender distinctions that divided stunt reporters and sob sisters from "real" reporters. Yet much of Ferber's most incisive fiction centers on the meanings and consequences of women's public roles. As her career unfolded, a central problem posed by the stunt reporters and sob sisters—the ways in which women's bodies were called upon to serve the commercial interests of a male-dominated public sphere—haunted her fiction with increasing intensity. By the time Ferber was writing *Giant* in the early 1950s, her interest in the effects of publicity on women had developed into an explicit critique of the ways in which white women's bodies were used to serve a racist, imperialist agenda. *Giant*'s narrative of Anglo-Mexican conflict, told through the consciousness of a white woman who also happens to be an extraordinary performer in her own right, advances a far more complex set of themes than *Dawn O'Hara*'s relatively narrow (and comparatively amateurish) tale of a newspaperwoman's struggles. But the trajectory is not incidental. Ferber's ironic interpretation of her own beginnings as a self-dramatizing Girl Reporter show that the journalistic work that launched her writing career gave her an education not just in fact-gathering but in the possibilities—and problems—of public embodiment for women.

Banishing the Reporter: Willa Cather

A noted Cather scholar once declared, "In the perspective of history, the world-renowned novelist that Willa Cather became must be joined with the young Nebraska newspaperwoman."[40] Yet Cather is rarely, if ever, remembered as a journalist. Cather—who began working for newspapers when girl stunt reporters were still making headlines—would not have minded. Unlike Ferber, she obscured her reportorial beginnings, shrugged off journalism as irrelevant to serious art, and mocked the realist impulse that sent writers "hunting among the ashcans" for material.[41] She rejected the male reporter-novelist model as firmly as Ferber welcomed it, and she never identified her journalism as a critical phase of her literary development.[42] Since she defined literary fiction in opposition to documentary realism, she had little interest in identifying herself as *any* kind of journalist, male or female. By refusing to link her authorship to her journalistic past, she expressed not only her sense of the limitations of reportorial realism but also her belief that for serious writers, mass-market newspapers could never be anything but a compromised venue.[43] Critics have mined Cather's early journalism for clues about her artistic development, finding evidence that newspaper and magazine writing allowed her to experiment with narrative voices, hone her prose style, inhabit alternative gender roles, even stumble upon story ideas.[44] Cather's authorial imagination has not been set, however, in the context of the sensational tradition of women's journalism. She wanted no part of an artistic model built on the spectacular bent of mainstream newspaperwomen, of course. Yet Cather's commitment to investing creative power in the female body inevitably led her to take up the newspaperwoman's legacy of public embodiment. But her literary imagination could make use of female bodies only after she had purged them of the self-dramatizing impulse of Ferber's Girl Reporter.

Cather shared more ground with the tradition of women's journalism than is initially apparent. Her attack on the realist ethos, particularly her rejection of "literalness, when applied to the presenting of mental reactions and of physical sensations," signals her skepticism about the artistic value of the news reporter's skills of precise, detached observation.[45] At the same time, it puts as much distance as possible between her writing practice and the mainstream newspaperwoman's practice of reporting on her own physical and emotional experiences. Yet her best fiction exalts the physical body as a source of desire, truth, and power. Her authorial vision, by finding authenticity in bodily truth, in some sense paralleled the intense body-consciousness of the female reporter, whose physical presence (and vulnerability) was so often central to the stories she told. This shared strategy also explains Cather's antipathy to sensational journalism. It threatened to undermine what Cather came to recognize as the very source of authentic artistic expression: the bodies of women.

Cather would not have said, as Ferber did, that her writing career accidentally began when she went to work for a newspaper. Essentially, however, that's what happened. The "major event" of her first year in college was the *Nebraska State Journal*'s publication of her essay on Thomas Carlyle.

Thrilled to see her words in print (her English professor had submitted the essay without telling her), Cather abandoned her plans to study science. Instead, she launched a career as a writer and editor that would sustain her for nearly two decades, taking her from Lincoln to Pittsburgh and then to New York. In 1894, while still a student, she was invited to help teach a journalism course. In 1896 she gave a speech on personal journalism at the first meeting of the women's auxiliary of the Nebraska Press Association.[46] Her first full-time job was editing a woman's magazine in Pittsburgh. During her years as a journalist, she "probably turned out more copy than appears in all of her collected works of the following thirty-five years," observes the biographer James Woodress.[47] She was always more of a theater and book critic than a hard-news reporter; most of her writing was not for the city desk. Yet she covered an assortment of news and feature stories, including the circus that came to Lincoln, the parade for President McKinley when he visited Pittsburgh, and the fortieth anniversary of the founding of a Nebraska river town that had fallen on hard times.[48] She also worked as telegraph editor for the *Pittsburgh Daily Leader,* editing and expanding foreign cables, and she wrote headlines on the sinking of the *Maine* in 1898.[49] In 1906 she began working for the fabled *McClure's* magazine, first as a writer and then as an editor.

Cather continued to pursue her literary writing during her years as a journalist: she published a book of poetry in 1903 and a short story collection in 1905, and placed several stories in national magazines. In 1908, in a well-known act of literary sisterhood, Sarah Orne Jewett wrote a letter urging Cather to get out of journalism to preserve her energies for art.[50] Three years later, Cather followed the advice, taking a leave of absence from *McClure's* to revise the manuscript of what would be her first novel, *Alexander's Bridge* (1912). She never returned to journalism. Instead she began writing some of her most important novels, including *O Pioneers!* (1913) and *My Antonia* (1918). Woodress observes: "When she died in 1947 her public was virtually unaware of this long foreground as a newspaper and magazine writer. She did not talk about it and regarded it as a closed part of her life."[51]

Although Cather's journalism career lasted considerably longer than Ferber's, we know almost nothing about her experience of it.[52] She did not write about it, although even Jewett, the mentor who admonished Cather to get out of journalism, included the newsroom on the very short list of potential topics she identified for Cather. "I want you to be surer of your backgrounds," Jewett wrote in that 1908 letter. "You have your Nebraska life,—a child's Virginia, and now an intimate knowledge of what we are pleased to call the 'Bohemia' of newspaper and magazine-office life."[53]

Cather's subsequent fiction proved Jewett correct in her belief that Cather's life experiences in Nebraska and Virginia would provide the foundation for her best work. But what Jewett called Cather's "intimate knowledge" of the bohemian landscape of journalism, presumably a site of alternative views and lifestyles, remains largely buried. She used a male reporter as the narrator of "Behind the Singer Tower," published in *Collier's* in 1912 as she was making the transition from magazine editor to full-time author, but the story is unsatisfying; Cather's lack of interest in the reporter himself leaves the tale disjointed and awkward.[54] None of Cather's novels takes up journalism as a subject, and there are no newspaperwomen among her heroines.

In an important study of Cather's artistic development, biographer Sharon O'Brien presents Cather's years in journalism as a time when she developed her writing skills in the company of men, a phase during which Cather was retelling "patriarchal myths and reinforcing stereotypes that denied women individuality, complexity, and power."[55] This explanation goes a long way toward explaining Cather's literary evolution. But O'Brien's analysis of Cather's "emerging voice," despite its sensitivity to the ways in which gender roles shape authorship, does not consider the newswoman as a cultural figure that may have discouraged Cather from continuing in journalism and shaped her imaginative treatments of women. The few women reporters Cather encountered in newspaper offices were unlikely to offer her empowering models, given their close identification with the mass-market venue Cather so distrusted. She had good reason to shun the sexually charged publicity associated with women reporters. In her break-through works of long fiction—*O Pioneers!* in 1913, *The Song of the Lark* in 1915, and *My Antonia* in 1918—Cather imagines a creative authority fueled by female sexual desire but, at the same time, resistant to the commodity culture that sought to appropriate that desire. The mainstream newspaperwoman whose femininity and sexuality were marketed along with her stories was anathema to that kind of creative authority. If Cather had known Nellie Bly, one scholar notes, she would have dismissed her as "theatrical and self-advertising."[56]

Yet Cather was no stranger to performances of gender. She cut her hair short and began wearing boys' clothes and calling herself William Cather in 1888, when she was fourteen years old, adopting a self-conscious masculinity that persisted for four years, through the beginning of her college career. Her defiant choice reveals just how aware she was of the implications of being female and especially of appearing in public as a woman. Her refusal to dress "like a girl" attracted attention in Red Cloud, her hometown, and in Lincoln, where she went to college.[57] Since her entry into journalism overlapped with the years of her "William Cather" mas-querade, she probably never stood much of a chance of being labeled a self-dramatizing *girl* reporter. Still, pursuing newspaper work was "a flam-boyant choice," as one critic observes, and in some ways a logical outgrowth of her pose as Billy Cather.[58] Yet unlike Ferber—or, as we shall see, Djuna Barnes—Cather would never assume a reportorial swagger and claim that she used to be a newspaperman.

Cather's account of a newspaper office encounter with Stephen Crane —a rare instance in which she talks about herself in the newsroom—shows her rejecting the reporter-novelist tradition and feminizing one of its stars. In 1893, while still in college, Cather began writing theatrical reviews for the *Nebraska State Journal.* She attended classes in the day, went to the the-ater in the evening, then rushed to the newspaper office to write (often scathing) reviews (see figure 11). It was an exhausting and exhilarating time. Stephen Crane, who was visiting the West to cover drought condi-tions in Nebraska, encountered Cather late one night at the *State Journal* office. Edith Lewis reports on their first meeting: "He was fascinated by the sight of a young girl—Willa Cather—standing *fast asleep.* He said it was the only time he had ever seen anyone asleep on their feet like that."[59] Tinged with both condescension and admiration, Crane's recollection offers a glimpse of Cather's newsroom presence as a young woman, highly visible and oddly vulnerable. Assuming her right to be there yet somehow still out of place, she appears not as a conscious person, capable of producing her own meanings, but as an unconscious body, the object of Crane's gaze.

Calling Crane "the first man of letters I had ever met in the flesh," Cather later recounted an exchange that, scholars have concluded, prob-ably did not occur.[60] In Cather's version, she hangs around the office, pes-tering Crane with questions until finally, late one night, he speaks to her seriously about his writing. Her fictionalized account, published in a Pitts-burgh periodical shortly after Crane's death in 1900, makes Crane's phys-ical person the object of scrutiny and effaces her own position as a curious newsroom phenomenon.[61] The girl reporter asleep in the newsroom, a spectacle in spite of herself, turns her gaze upon "this storymaker man," detailing his appearance of ill health, shaggy hair, shabby suit, and dusty, worn shoes. His slovenly, fragile self-presentation diverges from the popu-lar ideal of the manly newsman; Cather explicitly contrasts Crane with celebrity reporter Richard Harding Davis, "with his Gibson chin always freshly shaven."[62] The sickly, disheveled Crane—whose gloved hands are "long, white, and delicately shaped, with thin, nervous fingers"—confesses to the young Cather the secret of his writing career: that he pondered sto-ries for months before being able to write them, and that he wrote news

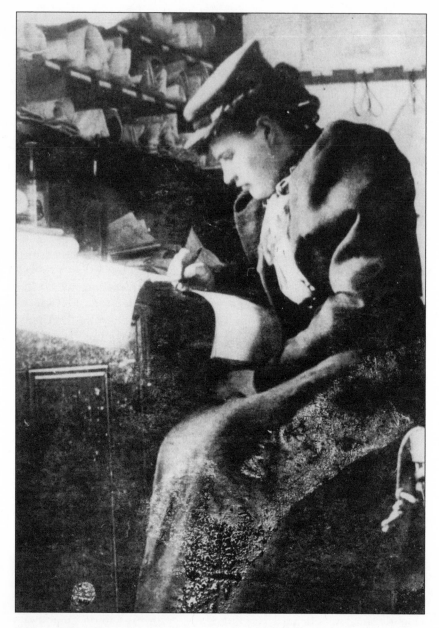

Figure 11. When she was in college in the early 1890s, Willa Cather began working at the *Nebraska State Journal*. (Nebraska State Historical Society Photograph Collections.)

articles only to make money. "I have often been astonished," Cather declares, "to hear Crane spoken of as 'the reporter in fiction,' for the reportorial faculty of superficial reception and quick transference was what he conspicuously lacked."[63] Crane's failure as a reporter authenticates his status as an artist. His "secret" confirms Cather's belief that journalism, which demanded a swift practice of writing, was opposed to literary art, which required refinement over time and careful winnowing of words and ideas. As O'Brien has argued, Cather gives Crane "her own literary aesthetic" and imagines "a rite of literary succession in which a male writer passes on the secret of creativity to the narrator, thus including him (or her) in the American literary tradition."[64] If this is a rite of literary succession, however, Cather makes it a very complicated one, refusing to align herself with the male reporter-novelist tradition even when she has the opportunity to do so. Instead, she bonds with Crane against it, imagining him as part of an alternative tradition to which the newsroom is, at best, incidental. She rescues him, and by extension herself, from what she saw as two artistic threats: the dead end of realism and a rigidly defined public role as a journalist.

Cather's rejection of journalism, particularly newspaper journalism, was part of her larger resistance to America's emerging mass-market culture, which promoted rapid circulation and consumption of information and products, tending to value speed of communication over depth of information and speed of production over product quality. Her first short story collection, *The Troll Garden* (1905), begins and ends with troubling portrayals of creative power tainted by consumerism. In both tales, newspaper reports act as a critical plot element. In "Flavia and Her Artists," a mean-spirited gossip column reveals the corruption of the artists who are the title character's guests, and in "Paul's Case," the teenager who has stolen money for a spree decides to kill himself after seeing an article on his theft. "Flavia and Her Artists," the opening story, depicts an artists' colony as a place of self-indulgence and professional self-interest, where the only things "in the making" are rude remarks and petty gestures. The professional art world acts as a devastating counterpoint to the fairy-tale aspirations of the young woman who serves as the story's center of consciousness. "Paul's Case," the collection's final story, pivots on a similar counterpoint: the jarring disjuncture between a teenager's aesthetic imagination and the business world he is being groomed to enter. Cather, however, reveals that disjuncture to be more apparent than actual, since Paul's pursuit of transcendence leads him only to the revelation that money is everything. Both stories unite Cather's sense of the fragility of the artistic impulse with her contempt for consumerism, and both cast newspapers as a corrosive force.

The visual culture of women's journalism could only have fueled Cather's antipathy, contributing to her dislike for news writing and diminishing her sense of the potential literary value of journalism. Although Cather had always been fascinated by women performers, particularly singers and actresses, she dismissed stereotypical visual images such as the Gibson Girl, a figure of womanhood that rose to national prominence in the early 1900s, as readily as she dismissed the new forms of mass-market fiction such as the Jesse James adventure Jim Burden reads in the opening pages of *My Antonia*. Cather disliked authorial celebrity intensely; she often refused to give interviews to reporters, and she expressed revulsion at the idea of selling her writing along with visual images of herself. This is exactly what many mainstream newspaperwomen were required to do, of course, since their pictures so often accompanied their reportage. *My Antonia*—the novel Cather was writing when she resolved to "banish the reporter" from her writing—evinces her desire to deflect such attention through its use of a male narrator.[65] Cather shifts the "Burden" of authorship onto Jim. And Jim, the novel's fictional author, scarcely appears in the illustrations. In his only illustrated appearance, he stands with Antonia looking at the sun, their backs to the viewer.

The drawings Cather commissioned and oversaw for *My Antonia* attack the very dynamic from which Ferber's "self-dramatizing Girl Reporter" evolved: the tendency to position white American middle-class girls and women as representative of the desires and curiosity of the mass public. Yet Cather also offers an alternative, in the form of working-class and immigrant women, whose images hold out the hope of redeeming the artist (writer and illustrator) from the corrupting influence of mass consumer culture. Her commitment to illustrating female desire both verbally and visually is evident in the drawings that accompanied the first edition of *My Antonia*. Cather commissioned them herself and fought to keep them from being replaced in later editions of the novel. She first met the illustrator W. T. Benda when she was managing editor of *McClure's* magazine. As a Polish immigrant who had lived in the American West, Benda had the kind of background Cather wanted. Cather chose him, according to one critic, because his work "*looked* like the old woodcuts" used before new technology began to reduce costs.[66] In an important analysis, Jean Schwind argues that Benda's illustrations correct Jim Burden's distorted vision, countering his romantic narrative with a realistic pictorial subtext.[67] Benda's illustrations value tradition, not technology, and they act as a realistic counterpoint to Jim Burden's romantic imagination. But by contextualizing Benda's images with the popular visual stereotypes of women appearing in newspa-

Figure 12. This illustration for *My Antonia* represents Lena as both sexy and preoccupied with her task of knitting. It resists conventional visual stereotypes and reinforces the novel's portrayal of Lena as both an object of desire and a determined pursuer of her own desires. (Willa Cather, *My Antonia*, illustrated by W. T. Benda [Boston: Houghton Mifflin, 1918], plate 7. Collections of the Library of Congress.)

pers and magazines, we can also appreciate them as a challenge to the mass-market imagery of women, particularly the commodification of women's sexuality. Benda depicts women not in self-dramatizing poses but intent on their daily activities. They appear anchored within landscapes, not as reproducible icons.

The newspaperwoman Dorothy Dix may have called this era "the Day of the Girl," but in her text and her illustrations, Cather insisted on portraying *women*. Four of the eight pen drawings in *My Antonia* depict solitary female figures. Antonia herself appears four times, first with her family, then alone in a field with her plow, then standing in a field watching the sky with Jim, and, finally, walking alone in a blizzard. Benda's last two drawings are particularly striking in their revision of conventional visual types. Both feature adult immigrant women working in poverty. In the first, a busty Lena stands with arms, legs, and feet bare, in a field, knitting in a dress with a plunging neckline (see figure 12). The illustration depicts Lena as an object of desire, but she looks down at her knitting needles, and her facial expression suggests concentration, not flirtation. Benda's drawing reinforces Cather's text, in which Lena insists that she can't help it that smitten men follow her around; her pastoral innocence seems to invite a sexually charged frolic. It is no wonder that Jim Burden later confesses that he has a recurring erotic dream about Lena. He wishes, he tells us, that he could have this "flattering dream" about Antonia, but he never does.[68]

Benda's final image of Antonia shows us why. Antonia drives unseen cattle in a blizzard, her illegitimate pregnancy concealed by a man's overcoat, her hair caught up in a man's hat (see figure 13).[69] This powerful, androgynous image pits woman against nature; Lena's pastoral frolic gives way to Antonia's heroic battle. Benda leaves Antonia's dark, vertical figure alone in an indeterminate landscape, including none of the surrounding detail he provides in the previous illustrations. Yet her facial expression appears merely intent, not much different from Lena's focus on her knitting needles. In the 1918 edition the text that appears opposite this image describes what Antonia is doing right after she drives the cattle home, namely, giving birth. The Widow Steavens tells Jim: "That very night, it happened. She got her cattle home, turned them into the corral, and went into the house, into her room behind the kitchen, and shut the door. There, without calling to anybody, without a groan, she lay down on the bed and bore her child."[70] Cather's textual description of Antonia in labor is juxtaposed with Benda's visual depiction of Antonia looking more manly than maternal. This merging of genders and labors—the combination of cattle-driving and childbirth—flouts the visual stereotypes of women and roots Antonia in a natural cycle of birth and death, literally bearing the consequences of her own sexuality. The cross-dressed Antonia is not playing at being a man or a woman; she is accepting her lot and creating new life. The playful voyeurism of Lena's image is replaced with the heroic intensity of Antonia's. The novel rewards both women, of course: Lena achieves business success and a carefree city life, while Antonia marries happily and has a large family. But Jim Burden's celebration of "his" Antonia leaves Cather's readers with no doubt about the picture that matters the most to Jim, the narrator, and to Cather, the author. Antonia, whose body bears the marks of her labors (not just childbearing but also the nurturing of her family and her farm), represents not the inchoate desires of an ultimately

Figure 13. The last of *My Antonia*'s four illustrations of its title character, this strikingly androgynous image of Antonia accompanies the scene in which she gives birth. It confronts readers with a portrait of a cross-dressed Antonia at the very moment when she is engaged in the most gender-specific of labors. (Willa Cather, *My Antonia*, illustrated by W. T. Benda [Boston: Houghton Mifflin, 1918], plate 8. Collections of the Library of Congress.)

unknowable mass public but rather a stalwart individual's ability to build and maintain a deep connection to her family and her environment.

Cather's 1920 short story "Coming, Aphrodite!" depicts the threat of mass consumer culture much more explicitly—and again adjoins the voyeuristic subtext of women's journalism—through a striking portrayal of a female character whose body is intensely public and powerful but painfully artificial, cut off from authentic desire and authentic artistic expression. Cather often allows female characters on the social margins— poor women, immigrant women, women like Antonia—to escape what she saw as the artificiality and emptiness of the public embodiment conferred on middle-class white women by the American media. This dynamic is apparent in "Coming, Aphrodite!," in which a male painter falls in love with an ambitious young opera singer who cannot understand why he prizes artistic integrity over commercial success. The story portrays the beautiful singer, Eden Bower, as an embodiment of the mass public that threatens to corrupt the painter. When Cather details her painter-hero's suspicious view of privileged women as false products of thoughtless consumerism, she specifically exempts women of the working classes from the indictment:

> He got on well with janitresses and wash-women, with Indians and the
> peasant women of foreign countries. He had friends among the silk-skirt fac-
> tory girls. . . . He felt an unreasoning antipathy toward the well-dressed
> women he saw coming out of big shops, or driving in the park. If, on his way
> to the Art Museum, he saw a pretty girl standing on the steps of one of the
> houses on upper Fifth Avenue, he frowned at her and went by with his shoul-
> ders hunched up as if he were cold. He had never known such girls, or heard
> them talk, or seen the inside of the houses in which they lived; but he be-
> lieved them all to be artificial and, in an aesthetic sense, perverted. He saw
> them enslaved by desire of merchandise and manufactured articles, effec-
> tive only in making life complicated and insincere and in embroidering it
> with ugly and meaningless trivialities. They were enough, he thought, to
> make one almost forget woman as she existed in art, in thought, and in the
> universe.[71]

The painter's criticism reflects Cather's own ambition to depict "woman as
she existed," not women as consumers or women who seem as mass-produced as the clothing and cosmetics they wear. But the story does not simply attack women as exemplars of materialism. The painter's commentary
on women appears in the text immediately after he has begun to spy on
his lovely neighbor through a knothole in the wall separating their apart-
ments, watching her perform her daily exercises naked. The context for
the passage, then, is the contrast between the painter's near-obsession with
Eden and his usual disinterest in women like her. Naked, she appears to
have escaped the "perverted" aesthetic of the well-dressed women whose
artifice so upsets him. As the painter watches Eden in her bower, his passion overwhelms him: "He could not understand it; he was no boy, he had
worked from models for years, and a woman's body was no mystery to him.
Yet now he did nothing but sit and think about one. . . . This brain held
but one image now—vibrated, burned with it. It was a heathenish feeling;
without friendliness, almost without tenderness" (368).

Through his voyeurism, the story suggests, the painter is enchanted,
swept up in "a vision out of Alexandria, out of the remote pagan past"
(366–67). But once they become lovers, Eden soon reminds him that she
is, in fact, not a magical link to an ancient past. Rather, she is very much a
product of her own publicity-mad era. When she offers to introduce him
to a successful commercial illustrator and he refuses scornfully, she responds in disbelief: "You mean you could make money and don't? That
you don't try to get a public?" When he affirms his contempt for the pub-

lic, she finally says: "I give up. You know very well there's only one kind of success that's real" (389). By endorsing the mass public as the arbiter of the "real," she reveals her failure to appreciate his most cherished goals, and he feels so betrayed that he cannot forgive her. Years later, Eden Bower, now a famous singer, returns to New York in a triumphant production of *Coming, Aphrodite!* and goes out of her way to learn that her former lover has had an influential career in art, although he has never earned popular acclaim. In the last paragraph of the story, Eden's face becomes "hard and settled, like a plaster cast; so a sail, that has been filled by a strong breeze, behaves when the wind suddenly dies. Tomorrow night, the wind would blow again, and this mask would be the golden face of Aphrodite. But a 'big' career takes its toll, even with the best of luck" (396). Unlike Antonia, who inhabits an Edenic orchard at the end of the novel that bears her name, Eden Bower finds no paradise.

In "Coming, Aphrodite!" Cather reinforces the association of women with mass culture. Eden Bower's art is based on the breezes of publicity, not on the integrity and beauty of her own body. The characterization contrasts sharply with Cather's earlier portrayal of Thea Kronborg, the opera singer protagonist of *The Song of the Lark* (1915), a bildungsroman that many critics read as the transitional work in which Cather's mature artistic vision first emerged. Thea's ecstatic union of body and spirit figures Cather's artistic ideal, while Eden's plaster-cast face proves just how wrong Eden is about which kind of success is "real." As Cather pursued her own ideal of success, she resisted the mass-mediated spectacle of the female body. Journalism, especially as practiced by women reporters, was worse than irrelevant to her writing. It was painfully threatening, a force that could wear away the vibrant possibilities of artistic expression, turning Eden Bower's talent and physical beauty into a golden mask. In Cather's view, the price of such a "'big' career" was emptiness.

Djuna Barnes, Stunt Girl

Years ago I used to see people. I had to, I was a newspaperman, among other things. (Djuna Barnes, 1971 interview)[72]

Djuna Barnes first entered a newspaper office twenty years after the heyday of the girl stunt reporters, but her flamboyant career in journalism featured exploits that rivaled Nellie Bly's most daring. Born almost a decade after Ferber and two decades after Cather, Barnes is the most unconventional of this chapter's reporter-novelists.[73] An author who rejected real-

ism and flouted cultural taboos, she staked her place as an artist on the social margin. In the 1910s and 1920s, Barnes surrounded herself with other
avant-garde writers and artists, living in Greenwich Village and then Paris.
Drawn to decadence and fond of satire, Barnes cultivated a personal image that went along with her radical perspective. She was tall and striking
and often wore a dramatic black cape.[74] She had both female and male
lovers, and, even more than Cather, she disrupted conventional gender
roles in her demeanor and in her writing.[75] Walter Winchell insisted that
she could spit better than most men. "Djuna Barnes, the femme writer, can
hit a cuspidor twenty feet away," he wrote in the late 1920s. Barnes denied
this, but she seemed to enjoy the rumor anyway.[76] Her books, not unlike
those of her friend and literary influence James Joyce, affronted middle-
class sensibilities, particularly with their frank treatment of sex and bodily
functions. Barnes's literary writings address poverty, suicide, child abuse,
rape, abortion, incest, and many variations of heterosexual and homosex-
ual sex. Although her best-known work is the experimental novel *Nightwood* (1936), she also produced visual art, poetry, and plays.

A history of bohemian New York cites Barnes as one of the women who
profited from the breakdown of exclusively male journalism. Christine
Stansell contrasts Barnes, who "could swagger around as a more-or-less
open lesbian-about-town in her job as a roving New York journalist, writing hermetic, involuted essays on Village life," with Nellie Bly, who in the
1890s "was so unusual as to make the news herself."[77] Although Stansell is
right to observe that by the 1910s women had become more likely to make
their way from journalism to literature, Bly and Barnes are best viewed not
in opposition but in progression. Literary history's neglect of women's
journalism has obscured the popular roots of Barnes's reporting persona
and kept readers from appreciating how she revised an existing tradition
of sensation journalism.[78] Assuming with a vengeance the newspaperwoman's role as vehicle of publicity, Barnes appropriated conventions of
female reporting to express a modernist aesthetic. Even as she developed
the ornate, difficult style of her most celebrated work, she continued to
reimagine the sensational bodily encounters that characterized women's
news writing.[79]

To be sure, Barnes's talent for aphorism, her splendid sense of rhythm,
and her idiosyncratic vision always distinguished her work from standard
newspaper writing. Her 1915 article about a visit to the International
Workers of the World headquarters opens by noting, "There are two classes
of people: those who wear caps and badges and those who wear hats and
canes." A few paragraphs later, Barnes turns the I.W.W.'s representative
color into a meditation on the struggle of laborers: "All revolt has a color;

the revolt of the mind is the same tint as the revolt of the body and the revolt of the soul. This color is red. Where one comes upon this color, one finds the hub of despair."[80] Short on factual content and long on philosophizing, this piece, published in the *New York Press,* describes the I.W.W. hall through a disorienting mix of concrete details and abstract statements. Writing with palpable ambition, Barnes seeks both to capture a scene—the dirty sheeting draped over the hall's twin doors, the gavel that sits on a little red stand, and the lank blond hair of a workman who speaks—and to make grand, ironic pronouncements on the condition of workers.[81]

Barnes, in short, took herself far too seriously as an artist to echo Ferber's casually ironic claim to being a self-dramatizing Girl Reporter. Yet Barnes may have been the most brilliantly self-dramatizing Girl Reporter of all. By taking up the mantle of the newspaperwoman, she inherited a contradictory legacy of publicity and female embodiment, one that upheld rigidly conventional views of womanhood even while it indulged in potentially subversive gender-bending. Like Ferber, Barnes was capable of appropriating the male identity of "newspaperman," as the quotation at the beginning of this section suggests. But in sharp contrast to Ferber's somewhat rueful fall into stunt reporting, Barnes refused to accept the bodily conventions through which mainstream newspaperwomen reported the news. She rejected the moralistic backdrop of reporting ventures like Ferber's; indeed, in Barnes's writing, one might say that the peepshow never closes down. She remained intrigued by the ways people look at bodies, and she explored voyeurism, especially the female body as a spectacle, in much of her work. Jean Gallegher argues that one of *Nightwood*'s singular achievements is the way it requires readers to abandon a detached, voyeuristic position and to apprehend bodies and sexuality in new ways.[82] Barnes's journalistic work anticipates this achievement.

Barnes scholars have frequently commented on her interest in manipulating the gaze. In an important analysis of spectacle in Barnes's journalism, Barbara Green argues that Barnes's fascination with the power of the gaze made stunt journalism a natural fit: "Given Barnes's position between spectator and spectacle, power and victimage, it seems almost inevitable that she would choose to write performative journalism, making a spectacle of herself by pinning her authority to her status as female image."[83] Such discussions of Barnes's journalism, illuminating as they are, tend to give her both too much and too little credit. Often her news writing has been interpreted as if she invented the subjective, embodied newspaperwoman when in fact she simply redefined it.[84] Mainstream stunt reporters, for the most part, acted as buffers, insulating newspaper readers from too much contact with their subjects. Barnes, however, placed herself at center stage to thrust an unsettling degree of contact upon her readers. Rereading her early reportage as part of a tradition of women's sensation journalism reveals her artful play on newspaper conventions. It also shows that when Barnes inhabited the newspaperwoman's body, she recognized it as both real and unreal, engaged in a circular process of becoming that resisted the very conventions that produced it.

Barnes began writing and drawing for the *Brooklyn Daily Eagle* in 1913, and for the next eight years she supported herself (and, at times, her mother, brothers, and grandmother) by freelancing for most of New York City's major newspapers.[85] She covered an occasional murder trial and a few other hard-news stories, but she specialized in features and interviews with artists, actresses, activists, celebrities of all types, and oddball characters such as the street-corner dentist "Twingeless Twitchell." Barnes was persistent, too; once, after a murder victim's grieving family threw her out of their house, she sneaked back in through an upstairs window to snap a photograph of the corpse.[86] Like Nellie Bly, Barnes often included commentary on her own charms in her interview write-ups, calling herself "Gunga Dul, the Pen Performer," and dramatizing herself along with her subjects.[87] She also performed her fair share of stunts, such as undergoing a force-feeding procedure, climbing into a cage to interview a gorilla, and being rescued by firefighters (three times, twice by rope and once by ladder) from the window of a tall building (see figure 14).[88] One editor even tried to get her to go for a ride in a homemade airplane.[89] Her newspaper career definitively ended, Barnes said, after an editor at the *Journal American* assigned her to interview a girl who had been raped six times. She sneaked past the guards to gain access to the victim's hospital room, tricked her into talking about the crime, and immediately regretted it. She refused to give the story to her editor and was promptly fired.[90] In the 1920s, Barnes opted for magazine journalism and the chance to live abroad, moving to Paris to write about the expatriate community for *McCall's*.[91] As her literary reputation grew, she took on fewer assignments; she wrote for *Theatre Guild* between 1929 and 1931, then effectively retired from journalism.

Barnes, like Cather, scoffed at writers who pandered to the mass public; she called her own journalism "rubbish."[92] As an artist, she disdained the average reader and sought recognition largely within an elite modernist circle that included James Joyce, Ezra Pound, T. S. Eliot, and Gertrude Stein.[93] She drew a firm line between journalism and literary work: the former paid the bills, the latter served art.[94] As one scholar of Barnes's journalism puts it, "She wrote newspaper and magazine journalism to survive, but she did not value it."[95] Barnes would never say, à la Ferber, that she

Figure 14. Djuna Barnes tested firefighters' rescue tactics in one of her newspaper stunts. (Djuna Barnes, "My Adventures Being Rescued," *New York World Magazine*, November 15, 1914. General Research Division, The New York Public Library, Astor, Lenox, and Tilden Foundations.)

learned to write in a newspaper office; when she went to work for the *Brook-lyn Eagle*, she had already published a poem in *Harper's Weekly*.[96] Earning money as a reporter kept her from depending on sales of her artistic and literary work for her livelihood, and in this way, her journalism career fostered creative independence, allowing her to experiment with style, form, and content.[97] More than one literary critic, however, has noted the irony that her "serious work" was not much appreciated, while "the journalism that came so easily and that she scorned was applauded."[98]

In part because of this irony, Barnes's early journalism has attracted scholars looking for insight into her self-consciously literary writing. They have found evidence of Pound's poetic theory in her reportorial style and traced her dualistic themes back to her choice of news topics.[99] One critic suggests that Barnes adapted the narrative conventions of journalism in her early short fiction, particularly in her use of stereotypes, her tendency to pack key information into introductory paragraphs, and her emphasis on action over characterization.[100] Another argues that some parts of *Nightwood* echo Barnes's journalism so clearly that her articles may well have provided source material for her greatest novel.[101] Her deliberate blurring of subject and object in her journalism and her persistent attraction to the grotesque and the deviant have been cited as early indicators of her avant-garde sensibility and her radical critique of societal conventions. So have her journalistic disruptions of gender identity and her pursuit of physical sensations as a means of truth-telling.[102] Such studies demonstrate convincingly that Barnes's literary inclinations shaped her journalism. They do not tell us much, however, about how inhabiting the charged role of the woman journalist may have shaped her literary inclinations.

Acknowledging Barnes's newspaper precursors allows us to see how she transformed the roles of stunt reporter and sob sister, contesting the terms through which the woman reporter's body was understood. Stunt reporters, as we have seen, carefully preserved the assumed virtue and sexual inviolability of the white, middle-class female body, thus containing their transgressions of cultural norms. Meanwhile, the tears of the sob sisters, the standard-bearers of sentimentalism in the popular press, signaled the depth of their womanly sympathy, so that their bodies acted as filters for a corrupt world. Barnes deployed many of the same strategies as these newspaperwomen—turning herself into an object of her own commentary, stressing her personal performance, narrating the process of her own objectification—but she refused to honor the essential definition of the female body that subtended them. This definition of white womanhood insulated female reporters when they risked their lives in subway tunnels and lion's dens or when they came into close contact with dirty, poor, exploited, or potentially corrupt urban dwellers. Barnes did more than reject this definition; she exploded it. She attacked the essential notion of white womanhood that cloaked the sharper edges of newspaperwomen's transgressions in the popular press. In effect, she performed as a stunt reporter without a net. Barnes flaunted the paradox of the sensational newswoman's body, which was called upon to be inviolable and permeable at the same time, to manifest the bedrock virtue of white womanhood and to act as a purifying filter through which crime and corruption could pass and then be presented, tidily, to newspaper readers.

Barnes's most famous stunt serves as a breathtaking example of her ability to reimagine the newswoman's body without a safety net of reassurances about that body's virtue and stability. Her report on being forcibly fed—inspired by the British government's policy of force-feeding suffragists who staged hunger strikes in jail—reveals the depth of her debt to women's sensation journalism, as well as her radical departures from its tradition. When the suffragists, imprisoned for civil disobedience, refused to eat to attract attention to their demand for the right to vote, prison authorities used steel gags and inserted feeding tubes between their teeth.[103] In fall 1914, Barnes subjected herself to a similar procedure (minus the steel gag) to write "How It Feels to Be Forcibly Fed," which appeared in the *New York World Magazine*. It was illustrated with multiple photographs of Barnes lying on a table, wrapped from head to toe in a sheet, being force-fed by a gowned and masked doctor and held down by three other men in rolled-up shirtsleeves. As she points out early in the story, she appeared, and felt, not unlike a corpse (see figure 15).[104]

Critics have rightly called attention to the way Barnes used her own body to protest the government policy of punishing suffragists, arguing that she "forced the state to enact its repressive politics on her body" and even that she enacted "the violation not only of the personal body, but of the body politic."[105] It is also worth noting, however, that the story follows the stunt reporter template established decades earlier by putting the newswoman's body at risk, stressing her vulnerability to violation, and using her suffering to encourage sympathetic identification with others who are similarly treated. Submitting to an invasive medical procedure, though reserved for the particularly bold, was nonetheless a standard stratagem in women's stunt journalism.[106] Recognizing its conventionality allows for a more rigorous reading of Barnes's avant-garde position—and a better understanding of how Barnes deployed her own body. Surely Barnes realized, for instance, that she could not simply defy consumer culture by acknowledging the tradition of marketing women's sensations as commodities.[107] The

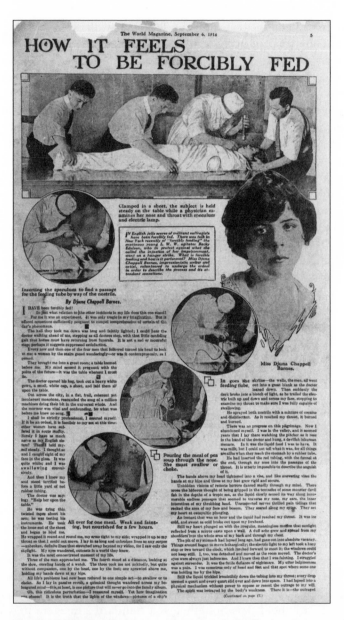

Figure 15. Horrified by the British government's treatment of suffragists who were on hunger strikes to protest women's lack of voting rights, Barnes arranged to undergo a force-feeding procedure so she could write about the experience. (Djuna Barnes, "How It Feels to Be Forcibly Fed," *New York World Magazine,* September 6, 1914. Special Collections Department, University of Maryland Libraries.)

staging of journalistic experience was nothing new by the time Barnes was doing it. What is remarkable about her reportage is not that she puts herself in danger, or that she challenges expert authority, but that she does so while shedding the armor of the conventional white middle-class female body which protected the stunt reporters—and their readers—from getting too close to the menaces their stories purported to document. In her stylized extension of the stunt reporting fad, Barnes takes on a tradition that combined a progressive veneer with ambivalent portrayals of people who operated outside cultural norms.

Barnes's revision of the standard medical procedure stunt begins with an exclamation—"I have been forcibly fed!"—and immediately emphasizes the difference between her experience and that of the British suffragists: "For me it was an experiment. It was only tragic in my imagination. But it offered sensations sufficiently poignant to compel comprehension of certain of the day's phenomena."[108] As we saw in chapter 1, it was conventional for stunt reporters to stress the uniqueness of their position and their essential difference from the roles they were assuming. Barnes, however, highlights not her difference from the suffragists but rather the difference between her choice to conduct an "experiment" and the suffragists' implicitly tragic lack of choice. At the same time, she offers her own physical sensations as a means to "compel comprehension" of the government's response to the jailed activists' hunger strike. Those sensations quickly take over the account, as Barnes describes her long walk down a hallway into the procedure room and pauses to recount her feelings:

> I shall be strictly professional, I assured myself. If it be an ordeal, it is familiar to my sex at this time; other women have suffered it in acute reality. Surely I have as much nerve as my English sisters? Then I held myself steady. I thought so, and I caught sight of my face in the glass. It was quite white; and I was swallowing convulsively.
>
> And then I knew my soul stood terrified before a little yard of red rubber tubing. (175)

The absurdity of any claim to strict professionalism is a primary target of Barnes's wit here. Instead of delivering an "acute reality" to her readers, she becomes a self-deprecating protagonist, narrating a tragedy that was, as she has already told us, tragic only in her imagination. Yet what she admits is "only" in her imagination becomes fiercely gripping as the article proceeds and her consciousness rebels against the procedure. She describes her growing loss of physical and psychological control at each step, as the doctor immobilizes her ("My eyes wandered, outcasts in a world they

knew" [176]), then examines and prepares her ("Now I abandoned myself. I was in the valley" [176]). Finally, he inserts the tubing through her
nose into her throat and pours milk into the funnel, and Barnes's narrative descends into nightmare:

> Unbidden visions of remote horrors danced madly through my mind.
> There arose the hideous thought of being gripped in the tentacles of some
> monster devil fish in the depths of a tropic sea, as the liquid slowly sensed its
> way along the innumerable endless passages that seemed to traverse my nose,
> my ears, the inner interstices of my throbbing head. Unsuspected nerves
> thrilled pain tidings that racked the area of my face and bosom. They seared
> along my spine. They set my heart at catapultic plunging.
>   An instant that was an hour, and the liquid had reached my throat. (177)

The ironic distance from her experience, so apparent in the article's opening, disappears. Documenting a loss of self, Barnes dispenses with any pretense of inviolability. Unlike the sob sisters, her body offers up no tears, no
moral filter, no soothing balm of sympathy in response to violence and suffering. And unlike the stunt reporters, Barnes declines to protect her readers from the dangers of overidentification.

Whereas the stunt reporters emphasized the disjunction between their
essential selves and their assumed roles, Barnes uses the performing self
to gain access to something essential within. She simultaneously expresses
her subconscious and articulates a politically charged vision, unifying personal experience with political conviction. Barbara Green argues that
Barnes forges her own spectacular power through this physical surrender:
Barnes portrays the procedure "as a crude and mechanical rape of the female body," Green writes, but her "professional discourse, her very writing
of the event, acts as a defense against medical invasion and allows her
to look again at the scene of her own blinding, to look back at the master-
ing physician."[109] This interpretation, compelling as it is, applies almost
equally to Nellie Bly's more pedestrian description in her 1888 *New York
World* article, "Visiting the Dispensaries: Nelly [sic] Bly Narrowly Escapes
Having Her Tonsils Amputated."[110] All stunt reporters found ways to "look
back" at medical experts and other professionals, juxtaposing the truth of
their physical sensations with the disinterested perspective of experts.
Barnes, however, goes beyond this paradigm, describing the invasion of
her mind and body with an intensity of detail that takes the narrative out
of the confines of doctor-patient, expert-layperson conflict into a crisis of
existential proportions.

Like other women reporters who are drawn into their stories as both objects and agents, Barnes calls her body into the service of public reality. In

this story, however, her body refuses to cooperate. Her report appears committed not to making the world seem less threatening to her readers but rather to forcing them to recognize its unmanageability. The public reality being served by her bodily experiment appears increasingly unreal, based only on the uncertain foundation of her own corporeality. As the milk slowly drips through the tubing into her belly, Barnes feels herself surrendering:

> The spirit was betrayed by the body's weakness. There it is—the outraged will. If I, playacting, felt my being burning with revolt at this brutal usurpation of my own functions, how they who actually suffered the ordeal in its acutest horror must have flamed at the violation of the sanctuaries of their spirits.
>
> I saw in my hysteria a vision of a hundred women in grim prison hospitals, bound and shrouded on tables just like this. (178)

Insisting upon both her artifice (her "playacting") and her complete loss of physical and psychological control, Barnes imagines her agony as a pale reflection of the pain of those "who actually suffered the ordeal," even as she slips into a vision of her own entrapment replicated a hundred times. Her personal "hysteria" is a mechanism of publicity itself, transmitting an image of oppressed women through her internal response to her own suffering.

The force-feeding story, despite its classic stunt reporting dimensions, may have more in common with the work of Ida B. Wells than that of Nellie Bly. In this and other writings, Barnes, like Wells, discredits the cherished ideal of the inviolate, inherently virtuous white female body. The fictionalized retellings of Barnes's own abusive family history in *Ryder* and *The Antiphon* constitute their own "red record" of violation. Barnes's force-feeding stunt also echoes the anti-lynching crusaders' emphasis on collective experience over individual achievement. Despite her already apparent interest in forging a unique artistic voice, Barnes celebrates not the singularity of her sensational suffering but its shared nature. In her self-described hysteria, Barnes conjures up her own fantastic counterpublic, made up of women in prison hospitals, shrouded on tables, laid out like corpses. "How It Feels to Be Forcibly Fed" does not, to be sure, stress the rationality of its author, as Wells and her sister anti-lynching activists were prone to do; but in its express hope that the author's sensations would "compel comprehension of certain of the day's phenomena," it calls out for public debate on the treatment of jailed suffragists.

In the article's final passage, Barnes rises shakily from the table:

I had shared the greatest experience of the bravest of my sex. The torture
and outrage of it burned in my mind; a dull, shapeless, wordless anger arose
to my lips, but I only smiled. The doctor had removed the towel about his
face. The little, red mustache on his upper lip was drawn out in a line of pleasant understanding. He had forgotten all but the play. The four men, having
finished their minor part in one minor tragedy, were already filing out at the
door.

"Isn't there any other way of tying a person up?" I asked. "That thing looks
like—"

"Yes, I know," he said gently. (179)

Concluding with a jab at the doctor, who "gently" acknowledges that his
force-feeding apparatus makes women look like shrouded corpses, Barnes
contrasts her wordless anger with the condescension of the red-mustached
expert, whose expression of "pleasant understanding" makes his efficient
supervision of the brutal procedure all the more horrifying. And Barnes
does not profess to have learned anything about herself at all, except perhaps that she cannot control her will, much less her body. Having taken
her readers deep within herself, having documented an almost unbearable
invasion of the so-called sanctuary of her spirit, she concludes with yet another artifice. She smiles.

In Barnes's writing, the self-dramatizing newspaperwoman becomes not
just an ironic figure but a tragic one, an index of the modern world's in-
humanity, a sign of the impossibility of self-knowledge, and evidence of the
elusive nature of identity itself. The doctor's gentle words of understanding are themselves an outrage, proof of the hypocrisy of sentimental culture's fetishizing of sympathetic identification. Barnes takes up the body
of the female reporter with a rigor that ultimately undermines the subject
position that makes her reporting possible. Under her ruthless self-inter-
rogation, the newswoman's public body itself becomes fragmentary, disin-
tegrating under the pressure of the very publicity that has called it into
being. Like Cather, Barnes entertained artistic ambitions that led her to
disdain journalism and distance herself from her early reporting. But her
revision of the mainstream newspaperwoman's sensational tactics, particularly her self-conscious flouting of reader expectations and her fascination with the spectacle of the body, prefigured her future work.

Many of Barnes's subsequent productions as a literary and visual artist
directly challenge the conventions that purport to govern female bodies
as they appear in public. The title of her first published collection of poems, *The Book of Repulsive Women* (1915), suggests her fierce opposition to
expectations about female appearance and behavior.[111] So does her visual

art. In *Ladies Almanack* (1928), a compendium of stories burlesquing her lesbian circle in Left Bank Paris, the "Windy March" chapter opens with an image of a woman holding a hand against another (presumably flatulent) woman's bared buttocks.[112] And in an image censored from the first edition of Barnes's novel *Ryder* (1928), a woman spreads her legs, lifts her skirts, and urinates in the street.[113] One critic calls the illustrations for *Ladies Almanack* and *Ryder* "the visual equivalent of sexually free writing."[114] The debates over censorship that her work inspired reenact the dynamic it seeks to interrogate—namely, the process that determines what bodily experiences are seen, felt, and narrated.[115] Unsettling assumptions about the relations between bodies and identities, surface and depth, publicity and intimacy preoccupied her throughout her career. Her unblinking approach to bodies and sex, her strategy of "making the familiar strange," and her carnivalesque mixing of styles and genres all served her subversive ends.[116]

The stunt reporters' role as urban guides—which itself revised the sensational "mysteries of the city" narratives of the mid-nineteenth century—informs the city wanderings of the characters of *Nightwood,* Barnes's melancholic tale of sexual obsession and loss.[117] Typically, however, Barnes denies her readers the reassurances that characterized mainstream newspaperwomen's encounters with the dark side of urban life, as she dismantles any notion of the white woman's body as inherently virtuous. An influential analysis argues that *Nightwood* deliberately constructs scenes of obscenity in order to challenge sexual orthodoxies.[118] Set in Paris, Vienna, and Berlin, with a final scene in upstate New York, *Nightwood*'s plot, such as it is, tracks the unhappy fate of three characters who, in relatively rapid succession, fall in love with an elusive young American named Robin Vote. Since Barnes gives Robin almost no voice in the novel, her politically charged name (one wonders, what rights does she have?) seems especially ironic. One of *Nightwood*'s most notorious elements is the explicit bestialization of its characters, especially Robin, who becomes a passionate object of desire for others while remaining indifferent not just to her lovers but to her own well-being.[119] In the novel's last scene, she crawls on the floor with a dog, barking, laughing, and crying.[120] Faced with such shocking disintegration, Barnes's readers are offered only one potential guide, in the figure of Dr. Matthew O'Connor, an endless talker whose favorite subject is the night.

We might read Dr. O'Connor, *Nightwood*'s most celebrated character, as a distant but recognizable parody of the sensational newspaperwoman, as Barnes's final devolution of the self-dramatizing Girl Reporter. Dr. O'Connor—cross-dresser, unlicensed gynecologist, storyteller, and the only character in the novel who seems able to explain anything to anyone else—professes a non-expert form of expertise. Like Nellie Bly, he is a performative amateur casual and a critic of scientific rationalism. And like the sob sisters, he is an emotionally expressive respondent to trauma, called upon to narrate and purify a corrupt world. In the surreal landscape of *Nightwood,* however, he can embody only the horror and failure of sob sisterhood. He converses constantly but purifies nothing, and he eventually collapses under the emotional burden. In his often cited last appearance in the novel, he screams with "sobbing laughter," overwhelmed by his role as explicator of the novel's many failed and abusive love matches. "'Love falling buttered side down, fate falling arse up! Why doesn't anyone know when everything is over, except me? . . . I've known everyone,' he said. 'everyone!'" Drunk, reeling, unable to understand or justify his own sympathy for the characters who have sought him out, he tries to stand and cannot. "'Now,' he said, 'the end—mark my words—now nothing, but wrath and weeping!'"[121] Pressed to ameliorate modernity's alienating effects, Dr. O'Connor explodes into hyperexpressiveness and disappears. By the time Robin Vote goes down on all fours in the novel's climax, he is already gone.

⁂

The alternative reporter-novelist traced in this chapter is defined less by bold inquiry or keen observation than by bodily self-consciousness. In her literary work, bodily experience offers a bulwark against the alienating effects of the mass media and a concrete means of grappling with the complexities of modern life. That experience is also shaped, however, by external demands, by commercial imperatives and gender conventions that exist outside the body. Bodily experience, even of the most intimate sort, is always potentially public, always somehow scripted and staged. Although women's bodies are critical to the alternative reporter-novelist's authorial vision, her most urgent conviction may well be an unsettling sense that those bodies are always being produced and reproduced, always serving multiple audiences, always engaged in the process of becoming the news. Her bodily consciousness unites her concepts of art and labor, figuring her authorship through the mass-market publicity that changed how and what Americans read in the late nineteenth and early twentieth centuries. Newswomen posited their bodies as sources of reality, but even as they did so, they were taking on the role of Ferber's self-dramatizing Girl Reporter, self-consciously producing, manipulating, and performing their bodies for public consumption. Barnes, more directly than Ferber or Cather, called attention to the paradoxical nature of the girl reporter's truth claims, foregrounding the essential unreality of the news transmitted by sensational newswomen. But all three of these writers kept some version of the newswoman's body in full view as they wrote, responding in their own ways to mass-market publicity's rendering of that body as both necessary and absurd.

Ferber, Cather, and Barnes—three writers who shared beginnings as newspaper workers but pursued very different literary careers—suggest the breadth of the newspaperwoman's legacy in American literary culture. Much of that legacy still remains unexplored. Recovering the work of mainstream newspaperwomen requires us to adjust our view of journalism in the United States, the role of women in mass culture, and the ways in which writers have responded to that culture. It also compels us to revisit our assumptions about the links between journalism and fiction in the American literary tradition. The path from news to novels, as I have noted, has never been particularly direct. Taking female reporters into account makes that path more crowded, more crooked, and more worth attending to than ever before. And while all the writers I have called upon to evoke an alternative reporter-novelist tradition are women, it is quite possible to imagine adding men to the group. To suggest otherwise would impose an inflexible model of gender on a tradition marked by fluid roles and flexible boundaries.

The figure of Dr. O'Connor, the cross-dressing pontificator of Barnes's *Nightwood,* gestures toward the gender-bending that has characterized the figure of the female reporter throughout this book. Although the gender identity of newspaperwomen acted as the very foundation of the "woman's angle" they were charged to provide, that identity itself was far from fixed. In an 1888 newspaper column titled "Nellie Bly's Odd Letters: Queer Communications Written by All Kinds of Strange People," New York's best-known girl stunt reporter introduces and quotes from a set of letters, including a "sweet and girlish" one that begs: "Please won't you tell me if you are a man or a woman? My chum's brother says you never existed at all, and I say you are a girl. Please decide for us. Inclosed find stamp for reply. P.S.—Do you play tennis?"[122] The column includes no response from Bly, so the letter receives no public answer; instead, it stands alone as a girlish grace note at the end of Bly's column. But we smile indulgently at the letter writer's naïve question at our own peril. Literary history has, essentially, taken the side of the chum's brother by discounting newspaperwomen so thoroughly that they might as well not have existed. Meanwhile, the implications of Bly's ambiguous gender identity—Is she a girl, a man, or a woman?—have escaped us. By printing the question, Bly invites readers to consider it themselves. Her refusal to decide "for" her reading public, as the letter writer requests, engages her readers in a sly game: Do they know the answer? If so, how? And if not, why not? Beneath these questions, of course, is the most daring one of all: What difference does it make? Until literary scholars acknowledge women's journalism as a vital and complex force in American letters, this question, too, will go unanswered.

Epilogue: Girl Reporters on Film

The same qualities that relegated newspaperwomen to the margins of literary history have made them especially appealing to filmmakers. The popular image of the female reporter whose body constantly came into play in her stories, whose presence at a news event was itself remarkable, whose emotionality and physical vulnerability generated as much narrative tension as the ostensible subjects of her reporting has translated readily into screenplays (and comic strips, as evidenced by the long-standing popularity of Lois Lane and Brenda Starr). From Jean Arthur's Babe Bennett in *Mr. Deeds Goes to Town* (1936) to Kate Winslet's Bitsey Bloom in *The Life of David Gale* (2003), women reporters have often been easier to find on screen than in actual newsrooms. Lying, crying, wisecracking, mending—and unmending—their ways, reporter-heroines like Babe and Bitsey have been celebrated and mocked, rewarded and punished, often in rapid succession. Taking a star turn as a reporter was almost a rite of passage for Hollywood actresses in the 1930s and 1940s. Joan Crawford goes undercover as a dancer to solve a gang murder in *Dance, Fools, Dance* (1931); Bette Davis gets a killer to confess and frees an innocent man in *Front Page Woman* (1935); Barbara Stanwyck concocts an elaborate stunt based on a fake suicide threat in *Meet John Doe* (1941); and Katharine Hepburn takes phone calls almost nonstop in her job as a political columnist (without ever seeming to cover an actual story) in *Woman of the Year* (1942).[1]

Film depictions of female reporters take up the body-conscious tactics of performative journalism, extending and occasionally unsettling the tra-

161

ditions of women's journalism I have explored in this book. In Frank Capra's *Mr. Deeds Goes to Town,* newspaperwoman Babe Bennett masquerades as a damsel in distress to trick a kindly small-town man (the Mr. Deeds of the title, played by Gary Cooper) who comes to the city after he unexpectedly inherits a fortune. They start dating and he falls in love while she writes front-page stories making fun of him. Babe thus encapsulates a primary dilemma for the newswoman: her professional success depends on her womanly appeal, but her performance as a sweet young thing unsettles the essential notions of womanhood that make her success possible. Could a real woman avoid falling in love with Gary Cooper? Of course not, says the film. Eventually Babe quits her job and devotes herself to making up for her deception.[2] Film characterizations of female reporters do more than illustrate the contradictions of being professional women, however. They dramatize the conditions of sentimental authorship, with its union of professionalism and emotionalism, its commitment to producing sentimental commodities in the form of narratives, and its dependence on female bodies as emotional conduits. And they often highlight how women writers' embodiment makes them especially vulnerable to victimization. At times, they even dismantle the assumed natural link between women writers and emotional news narratives, unlocking the bond between female bodies and expressions of affect.

The most famous film image of a newspaperwoman, Rosalind Russell's turn as the fast-talking Hildy Johnson in Howard Hawks's *His Girl Friday* (1940), both invokes and counters the sensational legacy of female reporters. The sentiment and spectacle that characterized mainstream women's journalism are everywhere apparent in *His Girl Friday.* But instead of identifying its newspaperwoman with these elements, the film insulates her from them. Hildy vacillates between two men: Walter (Cary Grant), her newsman ex-husband, who wants her to keep writing, and Bruce (Ralph Bellamy), her kind but dimwitted new fiancé. To keep Hildy from marrying Bruce, Walter involves her in a story about a hapless man who has been unfairly sentenced to death for an accidental shooting. Walter begs Hildy to interview the prisoner the day before his execution to try to save his life, but Hildy tells him to write the story himself. When Walter says, "You know I can't write that kind of thing. It takes a woman's touch, it needs that heart—" Hildy interrupts him with, "Don't get poetic. Get Sweeney—he's the best man you've got on the paper for that sob sister stuff." This exchange unravels the gender-specific nature of sob-sisterhood by suggesting that men can be at least as effective as women in writing that "stuff." It also treats the death row interview as a sentimental commodity; Hildy agrees to do it only after Walter promises to buy a big insurance policy from her fiancé.

Even more striking, however, is the way the film distances Hildy from the emotion and spectacle erupting around her. *His Girl Friday* uses not Hildy but Mollie Malloy, the sweetheart of the condemned murderer, to embody the sensational content of women's journalism. When Mollie enters the pressroom and pleads with the newsmen to help the imprisoned man, they ignore and insult her. While Mollie acts the part of the excessively emotional woman, Hildy observes from a distance, her fingers poised at her typewriter. Only after Mollie begins to sob uncontrollably does Hildy intervene and lead Mollie out of the room. She goes on to write a sentimental story about Mollie and the condemned murderer—a story so effective that when the newsmen sneak a look at it while it is still in her typewriter, they say they can't believe that anyone who writes so well would leave the business to get married. Because Hildy's ability to narrate Mollie's intimate connection to the condemned murderer is a professional asset, we might conclude that her success stems from her ability to identify as a woman with Mollie's suffering. But the scene resists this interpretation. Hildy and Mollie almost never appear in the same shot, and Hildy remains wedded to her typewriter, observing and calculating, while Mollie paces, gestures, and pleads. Hildy does not identify with Mollie, nor does she care more about the story than about her personal goals.

Later, when the distraught Mollie jumps out the pressroom window and tries to kill herself, Hildy is distressed—but not terribly so. And Hildy's story on Mollie and the murderer, affecting as it is, never appears in print. She rips it up to get back at Walter, who has continued to derail her plans to marry Bruce. Moreover, Hildy herself does not cry until the very end of *His Girl Friday*, when she thinks that Walter is sending her away from the newspaper business. And even then, her tears are for her lost career, not for the people she writes about. Hildy's character thus resists the model of authorship that typified the figure of the girl reporter in American culture. "You're getting a great newspaperman," the editor played by Cary Grant assures Bruce, the insurance salesman who is about to marry Hildy. By the end of the film, Hildy grows so frustrated by Bruce's attempts to get her attention while she is trying to write a breaking story that she exclaims, "I'm no suburban bridge player, I'm a newspaperman!"[3]

His Girl Friday is probably the best-known instance of explicit gender-bending in the history of images of newspaperwomen, since Russell's role in the film was based on a male character in Ben Hecht and Charles MacArthur's popular play *The Front Page* (1928).[4] In the original version, a male editor schemes to keep his best reporter, who is a man, from leaving the business to get married. By turning the male reporter of the original play into a woman, director Howard Hawks made *His Girl Friday* into a comic masterpiece. But Hawks did not change the story enough to make Hildy into a "real" newspaperwoman, on the order of a stunt reporter or sob sister. Instead, he staged the Hildy-Walter conflict as a heterosexual battle of equals. Such a battle required Hildy to be neither entirely a news-*man* nor entirely a news*woman*. Her dazzling androgyny has been difficult, if not impossible, for female reporters in subsequent films to achieve.[5]

Since *His Girl Friday,* a long list of reporter-heroines on screen has kept alive the sensational legacy of the stunt reporters and the sob sisters. In *Bridget Jones's Diary* (Miramax, 2001), the journalism career of Renee Zellweger's lovesick thirty-something is played strictly for laughs. The slightly overweight Bridget's first assignment as a television journalist is to slide down a firehouse pole wearing a miniskirt and a firefighter's helmet, for a report that features not her interview with firefighters but a shot of her exposed bottom on its way down the pole. Early in the sequel, *Bridget Jones: The Edge of Reason* (Universal, 2004), Bridget jumps out of an airplane to "investigate" the hobby of sky-diving and lands in a pigsty. When her boss orders cameramen to get "a close-up of the porker," they focus on her mud-splattered behind. In both films, Bridget's career takes a backseat to her search for a husband, a consistent theme even in recent films that give more attention to their heroines' work as journalists. The two plot lines that dominate films starring newswomen—the romantic hoax that backfires and the innocent man condemned to die—are perhaps most noteworthy for their stubborn insistence that for women, finding a mate continues to be a life and death proposition.[6]

But the popular iconography of the girl reporter may have been carried to its logical conclusion not in the movies but on television, in the wildly popular HBO comedy *Sex and the City.*[7] From 1999 to 2003, Sarah Jessica Parker starred as sharp-witted newspaper columnist Carrie Bradshaw, who reports weekly on New Yorkers' sex lives, including her own. She does "research" in bars, nightclubs, and high-end restaurants, documenting the characteristics of "toxic bachelors" and finding out for herself what happens when a woman has sex "like a man" (without feeling, she explains). Featuring an endless parade of designer fashions and explicit discussions about intercourse, *Sex and the City* revolves around women's material and sexual desires. Carrie embodies those desires in her writing and in her person, particularly when she is photographed for an advertisement in a sultry pose, wearing what she comes to call "the naked dress." Along with the title "Carrie Bradshaw knows good sex (and isn't afraid to ask)," the pho-

tograph appears on a bus billboard promoting her "Sex and the City" column.[8] In one episode, Carrie and her friends, armed with champagne,
gather on the sidewalk for their first glimpse of the bus billboard, but the
festive occasion falls flat when the billboard comes into view. The image
has already been defaced; someone has drawn a penis near Carrie's mouth,
so it looks as if she is about to perform fellatio on an oddly detached male
organ. Carrie's humiliation is short-lived; her friends console her, and she
is soon happily engaged in new dating dilemmas.[9] But the defaced billboard acts as a reminder of the vulnerabilities that subtend the woman
writer's public embodiment. By treating her own sexual intimacies as news
items, Carrie forges an authorial persona that transforms her life into a
kind of stunt, a performance of desire that can always be co-opted by her
audience. As cutting edge as her character appears, she might as well be
Nellie Bly; the shift from stunt girl to "postfeminist" sex columnist marks
not a revolution but the culmination of a long-established tradition. *Sex
and the City* has been celebrated for its portrayal of powerful, smart women
who pursue their desires with energy and humor.[10] Still, the newspaperwoman imagined at the turn of a new century expresses many of the same
possibilities and problems that she did at the turn of the last one.

Notes

Introduction

1. Bok, "Is the Newspaper Office the Place for a Girl?" 18.
2. Ross, *Ladies of the Press*, 3.
3. Ibid., 6.
4. William Dean Howells, "The Writer as Worker," in *Criticism and Fiction*, 305.
5. Scholarship on journalism and turn-of-the-century fiction in the United States focuses almost exclusively on male authors. Important studies such as Larzer Ziff's *The American 1890s* and Shelley Fisher Fishkin's *From Fact to Fiction* discuss newsmen exclusively. Christopher Wilson's study of American authors' quest for professional status suggests that the "masculine style" of Progressive Era journalism "put constraints upon many female novelists and journalists" (*Labor of Words*, 142). More recent work has made masculinity an explicit topic of inquiry. Keith Gandal's analysis of the slum as a literary spectacle argues for the "masculine nature of the turn-of-the-century interest in slums" and suggests that "the dogged city reporter" joined "the panoply of supermasculine figures that included the soldier . . . the cowboy, the hunter, and the Indian" (*The Virtues of the Vicious*, 10, 13). In his 1997 study of Stephen Crane's journalism, Michael Robertson makes a similar point. "The meaning of newspaper work for most journalists of the era," according to Robertson, "was tied to issues of male identity" (*Stephen Crane, Journalism, and the Making of Modern American Literature*, 4). John Dudley argues that male novelists wanted to be known as reporters in order to "camouflage" their potentially feminized role as artists (*A Man's Game*, 7, 60–62). Female reporters, even when noted as trendsetters, frequently merit only a few sentences. Mark Pittenger, in a wide-ranging study of Progressive Era social investigators he calls "down-and-outers," acknowledges that their "most exact predecessors were the sensational 'stunt girl' newspaper journalists such as Nellie Bly and her many imitators." But Pittenger mentions these women only in passing, to introduce the men who followed them ("A World of Difference," 30, 32–33). In his rich analysis of the class politics of Progressive Era social investigations, Eric Schocket makes a similar gesture, noting the female stunt reporters' role as initial "popularizers" of cross-class reporting without further comment ("Undercover Explorations of the 'Other Half,'" 112).

6. Crane's sketches appeared in the *New York Press,* "Misery" on April 22, 1894, and "Luxury" on April 29, 1894. On Crane, see Trachtenberg, "Experiments in Another Country"; and Robertson, *Stephen Crane,* 95–106. Another well-known journalist who wasn't above masquerading for a story was Julian Ralph, who once pretended to be a mayor's secretary to get a scoop. See Faue, *Writing the Wrongs,* 97. For more details on Ralph, see Lancaster, *Gentleman of the Press.*

7. Frazer, "The Sob-Lady," 41. Frazer, who published fiction in the *Saturday Evening Post* and *Good Housekeeping,* served as an ambulance service nurse and then as a war correspondent in France during the First World War.

8. Marzolf, *Up from the Footnote,* 32.

9. Gottlieb, "Grit Your Teeth," 58.

10. Helen MacGill Hughes's introduction to her classic study *News and the Human Interest Story,* first published in 1940, nicely sums up the general understanding of objective reporting. The reporter, she writes, "learns to look at events in a more or less impersonal way, seeing them as they are likely to look to his public and not as they would appear if interpreted from his own naïve point of view or that of any other normally egocentric individual" (unpaginated). Journalism historians have competing theories on the exact origins of the objective ideal in reporting, but most agree that journalistic objectivity emerged as a primary concern in the Progressive Era. By the 1890s, according to David T. Z. Mindich, all the standard elements of objectivity had come together—"detachment, nonpartisanship, the inverted pyramid writing style, and a reverence for facts and empiricism." Mindich also notes that objective journalism was viewed as "somehow a masculine endeavor" (*Just the Facts,* 113, 114–15, 130–31). Richard Kaplan, tracing shifts in the business practices of newspapers, comes to a similar conclusion, arguing that objectivity replaced partisanship in the late nineteenth and early twentieth centuries (*Politics and the American Press,* 17). Michael Schudson, however, suggests that objectivity was not widely accepted as an ideal until after World War I (*Discovering the News,* 122, 157). In a wide-ranging study of objectivity, Stephen J. A. Ward contends that although journalistic objectivity was invented as a doctrine in the 1920s, it had deep roots in Western culture and was anticipated by the professional movements of the late nineteenth century (*The Invention of Journalism Ethics,* esp. 204–57). See also Schiller, *Objectivity and the News;* Nord, *Communities of Journalism,* 4–5; and Chalaby, *The Invention of Journalism,* 128–40.

11. On the Pulitzer-Hearst fight, see Brian, *Pulitzer,* esp. 196–212.

12. Carey, "The Communications Revolution and the Professional Communicator." See also Baldasty, *The Commercialization of News,* which argues that attention to neutrality increased as the news began to be valued more as a commodity than for its civic function in advocating political positions. For another interpretation of the press in decline in the late nineteenth century, see Weaver, *News and the Culture of Lying,* esp. 35–52.

13. Brady, *Ida Tarbell,* 190–93; and Kochersberger, *More Than a Muckraker,* 87–90. For a detailed discussion of professional objectivity in Tarbell's work, see Sawaya, *Modern Women, Modern Work,* chap. 4, esp. 92–98.

14. Emotional connections between reporters and their stories have long shaped the exchange between journalism and fiction in American literary culture, of course. But literary newsmen have escaped the stigma of sob-sisterhood, even when their tears have inspired artistic revelations, as they do in "Nigger Jeff," one of Theodore Dreiser's early stories, adapted from his own coverage of an 1894 lynching in Missouri. On Dreiser's journalism, see Nostwich, "Historical Commentary"; Lingeman, *Theodore Dreiser,* 93–156; Robertson, *Stephen Crane,* 177–194; and Fishkin, *From Fact to Fiction,* 85–134.

15. On male realists' concern about their manhood, see, among others, Bell, *Henry James and the Past;* Habegger, *Gender, Fantasy, and Realism in American Literature;* Den Tandt, *The Urban Sublime in American Literary Naturalism;* Dudley, *A Man's Game;* and Auerbach, *Male Call.*

16. For a study of the consequences of the realist novelists' choice to write from the perspective of the disembodied narrator and to dispense with the convention of the knowable author, see Hochman, *Getting at the Author.*

17. Warner, *Publics and Counterpublics*, 30.

18. Ibid., 182–83.

19. For literary studies, see sources cited in note 5, as well as Trachtenberg, *The Incorporation of America*, esp. 122–26. An exception to literary historians' neglect of female journalists is Carol Batker's *Reforming Fictions*, which argues that women writers' reform politics were a driving force in journalism and literature of the 1910s and 1920s. For an invaluable guide to women's journalism in the United States, see Beasley and Gibbons, *Taking Their Place.* For a broad history of British and American women journalists from the nineteenth century to the present, see Chambers, Steiner, and Fleming, *Women and Journalism.* For other work on women journalists, see Burt, *Women's Press Organizations* and "Pioneering for Women Journalists"; Gottlieb, "Grit Your Teeth" and "Networking in the Nineteenth Century"; Beasley, "Women in Journalism"; Steiner, "Gender at Work"; and McGlashan, "Women Witness the Russian Revolution."

20. See chapter 5, note 10, for more details on writers for alternative presses, and chapter 2 for details on African American women journalists. On the suffragist press, see Solomon, *A Voice of Their Own*, esp. chap. 11, "Evolving Rhetorical Strategies/ Evolving Identities" by Linda Steiner (183–97). For a revealing study of a female labor journalist and a good overview of labor journalism at the turn of the century, see Faue, *Writing the Wrongs.* On women's reform journalism for Native American, African American, and Jewish presses, see Batker, *Reforming Fictions.*

21. Two important women's magazine writers were Sarah J. Hale, who edited the influential *Godey's Lady's Book* from 1837 to 1877, and Jane Cunningham Croly (Jennie June), who started as a fashion writer in 1856. Croly founded Sorosis, one of the nation's first women's clubs, in 1868 after being excluded from a New York Press Club dinner in honor of Charles Dickens. On Hale and Croly, see Gottlieb, "Women Journalists and the Municipal Housekeeping Movement." On African American women's magazines, see Rooks. For details on women's editions of newspapers—special issues that raised money for charity and became a fad in the mid-1890s—see Colbert, "Literary and Commercial Aspects of Women's Editions of Newspapers, 1894–1896." One women's page writer who went on to a long career as a writer of popular fiction was Sophie Kerr, who published more than two dozen books between 1916 and 1953 and who specialized in popular romances about businesswomen. See Honey, *Breaking the Ties That Bind*, 336.

22. To list just a few: Mary Katherine Goddard, publisher of the *Maryland Journal*, handled the first official printing of the Declaration of Independence in 1777. Anne Royall covered the U.S. Congress in 1831, and Lydia Maria Child wrote weekly letters for the *Boston Courier* in the 1840s. Margaret Fuller, best known as a member of Ralph Waldo Emerson's Transcendentalist circle, became the nation's first female foreign correspondent in the 1840s; Fuller reported on the siege of Rome in 1849. Fanny Fern (Sara Willis Parton) was one of her era's highest-paid newspaper columnists in the 1850s. Mary Ann Shadd Cary began editing the *Provincial Freeman*, an alternative to Frederick Douglass's abolitionist paper, in 1854. Mary Clemmer Ames started writing a "Woman's Letter from Washington" for the *New York Independent* in 1866. Kate

Field gained prominence as a correspondent in the 1860s; her reports on Charles Dickens's last American tour were so well received that she revised them into a book in 1868 (the same year Croly was banned from the New York press banquet for Dickens; see note 21). For an overview of women journalists, see Beasley and Gibbons, *Taking Their Place;* also Dickinson, "Women in Journalism." For details on Fern, see Warren, *Fanny Fern;* on Cary, see Rhodes, *Mary Ann Shadd Cary;* on Field, see Scharnhorst, "James and Kate Field" and "'It has served the truth without fear and without favor.'"

23. According to the U.S. Census for 1870, women made up only 35 of the 5,375 working journalists. See U.S. Bureau of the Census. It is likely, given the evidence of women's gradual movement into journalism in the mid-nineteenth century, that this figure underestimates the number of working newspaperwomen. It is probably best read as an indication of newswomen's lack of professional recognition and visibility, which was about to change.

24. Burt, *Women's Press Organizations,* xviii–xix.

25. Beasley and Gibbons, *Taking Their Place,* 64–73; Chambers, Steiner, and Fleming, *Women and Journalism,* 19–22.

26. Burt, *Women's Press Organizations,* xviii.

27. Beasley and Gibbons, *Taking Their Place,* 56; Mott, *American Journalism,* 490; Dickinson, "Women in Journalism," 137.

28. *The Journalist,* October 13, 1888, and January 26, 1889.

29. Dix's speech is quoted in "For a Broader Realm: Women Plead for Place in the Professions," *Washington Post,* February 14, 1902.

30. In 1880, the U.S. Census listed only 288 women (out of 12,308 total) as full-time journalists. In 1900 the number of women rose to 2,193 out of 30,038; in 1910 the figure was 4,181 out of 34,382; in 1920, 5,730 out of 34,197; in 1930, 11,924 out of 51,844. For a full census report, see U.S. Bureau of the Census. On the rise of women reporters in the United States, see also Beasley and Gibbons, *Taking Their Place,* 53; and Cairns, *Front-Page Women Journalists,* xi.

31. Mossell, *The Work of the Afro-American Woman,* 101.

32. See "Newspaper Women," 283–91, in Willard, *Occupations for Women.* Willard's title page acknowledges the assistance of two journalists, Helen M. Winslow and Sallie Joy White, in writing the book. For details on Willard, see Bordin, *Frances Willard.*

33. Harger, "Journalism as a Career," 220.

34. Shuman, *Practical Journalism,* chap. 11, "Women in Newspaper Work," 162, 148, and 151.

35. By 1950, women made up 32 percent of the profession (Cairns, *Front-Page Women Journalists,* 4). That figure has not changed significantly: in 2002, women accounted for about one-third of the working journalists in the United States. Chambers, Steiner, and Fleming, *Women and Journalism,* 84.

36. See, for example, Stead, "Young Women in Journalism"; and Crawford, "Journalism as a Profession for Women."

37. Only three of the forty-two women who responded to Bok's survey, and none of the thirty men who responded, said they would approve of their daughters working as newspaperwomen. Bok, "Is the Newspaper Office the Place for a Girl?" 18.

38. Winslow, "Confessions of a Newspaperwoman," 211. Winslow's tone contrasts sharply with the more upbeat treatment of journalism as a profession for women in Willard's *Occupations for Women* (1897), which Winslow helped to write.

39. Eliot, "Experiences of a Woman Reporter," 9. For an earlier article that expresses similar concerns, see Cahoon, "Women in Gutter Journalism."

40. See, for example, Boughner, *Women in Journalism* (1926); and Brazelton, *Writing and Editing for Women* (1927).

41. Ernst later became the mother of a legendary twentieth-century newspaper-woman, Katharine Graham, publisher of the *Washington Post* during the crises of Watergate and the Pentagon Papers. See Graham's Pulitzer Prize–winning autobiography, *Personal History,* 14.

1. Into the Madhouse with Girl Stunt Reporters

1. Because Bly was known primarily by her pen name throughout her life, I use it here. She was christened Elizabeth Jane Cochran when she was born in 1864. She began writing as "Nellie Bly" in 1885, when she went to work for the *Pittsburgh Dispatch.* (The pseudonym is a misspelled reference to Pittsburgh native Stephen Foster's popular song "Nelly Bly.")

2. Kroeger, *Nellie Bly,* 84–86. I am indebted to Brooke Kroeger's thorough research for many of my primary sources.

3. Bly's education was spotty at best. At fifteen she enrolled in a vocational school, but the family ran out of money after one semester and she left abruptly, never to return. Ibid., 23–26.

4. *New York World,* November 27, 1887; March 25, 1888; December 2, 1888; October 30, 1887; and July 11, 1894.

5. New York City newspapers, especially the *New York World,* led the way, but metropolitan dailies across the nation published "stunt girl" stories. In 1888, for instance, aspiring Minneapolis journalist Eva McDonald Valesh fished a dress "out of the rag-bag" to masquerade as a poor worker. Her series on workingwomen, published under the pen name Eva Gay in the *St. Paul Globe,* launched her career as a journalist and labor activist. On Valesh's career, see Faue, *Writing the Wrongs,* esp. 17–30. For two typical Valesh stories, see "Girls Make Cigars," *St. Paul Globe,* May 27, 1888; and "How Girls Clerk," *St. Paul Globe,* June 17, 1888. On stunt reporters in general, see Kroeger, *Nellie Bly,* 105, 120–25, and 148–49; Ross, *Ladies of the Press,* 48–63; Ghiglione, *The American Journalist,* 20; and Mott, *American Journalism,* 599. A less sensational precursor to Bly and Valesh was Helen Campbell, who wrote "Studies in the Slums" for *Sunday Afternoon* magazine in 1879, followed by "Prisoners of Poverty" in the *New York Tribune* in 1886 and 1887. On Campbell, see Henry, "'Reporting Deeply and at First Hand.'"

6. One history of women's journalism labels Nellie Bly "the most famous stunt reporter byline of all" and calls her globe-circling race "one of the greatest publicity stunts of all time." Beasley and Gibbons, *Taking Their Place,* 64–65. Bly's series was launched in "Across the Continent! The Route of Nellie Bly on the Homestretch of the Great Around-the-World Race against Time," *New York World,* January 23, 1890, 1. She soon had a rival, Elizabeth Bisland, who circled the globe in the opposite direction, seeking to beat Bly home. (Bly won.) Both women published book-length travelogues; see Bly, *Nellie Bly's Book;* and Bisland, *A Flying Trip around the World.* For an account by an author who prefers Bisland's more restrained style, see Marks, *Around the World in Seventy-two Days.*

7. Ross, *Ladies of the Press,* 60; Belford, *Brilliant Bylines,* 104; Abramson, *Sob Sister Journalism,* 44; and Furman, *Caroline Lockhart,* 9. "Annie Laurie" was the pen name used by Winifred Black early in her career.

8. For details on Elizabeth Banks, see Seth Koven's groundbreaking discussion in *Slumming,* esp. chap. 3, 140–80.

9. These include Pittenger, "A World of Difference"; and Schocket, "Undercover Explorations of the 'Other Half.'" An important exception is Koven's *Slumming.*

10. In the 1880s, reporters began to acquire new professional status; bylines ap-

peared more frequently, incomes rose steadily, and college degrees in journalism became more marketable. Mott, *American Journalism,* 488; Schudson, *Discovering the
News,* 65–69; Dicken-Garcia, *Journalistic Standards in Nineteenth-Century America,* 218.

11. Gandal, *The Virtues of the Vicious;* Wilson, *Labor of Words;* Robertson, *Stephen
Crane, Journalism, and the Making of Modern American Literature.*

12. In 1909 stunt reporting was still popular enough that future novelist Fannie
Hurst wangled a job in a shoe factory in order to write an exposé of its working conditions. The trick backfired when she tried to submit her story to an editor at the *St.
Louis Post-Dispatch,* who decided that Hurst was a better story on her own and sent a
reporter to interview her. Hurst, *Anatomy of Me,* 115–17. In the 1933 newspaper memoir *Gal Reporter,* Joan Lowell recalls assuming the roles of charwoman, taxi dancer,
homeless person, and factory worker. Lowell, *Gal Reporter,* 148, 104, 212, and 201.
Lowell even describes being assaulted by a "white slaver" who grabs her neck and
breasts (113). One of the best-known stunts of the second half of the twentieth century was feminist activist Gloria Steinem's report on her stint as a Playboy Bunny, first
published in *Show* magazine in 1963. And the tradition continues today. In June
2004, the Sunday *New York Times* printed a front-page story on a stunt that echoed
Nellie Bly's initial offer to go to Europe and return steerage class. The *Times* hired an
Ecuadorean woman reporter to join a group of Ecuadorans who were being smuggled
to Guatemala, in hopes of eventually making their way to New York City. The reporter
documented the filthy conditions, lack of food and water, and physical and sexual
abuse the desperate travelers suffered. She was even held hostage at one point. Gin-
ger Thompson and Sandra Ochoa, "By a Back Door to the U.S.: A Migrant's Grim Sea
Voyage," *New York Times,* June 13, 2004. Journalist-authors who have pursued similar
strategies include Ted Conover, who spent a year as a prison guard to write *Newjack:
Guarding Sing Sing* (2000); and Barbara Ehrenreich, who worked as a waitress, clean-
ing woman, and clerk to write *Nickel and Dimed: On (Not) Getting By in America* (2001),
then posed as a white-collar job-seeker for *Bait and Switch: The (Futile) Pursuit of the
American Dream* (2005).

13. I use the term "sensation heroine" in a broad sense here, to refer to the pro-
tagonists of nineteenth-century narratives that rely on the minute reporting of physical sensations, especially the sensations of a female body. Literary critics have applied
the category of "sensation fiction" to a wide range of popular texts. The two strands of
sensational writing most relevant to Bly's work are the novels that featured transgressive heroines who disguise themselves to serve their own desires (such as E. D. E. N.
Southworth's *The Hidden Hand* [1859] and Louisa May Alcott's *Behind a Mask* [1866])
and those that offered guided tours of the seamy side of urban life (such as George C.
Foster's *New York by Gaslight* [1840] and George Lippard's *The Quaker City* [1845]).
Stunt reporting drew on both of these traditions: the authors took on the characteris-
tics of the sensation heroine even as they revised the male-dominated genre of the ur-
ban guide narrative. See Brand, *The Spectator and the City;* Bergmann, "Panoramas of
New York, 1845–1860"; Blumin, "Explaining the Metropolis"; Denning, *Mechanic
Accents;* and Siegel, *The Image of the American City.*

14. Mott, *American Journalism,* 599.

15. I found no evidence that African American women journalists or other
women of color joined the stunt reporting trend. See chapter 2 for more on African
American newspaperwomen's relationship to white mainstream reporting.

16. Janet Steele reads Pulitzer's strategy in this manner in her analysis of the
World's redefinition of newspaper readers as consumers rather than producers. "Like
twentieth-century tabloids," Steele writes, "the *World* used sensationalism as bait; the
underlying message was prim enough to satisfy rigid Victorian mores" ("The Nine-

teenth-Century *World* versus the *Sun*," 569). While Steele's characterization of the paper's politics is accurate, she underestimates the capacity of sensationalism to carry underlying messages when she dismisses it as titillating "bait."

17. Even before Bly infiltrated the asylum, its public image was far from positive. Public outcry was relatively common; according to one scholar, "a new superintendent noted as one of his major accomplishments that the institution had managed to stay out of the news during 1880 and 1881." Grob, *Mental Institutions in America*, 121. Asylums across the nation were the targets of increasingly harsh criticism in the last third of the nineteenth century, as asylum superintendents faced declining public confidence. Many critics charged that the asylums were more custodial than therapeutic, pointing out that the period of rapid growth in the number of asylums coincided with substantial increases in immigration and in the urban population in general. Asylums like the one to which Bly was committed were remnants of a declining system; turn-of-the-century psychiatrists envisioned institutions more akin to hospitals than prisons. McGovern, *Masters of Madness*, 150; Perrucci, *Circle of Madness*, 32.

18. "Who Is This Insane Girl?" *New York Sun*, September 26, 1887.

19. Nellie Bly, "Behind Asylum Bars," *New York World*, October 9, 1887.

20. Two weeks after Bly's story appeared, the assistant district attorney led a grand jury investigation of asylum conditions. Later that year, a city board approved a 57 percent increase in the budget for the Department of Public Charities and Corrections, the largest increase granted any city department. The board earmarked a substantial portion ($50,000) of the increase for the asylum where Bly was confined. Kroeger, *Nellie Bly*, 96–98. See also Brian, *Pulitzer*, 124–27 and 144–48.

21. Although it was unusual for writers to have themselves committed to mental institutions *on purpose*, by this period the asylum exposé written by a former mental patient was a recognizable genre. The earliest such stories appeared in the 1830s, but the best-known exposés were by Mrs. E. P. W. Packard, who charged that her husband had wrongly had her committed to the Illinois State Hospital for the Insane for three years. Packard launched one of the first personal freedom crusades for individuals involuntarily committed to mental hospitals Grob, *Mental Institutions in America*, 263. See *Mrs. Packard's Reproof to Dr. McFarland* (1864); *Great Disclosures of Spiritual Wickedness!!* (1865); and *Modern Persecution, or Insane Asylums Unveiled*, 2 vols. (1873).

22. *New York World*, October 9, 1887.

23. *New York Times*, September 26, 1887.

24. Bledstein, *The Culture of Professionalism*, 79.

25. Published five years before "The Yellow Wallpaper," Charlotte Perkins Gilman's well-known critique of S. Weir Mitchell's rest cure, Bly's report seems to forecast the complaints of Gilman's distraught narrator. Bly laments her forced inactivity: "I was never so tired as I grew sitting on those benches. . . . What, excepting torture, would produce insanity quicker than this treatment? Here is a class of women sent to be cured? . . . I would like the expert physicians who are condemning me for my action, which has proven their ability, to take a perfectly healthy and sane woman, shut her up and make her sit from 6 a.m. to 8 p.m. on straight-back benches, do not allow her to talk or move during those hours, give her no reading and let her know nothing of the world or its doings . . . and see how long it will take to make her insane. Two months would make her a mental and physical wreck." Bly, *New York World*, October 16, 1887.

26. Kroeger, *Nellie Bly*, 105.

27. *New York World*, October 9, 1887.

28. Kroeger, *Nellie Bly*, 104.

29. See Pittenger, "A World of Difference"; and Schocket, "Undercover Explo-

rations." Eric Schocket coins a provocative term for these masquerades—"class-trans-vestite narratives"—without explaining how the gendered meaning of the term might apply. Confining his analysis to class-switching, not gender-bending, Schocket traces a process he calls "containment through embodiment" (111); he argues that these "class transvestites" saw their own bodies as both objects of social forces *and* sources of social knowledge. Through their impersonations, he contends, these writers "attempted to move 'inside' and collapse the distance between subject and object into one performative, narrational 'body'" (110). For a complementary reading of transgression in urban sensation novels as reactionary, see Looby, "George Thompson's 'Romance of the Real.'"

30. Briggs, "The Race of Hysteria."

31. A few years later, Bly's white, middle-class body indicated racial, cultural, and technological superiority in the most concrete way possible when she staged her most ambitious stunt of all: her 1890 race to circle the globe faster than Jules Verne's fictional hero, Phileas Fogg. Her travelogue, supplemented by a contest to guess her time and an array of Nellie Bly merchandise from coats and hats to board games, graphically contrasted her own cultural superiority with the picturesque but inferior peoples she encountered. See note 6.

32. Before Bly's deception was discovered, the *New York Herald* interviewed one of her doctors about the mysterious insane girl. The soon-to-be-red-faced expert explained his diagnosis: "Her delusions, her dull apathetic condition, the muscular twitching of her hands and arms and her loss of memory all indicate hysteria." *New York Herald,* September 15, 1887.

33. Bly, "Behind Asylum Bars."

34. Showalter, *The Female Malady,* 145.

35. The case of Freud's Dora, perhaps the most famous hysteric of the twentieth century, is emblematic. As Charles Bernheimer and Claire Kahane note in their introduction to *In Dora's Case: Freud—Hysteria—Feminism,* critical interest in the case often centers on Freud's description of his own attempts to create a scientific narrative from Dora's disjunctive speech (18).

36. Beizer, *Ventriloquized Bodies,* 11–12.

37. Lunbeck, *The Psychiatric Persuasion,* 211.

38. In an analysis of medicine's professionalization, the sociologist Magali Sarfatti Larson attributes much of doctors' extraordinary power to their success in insulating medical experts from the public. "The privacy of the consulting room," Larson observes, "makes the physician's services impenetrable to public scrutiny: in the actual transaction itself, the patient faces the physician alone" ("The Production of Expertise and the Constitution of Expert Power," 22). Bly denies this privilege to the Blackwell's Island experts by taking the public with her into the consulting room.

39. Bly, "Behind Asylum Bars.".

40. For an illuminating discussion of how a proper appearance protected women who ventured into city streets, see Kasson, *Rudeness and Civility,* 128–36.

41. Bly, "Behind Asylum Bars.".

42. The peripheral news coverage generated by Bly's stunt had less to gain by protecting her sexual purity than her first-person reports. It is even possible that the authors of these articles sought to heighten their appeal by stressing the titillating aspects of Bly's incarceration.

43. *New York World,* October 10, 1887.

44. Carol Groneman's survey of more than one hundred case studies in American and European medical journals and texts showed that experts diagnosed women as nymphomaniacs in the late nineteenth and early twentieth centuries whose "symp-

toms" were committing adultery, divorcing their husbands, flirting, or feeling more passionate than their male partners. This diagnosis was often not easily distinguished from hysteria. Groneman, "Nymphomania," 341.

45. *New York World*, October 10, 1887.

46. Quoted in Kevles, *In the Name of Eugenics*, 107.

47. Block, "Sexual Perversion in the Female," esp. 4.

48. Lunbeck, *The Psychiatric Persuasion*, 185–201.

49. *New York World*, November 27, 1887.

50. Ibid., March 25, 1888.

51. Ibid., July 11, 1894.

52. Ibid., December 2, 1888.

53. In "Dr. Cooley's Cure Factory: Nell Nelson Spends a Week at a Queer Sanitarium in Jersey," Nell Nelson writes, "There wasn't a thing the matter with me but a spirit of investigation and I weighed 125 pounds. Now I can scarcely make a nickel register 118, and I have a terrible hollowness of the stomach." Writing from the perspective of the pampered patient, Nelson recounts sexually charged encounters with doctors and submits to "stomach shaking" treatments, sweat baths, and lectures on her sinful nature, eventually concluding that no cures were to be found at Dr. Cooley's. See *New York World*, December 16, 1888. Nell Nelson was the pen name of Nell Cusak.

54. *New York World*, November 27, 1887.

55. In "Trying to Be a Servant," Bly makes a similar point in an exchange with the supervisor of an employment agency. The commodity value of being "nice-looking" is explicit:

> "Well?" he said to me in a questioning manner, as he glanced quickly over my "get up."
> "Are you the man who gets good places for girls?" I asked. . . .
> "What did you work at last?"
> "Oh, I was a chambermaid. Can you get me a position, do you think?"
> "Yes, I can do that," he replied. "You're a nice-looking girl and I can soon get you a place. Just the other day I got a girl a place for $20 a month, just because she was nice-looking. Many gentlemen, and ladies also, will pay more when girls are nice-looking." *New York World*, October 30, 1887.

56. Ibid., November 25, 1888.

57. For another installment of Nelson's white slave series, see "Fingers Worn to the Bone: White Slaves of the Bookbinderies Working at Starvation Wages," *New York World*, November 18, 1888. Like the rest of the series, this story details the workers' illnesses, poor wages, and dangerous working conditions.

58. *New York World*, December 11, 1887. For another beggar impersonation story, see Meg Merrilies, "In the Guise of a Street Sweeper," ibid., February 11, 1894.

59. Ibid., February 12, 1888.

60. Nell Nelson similarly distances herself from her subjects in "A Luxurious Opium Joint." Early in the article, Nelson recalls her entrance in first person, present tense: "I have an escort of two gentlemen and a wisdom-loving chaperon. Still I am afraid, and my trepidation increases when 'the fiend,' as our guide calls himself, draws my hand through his arm, pulls my veil in wrinkles over my face to save me from possible recognition and whispers, 'Don't let surprise betray you.'" With this ominous beginning, Nelson ushers her readers into a large, hazy room where men and women lie on dozens of bunks. After this exchange, however, she tells her readers

almost nothing about what she did or what happened to her; we learn only that she was afraid, that she sat down on a bunk, and that she could barely stand to look around (although she obviously did). Slipping into past tense and away from first person, she describes an erotic scene, including "a beautiful girl, her head resting on one man's breast, her feet across the knees of another. . . . [H]er dress was unfastened, her hair fell about her face and neck and her eyes were closed as she inhaled the burning pill," and six men who "were coiled about one another like human snakes in a third bunk and all were partially undressed." She reports no direct interaction with anyone after the initial exchange with her guide. Just as Bly protects her body from a direct link to sex workers, Nelson protects hers from the sensual drug-users. See *New York World*, March 3, 1889.

61. Reagan, *When Abortion Was a Crime*, 47, 56, 60; for a thoughtful analysis of this "stunt," see 46–61. See also *Chicago Times*, December 12, 1888–January 23, 1889. Bly wrote a tamer version of the same story when she toured adoption agencies and masqueraded as an unwed mother, telling people that she had "a baby I want to dispose of." See "What Becomes of Babies," *New York World*, November 6, 1887.

62. Schilpp and Murphy, *Great Women of the Press*, 150.

63. Black, "Rambles through My Memories," 214. Black's subsequent stunts included an "undercover stint in a Southern cotton mill; a job at a local fruit canner for twenty-six cents a day; interviews with the proprietress of a brothel; and a role as a Salvation Army angel." Schilpp and Murphy, *Great Women of the Press*, 150. A decade after her first stunt, Black disguised herself as a boy to slip past the guarded perimeter of Galveston, Texas, after a tidal wave disaster took seven thousand lives. The first reporter from outside the city to view the carnage, she began her report by dramatizing her own success at getting into Galveston: "I begged, cajoled, and cried my way through the lines of soldiers with drawn swords who guarded the wharf at Texas City and sailed across the bay on a little boat which is making irregular trips to meet the relief trains from Houston." Her stunt story, however, immediately gives way to moving descriptions of the catastrophe. See Black, "Corpse-Laden Waters"; reprinted in Belford, *Brilliant Bylines*, 110–13.

64. Ross, *Ladies of the Press*, 69.

65. *New York American*, April 22, 1894.

66. Bly's fame made her opinions themselves newsworthy. In "Should Women Propose? Nellie Bly Advances Arguments in the Affirmative," *New York World*, November 11, 1888, she argued not only that women should propose to men but also that there would be fewer unhappy marriages if they did.

67. Kroeger, *Nellie Bly*, 224. The name was probably intended as a mocking reference to the prophetic old gypsy woman who served as the heroine of Sir Walter Scott's 1815 novel *Guy Mannering*. John Keats, apparently inspired by Scott's Meg Merrilies, wrote a widely anthologized poem about an "Old Meg" who "liv'd upon the Moors." In jarring contrast to the frivolous antics of the stunt reporters whose work appeared under the Meg Merrilies byline, the fictional Meg of Scott's novel and Keats's poem is heroic in her isolation, strength, and weirdness. I am grateful to Hugh Ormsby-Lennon for calling my attention to Meg's literary provenance.

68. Meg Merrilies, "Down under the East River," *New York World*, April 22, 1894.

69. For more Meg Merrilies stories, see "How Easy It Is to Be an Actor," *New York World*, January 28, 1894; "A Night in the U.S. Treasury," ibid., April 5, 1894; "A Week in Trouserettes," ibid., March 4, 1894; and "Another Week in Trouserettes," ibid., March 11, 1894.

70. Pittenger, "A World of Difference," 44–45.

71. Steele, "The Nineteenth-Century *World* versus the *Sun*," 597; Schudson, *Discovering the News*, 119; Emery, Emery, and Roberts, *The Press and America*, 173–75; Juergens, *Joseph Pulitzer*, xii, 46–47, 59.

72. Barth, *City People*, 62–63.

73. Emery, Emery, and Roberts, *The Press and America*, 176.

74. The urban environment may also have contributed to anxieties about hypersexuality. In 1907 the editor of an important American medical journal "explicitly linked the appearance of perversion and lust-murder to the size of the cities." Birken, *Consuming Desire*, 130.

75. Bergmann, "Panoramas," 119 and 128; Siegel, *The Image of the American City*, 34.

76. The stunt reporters' role as vehicles of publicity embodies and helps to defuse the threat William Dean Howells illustrates through the character of Isabel March in *A Hazard of New Fortunes*, a novel set in New York City and published in 1890, in the heyday of the stunt reporters. After moving to New York, the resolutely middle-class Isabel confesses that the specter of the urban poor disturbs her: "'I'm beginning to feel crazy. . . . I don't believe there's any *real* suffering—not real *suffering*—among those people; that is, it would be from our point of view, but they've been used to it all their lives and they don't feel their discomfort so much'" (56). Isabel associates insanity with overidentification with "the other half." As Amy Kaplan observes, "The fear of being like 'those people' threatens Isabel's sanity because it blurs the boundaries of her self-image" ("'The Knowledge of the Line,'" 73). Stunt journalism targeted readers with concerns just like Isabel's, while also campaigning for recognition of the sensibilities of the urban poor themselves.

77. See, for instance, George Miller Beard's *Practical Treatise on Nervous Exhaustion* (1881) and S. Weir Mitchell's novel *Characteristics* (1892).

78. *New York World*, October 16, 1887.

79. Nell Nelson also notes the threat of infection in her white slave series. In her cigarette factory exposé she reports, "I spent a day at this loathsome work, stained my hands a rich brown, coughed till my throat was sore [the foreman smoked all the time], and got so thoroughly permeated with the dust and smell that I had to be disinfected before I could mingle with any of my friends again." *New York World*, November 25, 1888.

80. Roseboro's masquerade as a beggar suffers from a similar problem. "Begging as an Avocation," *New York World*, December 11, 1887.

81. A huge drawing of Bly atop an elephant adorns the front page of the *World*'s Sunday magazine section, February 23, 1896. The uninspired story begins: "I tried to train an elephant last week. The elephant was scared. So was I. Neither of us mentioned it at the time. But I have thought of it since and doubtless so has he."

82. Stunt reporters never entirely disappeared, of course. Chapter 4 traces their appearances in fiction, and chapter 5 deals with two writers who engaged in "stunts" after Bly's heyday had passed: Edna Ferber and Djuna Barnes. See also note 12.

83. Pittenger, "A World of Difference," 38–39.

2. The African American Newswoman as National Icon

1. Wells initially won a $500 verdict, but it was overturned on appeal. My account is based on Linda O. McMurry's detailed description in her biography of Wells, *To Keep the Waters Troubled*, 24–31. See also Royster, intro. to *Southern Horrors and Other*

Writings, esp. 16–17; and Wells-Barnett, *Crusade for Justice.* My discussion of Wells is indebted to scholarship by McMurry, Sandra Gunning, Patricia Schechter, and Jacqueline Goldsby.

2. Although no published study analyzes the stunt reporters and the anti-lynching crusaders together, Sue Davidson's young adult book *Getting the Real Story: Nellie Bly and Ida B. Wells* offers parallel biographies of the two writers. Goldsby's dissertation, "After Great Pain," reads Wells's writing as a parody of stunt reporting. See "After Great Pain," 121–23 and 128–43.

3. Evidence suggests that moving to the second-class car could have threatened more than Wells's dignity. One of Wells's contemporaries, Mary Church Terrell, documented her struggles to fend off sexual assaults in second-class train cars in her autobiography, *A Colored Woman in a White World,* 335–46; see also 45–46, 135–36, and 290. The literary scholar Elizabeth McHenry has found that Terrell based an unpublished short story on her experience riding Jim Crow cars in the South ("Toward a History of Access: The Case of Mary Church Terrell," symposium on Print Culture and American Literary History, University of Illinois at Urbana–Champaign, September 26, 2005).

4. On Matthews, see chap. 7, "Victoria Earle Matthews," in Logan, *With Pen and Voice,* 120–25. More than a half-century after Wells's crusade, Marvel Cooke may have performed the first "stunt" by a black newswoman when she joined what she called a modern slave market in New York City. After standing with unemployed city-dwellers who congregated on a Bronx street corner to seek temporary work from passersby, Cooke reported on the humiliating experience. See "'Mrs. Legree' Hires Only on the Street, Always 'Nice Girls,'" *The Compass,* January 11, 1950. For an interview in which Cooke discusses the story, see Beasley and Gibbons, *Taking Their Place,* 112–16.

5. It is precisely this tension that Frances Harper and Pauline Hopkins fictionalized in their reimaginings of the tragic mixed-race heroine. But black journalists seeking to establish their own authority did not take similar risks in their self-presentations.

6. The invitation came via telegram, sent by a Memphis daily to a white newspaper in Chicago that had hired Wells. She quotes the telegram in one of her pamphlets, exposing it as a shocking display of power and cruelty: "MEMPHIS, TENN., July 22, To Inter-Ocean, Chicago. Lee Walker, colored man, accused of raping white women, in jail here, will be taken out and burned by whites tonight. Can you send Miss Ida Wells to write it up? Answer. R. M. Martin, with Public Ledger." Two white women claimed that Walker had asked the women for something to eat and then threatened to assault them, although he ran away without hurting them. The night Wells received the invitation, a lynch mob battered down the prison door with an iron rail and grabbed Walker, who fought desperately, biting and scratching. While the Memphis sheriff watched, the mob beat and stabbed Walker, hanged him from a nearby telegraph pole, built a fire in the middle of the street, and threw his body onto the pyre. After the fire died, they collected teeth and fingernails as souvenirs, dragged the burned body down Main Street, and hoisted it aloft again so that it dangled from a central pole in front of the courthouse. See Ida B. Wells, *Red Record,* reprinted in *Southern Horrors and Other Writings,* 113–16.

7. Gates, "The Trope of a New Negro and the Reconstruction of the Image of the Black."

8. Jacqueline Dowd Hall's *Revolt against Chivalry* remains one of the most important analyses of lynching and the social order. Other excellent sources on Wells are Patricia Schechter's "Unsettled Business" and her book-length study *Ida B. Wells-Bar-*

nett and American Reform, 1880–1930. See also W. Fitzhugh Brundage's edited collection *Under Sentence of Death.*

9. Whites, "Rebecca Latimer Felton and the Wife's Farm."

10. On lynching rationales and white press coverage, see Beasley, "The Muckrakers and Lynching"; Mindich, *Just the Facts;* and Goldsby, "After Great Pain." On white supremacist fiction, see Stokes, *The Color of Sex.* On lynching as spectacle, see Hale, *Making Whiteness.* For more general studies of lynching, see, among others, Dray, *At the Hands of Persons Unknown;* Litwack, *Without Sanctuary;* and Tolnay and Beck, *A Festival of Violence.*

11. McMurry, *To Keep the Waters Troubled,* 145.

12. For an incisive analysis of how Wells's attack on white women isolated her, see Schechter, *Ida B. Wells-Barnett,* esp. chap. 3, "The Body in Question," 81–120.

13. Terrell, "Lynching from the Negro's Point of View," 853–68. More than two decades later, Alice Dunbar-Nelson protested lynching as a columnist for African American newspapers. See *The Works of Alice Dunbar-Nelson,* 115 and 122.

14. Many women fought lynching not by writing for the press but by joining black women's clubs to promote social reform and raise money for activist efforts. Wells's first pamphlet, *Southern Horrors: Lynch Law in All Its Phases* (1892), was funded by a testimonial dinner organized by two black club women, one of them a journalist. See McMurry, *To Keep the Waters Troubled,* 171; Royster, intro. to *Southern Horrors,* 23–25. On black women's role as "the backbone of the anti-lynching crusade," see Terborg-Penn and Brown, *Eradicating This Evil,* 148. See also Carby, *Reconstructing Womanhood;* Schechter, *Ida B. Wells-Barnett;* and Perkins and Stephens, *Strange Fruit.*

15. Simmons, *The African American Press,* 6.

16. See Gunning, *Race, Rape, and Lynching,* 86; and Schechter, *Ida B. Wells-Barnett,* 114 and 59–63. Building on Sandra Gunning's discussion of the last lynching victim mentioned in *Southern Horrors*—a black girl, thirteen-year-old Mildred Brown, who was hanged for allegedly poisoning a white baby—Schechter argues that Wells highlighted a girl victim in order to shield black women from potentially damaging exposure. Gunning, *Race, Rape, and Lynching,* 87; Schechter, *Ida B. Wells-Barnett,* 114.

17. Women who took on leadership roles worked especially hard to appear ladylike. Claudia Tate writes: "Even though the black Victorian model permitted professional activity outside the home for the wife and other females of the household, modesty and reserve were essential. Those middle-class women (like Mary Church Terrell and Ida B. Wells) who asserted positions of leadership, thus resisting that decorum, were often regarded as aggressive and immodest" (*Domestic Allegories of Political Desire,* 151–52).

18. See Fraser, "Rethinking the Public Sphere," 123.

19. "British Anti-Lynchers," *New York Times,* August 2, 1894.

20. See, among others, Simmons, *The African American Press,* 1; and Harris, *Exorcising Blackness,* 5–7.

21. Simmons, *The African American Press,* 21.

22. "Do You Read Negro Papers?" *New York Age,* October 22, 1914.

23. "For black Americans the periodical press could not afford to be ephemeral," contends C. K. Doreski in *Writing America Black: Race Rhetoric in the Public Sphere.* "It had consciously to shape and nurture its nascent history" (4).

24. Holt, "Afterword," 327.

25. Wade-Gayles, "Black Women Journalists," 139.

26. Delilah L. Beasley became the first black woman to write on a regular basis for a mainstream white newspaper when she began contributing to the *Oakland Tribune* in

1886. Streitmatter, *Raising Her Voice*, 74. For details on Beasley, see Crouchett, "Delilah Leontium Beasley"; and Davis, *Lifting as They Climb*, 188–95.

27. Wade-Gayles, "Black Women Journalists," 143–44; Bullock, *The Afro-American Periodical Press*, 329.

28. Smith, "Some Female Writers," 39–44; Penn, *The Afro-American Press*, 367–427, esp. 398 and 426.

29. The trade press, in contrast to mainstream publications, tended to treat the work of both white and African American newspaperwomen more positively. See Gottlieb, "Grit Your Teeth." The sympathetic reports of the trade press on women's growing acceptance as professional journalists, however, lacked the urgency and depth of the black press's celebration of African American newspaperwomen.

30. Wade-Gayles, "Black Women Journalists," 147.

31. On attacks between black journalists, see McMurry, *To Keep the Waters Troubled*, esp. 100–101 and 155. For a thorough treatment of black women and reform in this era, see Schechter, *Ida B. Wells-Barnett*.

32. Bullock, *The Afro-American Periodical Press*, 166.

33. T. Thomas Fortune quoted in "The Race in Literature: Our Newspaper and Book Makers," *New York Age*, February 2, 1888.

34. Penn, *The Afro-American Press*, 407.

35. *New York Freeman*, May 8, 1886.

36. Gertrude Bustill Mossell, "To Make Our Papers Pay: A Woman's Suggestion of Ways and Means," *New York Age*, February 16, 1889.

37. See Burt, *Women's Press Organizations*.

38. Gertrude Bustill Mossell, "Our Woman's Department," *Indianapolis World*, August 6, 1892.

39. *New York Age*, June 29, 1889.

40. Mossell, *The Work of the Afro-American Woman*, 98–99.

41. Ibid., 100.

42. Braxton, intro., ibid., xxviii.

43. Gertrude Bustill Mossell, "Women and Journalism," *New York Freeman*, May 8, 1886.

44. Mossell, *The Work of the Afro-American Woman*, 100–101.

45. Even newswomen who painted a less cheerful picture of professional acceptance recognized the special value of African American women writers in the public sphere. In 1896 the black newspaper *Richmond Planet* printed two articles by Amelia Johnson documenting her struggle to place a story in the *Youth's Companion*, a national children's magazine with a primarily white audience. After an exchange of letters in which Johnson accused the editors of racism, they paid her twenty dollars for one of her submissions, but they never published it, according to her report. See "The History of a Story: How I Wrote A Story for the *Youth's Companion* and Why It Has Not Appeared," *Richmond Planet*, February 22 and 29, 1896. Johnson's story merited retelling precisely because she framed it not as an individual rejection but as a fight to represent her race. As Wendy Wagner argues in her analysis of the incident, "Johnson clearly saw herself as a spokesperson for her race, as an author by whose works the entire race would be judged" ("Black Separatism," 100).

46. Smith directed publication of *Our Women and Children*, published in Lexington, Kentucky, beginning in 1888, and she edited the "Women and Women's Work" department. She also wrote for the *Indianapolis Freeman*. For details, see MacFarlane, "Lucy Wilmot Smith."

47. Lucy Wilmot Smith, "Some Female Writers of the Negro Race," *The Journalist*,

January 26, 1889. This article, which was reprinted in the *Indianapolis Freeman*, February 23, 1889, appears in Beasley and Silver, *Women in Media*, 38–44.

48. Ibid., 39.

49. Streitmatter, *Raising Her Voice*, 148–49. See also Wade-Gayles, "Black Women Journalists"; Snorgrass, "Pioneer Black Women Journalists"; and McMurry, *To Keep the Waters Troubled*.

50. Streitmatter, "African American Women Journalists and Their Male Editors," 78.

51. Carrie Langston, "Women in Journalism," *Atchison Blade*, September 10, 1892.

52. Ibid.

53. Tucker, "Miss Ida B. Wells and Memphis Lynching," 113; McMurry, *To Keep the Waters Troubled*, 110.

54. Quoted in McMurry, *To Keep the Waters Troubled*, 100; Lucy Wilmot Smith, "Women as Journalists," *Indianapolis Freeman*, February 23, 1889.

55. Penn, *The Afro-American Press*, 426.

56. Wells scholars are unclear on the origin of the pseudonym. It may have been a misreading of the letters of her first name, Ida. Royster, intro., 16.

57. Ida B. Wells, *United States Atrocities: Lynch Law* (London: Lux Publishing, 1894).

58. For another relevant study of Wells, see Diggs-Brown, "Ida B. Wells-Barnett."

59. Royster, intro., 19 and 28.

60. On how Wells's radicalism isolated her and how more conventionally minded reform movements reacted to her, see Schechter, *Ida B. Wells-Barnett*, esp. 118.

61. Quoted in McMurry, *To Keep the Waters Troubled*, 114.

62. *Freeman*, August 24, 1889.

63. See McMurry, *To Keep the Waters Troubled*, 115–17, for details on how Wells's male colleagues treated her. "Given the venomous verbal assaults male journalists exchanged, turning their poisoned pens on Wells was actually recognition of her being accepted as part of the 'fraternity,'" McMurry notes. "At the same time, however, many couched their criticisms of Wells in sexist terms that belittled her" (115).

64. On the black dandy's significance as a figure for the black male intellectual, see Miller, "W. E. B. DuBois and the Dandy."

65. On the origins and meaning of the cakewalk, see Sundquist, *To Wake the Nations*, 271–94.

66. See Wells-Barnett, *Crusade for Justice*, 80. On Wells's relation to the stage, see Gunning, *Race, Rape, and Lynching*, 88–89; and Schechter, *Ida B. Wells-Barnett*, 18–23. Schechter suggests that Wells may have staged her dramatic exile from Memphis; at the very least, she was well prepared to take advantage of its consequences (*Ida B. Wells-Barnett*, 78–79). In her autobiography, Wells recalls that her tears moved her audience powerfully when she gave the lecture that raised money for her to publish her first pamphlet, but she immediately adds that she had not planned to cry (*Crusade for Justice*, 79–80).

67. Quoted in McMurry, *To Keep the Waters Troubled*, 116.

68. Carby, *Reconstructing Womanhood*, 118.

69. Harris, *Exorcising Blackness*, 15 and 5.

70. Historian Gail Bederman observes, "Wells recognized that behind middle-class gender lay a fundamental assumption that all pure women and manly men were white" (*Manliness and Civilization*, 76). For cogent analyses of how Wells manipulated dominant definitions of manhood, race, civilization, and sex, see ibid., 45–76; and Davis, "The 'Weak Race' and the Winchester," 85–92.

71. Wells, *Southern Horrors,* 78.
72. Ibid., 50.
73. Wells liked the Samson analogy well enough to repeat it in the pamphlet's first chapter. Ibid., 53.
74. Ibid., 50.
75. Ibid., 5.
76. McMurry, *To Keep the Waters Troubled,* 125.
77. Wells, *A Red Record,* 82.
78. Davis, "The 'Weak Race' and the Winchester," 77.
79. Wells, *Red Record,* 121–22.
80. Ibid., 122. This same passage appears in slightly shorter form in *Southern Horrors,* 55–56.
81. Wells, *Red Record,* 82. Carby argues that Wells cited white newspapers "not only to avoid accusations of exaggeration or fabrication" but also because Wells believed that murderers would (and should) be condemned by their own words (*Reconstructing Womanhood,* 111).
82. See, for instance, the outburst in the entry of September 4, 1886, in Wells, *Memphis Diary,* 102.
83. Wells, *Red Record,* 139.
84. Ibid., 139.
85. Mindich, *Just the Facts,* 132; for a compelling discussion of how Wells resisted such dismissals, see esp. 134–36.
86. The cover of the British version, *United States Atrocities: Lynch Law,* also featured an etching of Wells.
87. Wells, *Southern Horrors,* 52.
88. Ibid., 52.
89. Gunning, *Race, Rape, and Lynching,* 85. For a related analysis of the black body's role as a medium of political messages in lynching discourse and in Wells's journalism, see Davis, "The 'Weak Race' and the Winchester," 82–83.
90. For a complementary reading of Wells's choice to reproduce this case of mistaken gender identity, see Clymer, *America's Culture of Terrorism,* 128–30.
91. McMurry notes, "Rumors of her immorality haunted her entire single life" (*To Keep the Waters Troubled,* 30).
92. "British Anti-Lynchers."
93. Baker, "Critical Memory and the Black Public Sphere," 13–14.

3. The Original Sob Sisters

1. Before the Thaw trial, the few women who reported trials usually worked alone. In 1875 the *San Francisco Chronicle* sent a female correspondent to Henry Ward Beecher's trial. Fox, *Trials of Intimacy,* 92. Elizabeth Jordan recalled being the only woman reporter at the 1893 trial of Lizzie Borden (*Three Rousing Cheers,* 119). Jordan's articles regularly appeared on the front page but without bylines or the aggressive marketing that characterized reports of the Thaw trial. See, for example, *New York World,* June 8, 9, and 13, 1893. One drawing, captioned "Talking It Over with the Reporter," shows two female spectators talking to Jordan (*New York World,* June 18, 1893). Better known is Susan Glaspell, who wrote "A Jury of Her Peers" and *Trifles,* based on her coverage of a 1901 murder trial in Iowa. Glaspell, too, was apparently the only newswoman in court. Ben-Zvi, "'Murder, She Wrote'"; Bryan, "Stories in Fiction and in Fact," 1293–1364.

2. Although these four were responsible for most of the female-authored reports, at least eight other women received bylines for trial accounts.

3. Ross, *Ladies of the Press,* 65. Journalism historians, citing Ross's 1936 account, give Cobb credit for christening the sob sisters. He remains a likely candidate, although my research of the trial coverage did not authenticate his coinage. Reviewing reports from mid-January to mid-March 1907 in the *World, Evening World, New York American, New York Times,* and *New York Evening Journal,* I found many references to the newswomen, including "pity platoon," "sympathy squad," "female railbirds," and "lady muckrakers," but no specific "sob sisters" reference.

4. See Schilpp and Murphy, *Great Women of the Press,* 116. Dictionaries agree that "sob sister" came into use in the 1910s. Mathews, *Dictionary of Americanisms,* 1588; Chapman, *Dictionary of American Slang,* 516. Sometimes the phrase also signified an advice columnist, a role that would later make one of the newswomen, Dorothy Dix, a household name.

5. Belford, *Brilliant Bylines,* 106.

6. One of the first novelists to earn the dubious label was Fannie Hurst, who titled a 1916 short story "Sob Sister." She later became good friends with Ada Patterson, one of the Thaw trial reporters. Salpeter, "Fannie Hurst." On how being called a "sob sister" injured Hurst's literary reputation, see Thompson, *Influencing America's Tastes,* 159. The term was occasionally used to denigrate male writers as well. Decades after the Thaw trial, in a disparaging review of Truman Capote's true-crime narrative *In Cold Blood* Sol Yurick called it "sob sister gothic."

7. Former newspaper reporter Mildred Gilman's 1931 novel *Sob Sister* illustrates the term's negative connotations. Gilman characterizes the career of her spunky protagonist, Jane Ray, as misguided and hypocritical: "Here was her chance to harden herself to everything in life, to every shock and emotion and human sentiment. [Jane] struggled to become a hard-boiled sob sister. . . . She carefully schooled herself to promise freedom to criminals and false hopes to those in distress, to deceive the mothers of murdered girls and steal pictures from them. And at last, Jane Ray, without seeming to feel anything herself, could pour more anguish into her copy, more deep emotional feeling, than any other sob sister" (19). For another disparaging portrayal of a sob sister, see Maurine Watkins's 1927 Broadway smash *Chicago,* in which newspaperwoman Mary Sunshine is fed stories to inspire sympathy for murderer Roxie Hart.

8. Nancy Glazener's study of debates over literary realism in elite journals at the turn of the century shows that weeping and sentimentalism were often imagined as synonymous. Glazener also demonstrates that tears could signal not only sentimentalism but also transgressive female sexuality—a link that helps to explain why the newswomen who covered the sexually charged Thaw trial ended up being known for their tears. See Glazener, *Reading for Realism,* 121–30.

9. For an excellent synthesis of approaches to genre in early-twentieth-century fiction, see Howard, *Publishing the Family,* esp. chaps. 5–6. On modernism and mass culture, see Strychacz, *Modernism, Mass Culture, and Professionalism,* esp. chaps. 1–3; on sentimentalism, see Clark, *Sentimental Modernism;* on sentimentalism and realism, see Glazener, *Reading for Realism* and Hoeller, *Edith Wharton's Dialogue with Realism.* For a reading of the Progressive Era as sentimental, see Harker, "'Pious Cant' and Blasphemy," 56–57.

10. With the notable exception of Martha Merrill Umphrey's study of sensationalism in the *Evening Journal*'s trial coverage, the Thaw case has received scant scholarly attention. Even Phyllis Abramson's *Sob Sister Journalism* has no sustained analysis of the reportage. The case has inspired several popular history books, however. See Lessard, *The Architect of Desire;* Mooney, *Evelyn Nesbit and Stanford White;* and Langford, *The Mur-*

der of Stanford White. One historical study cites the case as proof that celebrity journalism had burst into full bloom by the early 1900s. See Ponce de Leon, *Self-Exposure,* 49–50.

11. Gottlieb, "Grit Your Teeth," 58.

12. Mindich, *Just the Facts,* 129–32.

13. Recent studies have argued against the dichotomy between information and entertainment journalism and challenged the assumption that the yellow press corrupted fact-based journalism to cater to the uneducated tastes of poor and/or immigrant readers. See Campbell, *Yellow Journalism;* and Sumpter, "Sensation and the Century."

14. Sanchez-Eppler, *Touching Liberty,* 26–27; and Dobson, "Reclaiming Sentimental Literature," 266–67.

15. Howard, *Publishing the Family,* 245.

16. On men's neglected roles as producers and consumers of sentimentality and melodrama, see Chapman and Hendler, *Sentimental Men;* Travis, "The Law of the Heart"; Williams, "Melodrama Revised"; and Lutz, "Men's Tears."

17. Warner, *Publics and Counterpublics,* 179.

18. Because the age of consent in New York at this time was sixteen, Evelyn's coerced sex with White would not have been considered statutory rape in a court of law. Odem, *Delinquent Daughters,* 30–31.

19. Eventually Thaw was found not guilty by reason of insanity and committed to an asylum, where his conditions of imprisonment were improved by family cash. When he was declared sane and acquitted of all charges in 1915, he immediately divorced Evelyn on grounds of adultery. Mooney, *Evelyn Nesbit,* 287. For a detailed analysis of Thaw's defense strategy and a different reading of its implications, see Umphrey, "Media Melodrama!"

20. William Hoster, "Mrs. Thaw Shows White a Villain," *New York American,* February 8, 1907.

21. For a similar passage, including the claim that "nothing more sickening, more appalling has ever been seen in a court-room than this slow, piecemeal stripping naked of a woman's soul," see Samuel Hopkins Adams, "Not All an Innocent Butterfly," *New York World,* February 22, 1907.

22. Nixola Greeley-Smith, "Countess of Yarmouth a Great Beauty," *New York Evening World,* January 29, 1907.

23. Schilpp and Murphy, *Great Women,* 151–52.

24. Nixola Greeley-Smith, "Thaw in Court as Seen by a Woman," *New York Evening World,* January 23, 1907; and Emma H. deZouche, "Actors in Thaw Tragedy Seen by Woman's Eyes," *New York World,* January 24, 1907.

25. Although bylines were increasingly common by 1907, most articles still appeared without them. If no author is cited for a news article, the reader should assume it had no byline.

26. *New York Evening Journal,* February 1, 1907 (Dix); *New York American,* February 9, 1907 (Black).

27. Advertisement, *New York American,* January 27, 1907.

28. Beatrice Fairfax, "Calls Thaw Case Tragedy," *New York Evening Journal,* February 8, 1907. This rhetoric obscured the fact that not all women writers found emotional resonance in the trial. Blanche Walsh, for instance, dismissed it as a shallow spectacle: "The Thaw trial is an animated iceberg. Feeling and emotion do not enter into it for one minute" ("Six Lawyers Always Ready," *New York Evening Journal,* February 9, 1907). Unsurprisingly, I found no more Walsh bylines during the trial.

29. Viola Rodgers, "Remarkable Interview," *New York American* January 26, 1907.

30. Nixola Greeley-Smith, "Evelyn Nesbit Thaw Now Only the X-Ray Picture of a

Famous Beauty," *New York Evening World,* January 25, 1907; Winifred Black, "The Mother's Is the Greatest Tragedy," *New York American,* January 29, 1907; Samuel Hopkins Adams, "Mrs. Harry Thaw Tells Jury of Her Relations with Stanford White," *New York World,* February 8, 1907.

31. Richard Dyer observes in his study of racial whiteness, "In Western tradition, white is beautiful because it is the colour of virtue" (*White,* 72).

32. Although the violence that Ida B. Wells and others protested began to decline after 1890, historians have argued that the cultural impact of lynching actually increased, because images and information about the murders circulated more widely as they became less common. Hale, *Making Whiteness,* 201. One of the most notorious portrayals of white womanhood under threat is D. W. Griffith's popular 1915 film *Birth of a Nation,* an adaptation of Thomas Dixon's novel *The Clansman* (1905).

33. On Wells's anti-lynching crusade and the embattled position of African American women, see chapter 2.

34. *New York American,* February 8, 1907.

35. "Mrs. Evelyn Nesbit Thaw Describes How Stanford White Wronged Her," *New York Evening World,* February 7, 1907.

36. "Evelyn Thaw Tells Her Story," *New York Times,* February 8, 1907.

37. "Thaw Trial Begins," *New York Times,* January 24, 1907.

38. William Hoster, "Complete Story of the Day in the Courtroom," *New York American,* January 24, 1907.

39. Maurice Ketten, *New York Evening World,* January 23, 1907.

40. This strategy was not original. A quarter-century earlier, similar policing efforts occurred in the Henry Ward Beecher–Theodore Tilton trial. See Fox, *Trials of Intimacy,* 92–95.

41. "Thaw Stirred to Wrath," *New York Times,* January 28, 1907.

42. "Evelyn Thaw Tells Story," *New York Times,* February 8, 1907.

43. "Object to Thaw Testimony," *New York Times,* February 10, 1907. For related incidents in Wisconsin, Ohio, and Kentucky, see "Crazy over Thaw Case," *New York Times,* February 15, 1907.

44. "Roosevelt Plans Thaw Censorship," *New York Times,* February 12, 1907. In New York City, the U.S. district attorney warned that he would prosecute violations of federal statutes prohibiting the mailing of "obscene matter." See "Jerome Checks Thaw Defense," *New York Times,* February 12, 1907.

45. "More than a score of women fought through the crowds," according to one report. "Crowd at Court Breaks Record," *New York Evening Journal,* February 7, 1907. Two days later an article reported that the number of women in court had tripled. Emma H. deZouche, "Rush of Women to Court," *New York World,* February 9, 1907.

46. "What Girls May Learn from the Thaw Case," *New York Evening Journal,* February 2, 1907.

47. The sob sisters were not the only women who wanted to see the trial. My survey suggests that out of about three hundred people in court on a given day, around twenty were women, and sometimes the number was much higher. Only four to six of these women were news reporters.

48. Winifred Black, "Testimony Too Tame," *New York American,* February 6, 1907.

49. Ibid.

50. "Types of Women," *New York Evening World,* February 9, 1907.

51. Charles Somerville, "Crowd Fights to Hear Evelyn Thaw," *New York Evening Journal,* February 19, 1907.

52. "Mrs. Thaw Sobs Out Her Life's Secrets," *New York American,* February 22, 1907.

53. Doctorow, *Ragtime,* 5.

54. "Thaw Has Crown of Women's Love," *New York American*, January 23, 1907.

55. "Sympathy Grows for Evelyn Thaw," *New York Evening Journal*, February 18, 1907.

56. While the other major players in the case were also pictured, my survey of the coverage suggests that images of Evelyn outnumbered images of everyone else by more than four to one. For more details and a complementary analysis of Evelyn's role in the trial, see Umphrey, "Media Melodrama."

57. *New York Evening World*, January 28, 1907.

58. "All Against Her, Evelyn Thaw Turns to Woman of Ice," *New York Evening Journal*, February 26, 1907.

59. "The Vivisection of a Woman's Soul," *New York Evening World*, February 22, 1907.

60. Ibid.

61. "Mrs. Thaw's Great Sacrifice," *New York Evening Journal*, February 1, 1907.

62. "Thaw Trial Begins," *New York Times*, January 24, 1907.

63. "Remarkable Interview," *New York American*, January 26, 1907.

64. "Evelyn Thaw Pitiful Plaything of Fate," *New York Evening Journal*, February 26, 1907.

65. "Evelyn Thaw Tells Her Story," *New York Times*, February 8, 1907.

66. "People Were Stilled," *New York American*, February 8, 1907. Dix used the same terms: "She held herself under wonderful control and told her story in a level monotone, sadder than any tears could have been." Dorothy Dix, "Evelyn Thaw's Story," *New York Evening Journal*, February 8, 1907.

67. "Bared Her Life's Secrets without Quiver of Eyelid," *New York World*, February 8, 1907.

68. "Evelyn Nesbit's Diary Read in Court," *New York American*, February 27, 1907.

69. "Witness Blushes," *New York Times*, February 27, 1907.

70. This view of complexion as a moral barometer echoes the sentimental typology Karen Halttunen finds in middle-class conduct manuals of the 1840s (*Confidence Men and Painted Women*, 88). Although Halttunen argues that the conduct rules were soon recognized not as guarantees of sincerity but rather as scripts for genteel performances, the reports of Evelyn's blush suggest that even in the early 1900s, sentimental typology was familiar enough for writers to invoke it with confidence.

71. "School Diary Casts New Light," *New York World*, February 27, 1907.

72. "Evelyn Thaw Has Triumphed," *New York Evening Journal*, February 27, 1907.

73. "Evelyn Thaw's Schoolgirl Diary," *New York Evening World*, February 27, 1907.

74. Although white people are not unique in their ability to blush, the news accounts rely on a trope that imagines moral response as racially specific, so that the blush signals both the blusher's whiteness and her ability to feel shame. For a provocative reading of the moral and racial meanings of blushing, see O'Farrell, *Telling Complexions*, esp. 84 and 166.

75. On white women's paradoxical place in the discourse of racial dominance, see Dyer, *White*, esp. 29.

76. Abramson, *Sob Sister Journalism*, 51.

77. Women were not eligible to serve on juries in New York until 1937. The state policy allowing women to be exempted easily from jury duty did not end until the mid-1970s, and lawyers were permitted to use peremptory challenges to screen jurors on the basis of gender until 1994, when the U.S. Supreme Court banned the practice. See Kerber, *No Constitutional Right to Be Ladies*, chap. 4, esp. 136–41.

78. "The Room of Weary Waiting," *New York American*, January 27, 1907.

79. "Calls Thaw Case Tragedy," *New York Evening Journal*, February 8, 1907.

80. *New York Evening Journal,* February 16, 1907.

81. Ibid.

82. "Nixola Greeley-Smith Pictures the Prisoner," *New York Evening World,* February 1, 1907.

83. See, for example, Ella Wheeler Wilcox, "He Killed in Interest of Society," *New York Evening Journal,* February 25, 1907.

84. Winifred Black, "Juror Voting to Convict Deserves Divorce," *New York American,* February 9, 1907.

85. Dorothy Dix, "Thaw Would Be Acquitted," *New York Evening Journal,* February 1, 1907.

86. Korobkin, *Criminal Conversations,* 89.

87. Mooney, *Evelyn Nesbit,* 83.

4. A Reporter-Heroine's Evolution

1. James, *The Portrait of a Lady,* Norton Critical Edition, 55. This edition includes James's 1908 revision and an appendix with the original text from 1881. Subsequent references to both versions are from this source and are cited parenthetically in the text.

2. Even a sympathetic 1989 study refers to Henrietta as "a minor character who demands too much." Miller, "The Marriages of Henry James and Henrietta Stackpole," 16.

3. The emergence of the "little magazines" is just one example of the effort of modernist writers to define their own venues outside mass-market demands. The boundaries between high art and popular literature were often more permeable than anxious artists or critics would admit; the so-called High Modernists engaged in a lively dialogue with mass culture, despite their hostility toward its easily consumable products. On the interdependence of modernism and mass culture, see Dettmar and Watt, "Introduction: Marketing Modernisms." For an account of how the high/low division developed in the nineteenth century, see Levine, *Highbrow/Lowbrow.* On women writers seeking recognition as artists, see, among others, Ammons, *Conflicting Stories,* 3–19; Brodhead, *Cultures of Letters,* 173–76; and Sofer, "'Carrying a Yankee Girl to Glory.'"

4. See, among others, Moers, *The Two Dreisers;* Ziff, *The American 1890s;* Fishkin, *From Fact to Fiction;* Wilson, *Labor of Words;* Kaplan, *The Social Construction of American Realism;* Strychacz, *Modernism, Mass Culture, and Professionalism;* Robertson, *Stephen Crane, Journalism, and the Making of Modern American Literature;* and Salmon, *Henry James and the Culture of Publicity.*

5. Conn nicely encapsulates James's horror of journalism when he concludes: "For James the richest life is lived inwardly. The growing dominion of the newspapers, in whose columns life is stripped of its interiority altogether and presented in simplified outwardness, is thus not merely a symptom of cultural decay; it is decay's monument" (*The Divided Mind,* 21).

6. In *Henry James and the Past,* Bell argues that James's engagement with the culture of publicity allows him "to recognize a radically new liberty for the self" (11). Anne Margolis calls James's prefaces "quite devious" in their portrait of a Master who cared nothing for popular taste, arguing that James displayed keen interest in cultivating an audience throughout his career, despite his tendency to celebrate the taste of the few and denounce the public as puerile. Margolis reads Henrietta as comic relief and "an easy target" for James's "prejudices against that 'vulgar' phenomenon, the fe-

male journalist" (*Henry James and the Problem of Audience*, 47). On James's fascination with the mass market and literary publicity, see also Jacobson, *Henry James and the Mass Market*. In a close reading of *The Bostonians*, Michael Robertson argues that James's characterization of Matthias Pardon distorts the historical reality of male-dominated newspapers. Robertson suggests that James compensates for his assumed lack of masculinity by reversing "the gender orientation of journalism and fiction"; thus James asserts the maleness of his own authorial position by feminizing journalism and making the novel "a forum for Basil Ransom's patriarchal views" (*Stephen Crane*, 37–38). For more analyses of newsmen in James, see Salmon, *Henry James*, esp. 14–45; Strychacz, *Modernism*, esp. 45–61; and Hahm, "Henry James and the Devouring Publicity of Life."

7. Henrietta Stackpole holds but a minor place in this criticism, and the history of newspaperwomen not even that. Although Howard Bight of James's short story "The Papers" is part of a news-reporting couple, his love interest, Maud Blandy, has received almost no attention. Recent readings of Henrietta Stackpole are limited by their failure to consider the historical particulars of her profession; she is often read as more of an anomaly than she actually was, particularly by 1908. In an otherwise compelling essay on Henrietta's character, for instance, Carolyn Mathews misleadingly refers to her as "a female assuming a male work role" ("The Fishwife in James's Historical Stream" 197). In a now dated study of James's attitudes toward daily journalism, Abigail Hamblen mentions female reporters only in passing and notes that in the 1880s, "women reporters began to sob" ("Henry James and the Press," 171).

8. See entry for November 17, 1887, in James, *The Complete Notebooks*, 40–41.

9. Henrietta's is not the only characterization James revised; he made thousands of changes, developing, for instance, Isabel's subtle consciousness and stressing her desire for imaginative freedom. For analyses of the revisions as a whole, see Matthiessen, "The Painter's Sponge and the Varnish Bottle"; and Baym, "Revision and Thematic Change in *The Portrait of a Lady.*"

10. Gary Scharnhorst ("James and Kate Field") makes a painstaking case for Field as the primary model for Henrietta Stackpole. Mathews ("The Fishwife") nominates Woolson as the most likely candidate (190–91). James's biographer Leon Edel posits "Miss Hillard," an aggressive woman James encountered, as a possible inspiration (*Henry James: A Life*, 261).

11. At least one scholar has argued that James cared too much about the symbolic value of journalists—and too little about their historical circumstances—to create any convincing portraits of journalists, male or female. See Habegger, *Gender, Fantasy, and Realism in American Literature*, 93–95. But James's lack of interest in the details of American workers' lives would not have precluded his observing the increasing visibility of American newspaperwomen.

12. For details on black newspaperwomen, see chapter 2.

13. For examples of this phenomenon, see chapters 1 and 3.

14. Habermas, *The Structural Transformation of the Public Sphere*, esp. 24–26 and 28–31.

15. Baym, "Revision and Thematic Change," 627. In an analysis of Jamesian newsmen, Robertson observes that James is kinder to Henrietta as a character than to the male reporters he creates (*Stephen Crane*, 53). Although I would not call the revisions to Henrietta's character kind, Robertson is surely right that James gives her a more complex characterization than he gives his newspapermen.

16. Robertson, *Stephen Crane*, 31. In *Writing Realism*, Daniel H. Borus reads Henrietta in this way, calling her an instance of James's "most damning criticism of the publicity-mad new journalism" (130).

17. Baym, "Revision and Thematic Change," 628.

18. Henrietta's "'unnatural' womanhood and her 'vulgar' social class smack of a tasteless, monstrous modernity," Mathews writes, but "readers are nonetheless led to regard modernity in a positive light" ("The Fishwife," 196).

19. For Ralph's "monster" reference, see the Norton Critical Edition, *79;* for Gilbert's, see 409. The narrator also tells us that Gilbert views Isabel's alliance with Henrietta as "a kind of monstrosity" (328).

20. James, *Notebooks,* 16.

21. See Davis, *Gallegher and Other Stories.* At the story's end, the managing editor takes Gallegher into his lap and thinks of his own son at home in bed (56–57). Arthur Lubow writes that the story's publication in August 1890 made Davis "Byronically famous overnight" (*The Reporter Who Would Be King,* 68).

22. Newspaperwomen tend to be dismissed as anomalies. Howard Good calls the female protagonist a "rare specimen in newspaper fiction" (*Acquainted with the Night,* 35), while Loren Ghiglione laments that women journalists are rarely portrayed as complex human beings (*The American Journalist,* 124–27). One study observes that "the dogged city reporter" joined the "panoply of supermasculine figures" in this era; see Gandal, *The Virtues of the Vicious,* 13. Women receive limited attention in studies by Ziff, Wilson, and Robertson, and in Hardt and Brennen, *Newsworkers.* A notable exception is Maurine H. Beasley and Stacy L. Spaulding's "Crime, Romance, and Sex: Washington Women Journalists in Recent Popular Fiction."

23. Women journalists occasionally appeared in fiction before this era, of course. The title character of Fanny Fern's popular mid-nineteenth-century novel *Ruth Hall* (1854) becomes a successful columnist, conquering the male-dominated newspaper business with talent, grace, and determination. Lillie Devereux Blake's suffragist novel *Fettered for Life* (1874) features a cross-dressing newspaperwoman, a gallant young reporter named Frank Heywood who rescues the heroine from being raped early in the book. (Frank's secret identity as a woman is revealed about three hundred pages later.) See Blake, *Fettered for Life,* 10–25, 53–54, and 364–68. And Rebecca Harding Davis's novella *Earthen Pitchers* (1874) includes a character, Jane Derby, who supports herself as a journalist.

24. London, "Amateur Night," 712. This story appeared in *Moonface and Other Stories* (1906) and in *Jack London's Stories for Boys* (1936).

25. Hoyt, "The Newspaper Girl"; see also Gottlieb, "Grit Your Teeth," 56. In a 1905 short story about a young woman's struggles to succeed as a reporter in New York City, the narrator observes: "The same expectation possesses the souls of hundreds in the army of girls that throng into New York every year. The hard, strenuous reality of an overcrowded market, and their mistaken estimate of their own ability, send many away with heavy hearts and broken hopes." Fallows, "The Journalistic Career of Evelyn," 362.

26. Ferber, *A Peculiar Treasure,* 115.

27. Hickok, perhaps best known today as Eleanor Roosevelt's companion, mimicked the hot chocolate–drinking habits of Dawn O'Hara when she began her journalism career in the Midwest. Ross, *Ladies of the Press,* 205. For details on Hickok's life, see Beasley, "A 'Front Page Girl' Covers the Lindbergh Kidnapping."

28. Ross, *Ladies of the Press,* 486.

29. Good, *Acquainted with the Night,* 91.

30. Michelson, *A Yellow Journalist* 169. The serial was first published in the *Saturday Evening Post* beginning January 14, 1905.

31. Tarkington based his editor-heroine on his sister, Haute Tarkington Jameson, a journalist who put her persuasive skills to use to advance her brother's career. Ap-

parently it was she who got S. S. McClure to agree to read the manuscript of *Gentleman from Indiana* in the first place; according to Tarkington family legend, the indomitable Haute "contained the force of a juggernaut." Mayberry, *My Amiable Uncle*, 23.

32. Michelson, *A Yellow Journalist*, 175.

33. Atherton, *Patience Sparhawk*.

34. For a later example of a woman journalist becoming a celebrity, see Anzia Yezierska's *Salome of the Tenements* (1923). In the opening scene, the heroine interviews a millionaire to write an article about him for *Ghetto News*, then uses the encounter to spark an unlikely romance and eventually a widely publicized marriage. Yezierska modeled the character after a real woman journalist, Rose Pastor Stokes, a Russian immigrant who met her future husband, millionaire Graham Stokes, while on assignment for a Jewish daily.

35. Journalism historian Howard Good has observed that newspaper fiction often dramatizes the difficulty or impossibility of writing literature while being a journalist (*Acquainted with the Night*, 9–12). On some classic denials of journalism's literary value, see Tichi, *Exposés and Excess*, 12–14.

36. Howells, *A Modern Instance*, 320.

37. Two noteworthy exceptions are the reporter-heroines of Edna Ferber's *Dawn O'Hara* (1911) and Jordan's *May Iverson's Career* (1914), who do both.

38. Jordan, *Tales of the City Room*, 231–32.

39. Isabel's indulgent smile at Henrietta turns "cold" in the 1908 edition (92).

40. For more on stunt reporters and Meg Merrilies, see chapter 1.

41. Although the Norton Critical Edition is cited, this passage is most easily read by consulting an edition of the 1881 text. See James, *The Portrait of a Lady* (1995), 77.

42. Jordan details her acquaintance with James in her autobiography and even suggests that at one point, friends in London wrongly assumed they were romantically involved. See Howard, *Publishing the Family*, 35–36; and Jordan, *Three Rousing Cheers*, esp. 208–12 and 216–20.

43. For a thoughtful historical analysis of the Borden case, see Robertson, "Representing 'Miss Lizzie.'"

44. See, for example, Elizabeth G. Jordan, "This Is the Real Lizzie Borden," *New York World*, June 18, 1893, 13.

45. Ross, *Ladies of the Press*, 177.

46. Jordan, *Three Rousing Cheers*, 23. Jordan was explicit on this point: "I had warned [editor] Colonel Cockerill that I was not up to 'stunt' reporting and I did not like it." Ibid., 23.

47. Ibid., 31–35.

48. For details, see Howard, *Publishing the Family*, 179–212.

49. Ibid., 180.

50. Gertrude Atherton played a key role in launching Jordan's literary career. Although Atherton never worked as a daily newspaper reporter, while she was writing *Patience Sparhawk* she persuaded the *New York World*'s managing editor to allow her to sit at a desk in the newspaper's building so she could meet reporters and "absorb atmosphere." Leider, *California's Daughter*, 145–46. During her time there, she befriended Jordan, who solicited Atherton's criticism of her first short story, which also featured a reporter-heroine. Atherton liked it so much that she sent it to a *Cosmopolitan* editor, who agreed to publish it. Jordan, *Three Rousing Cheers*, 110. Later the story opened her first story collection, *Tales of the City Room*.

51. Jordan, *Tales of the City Room*, 19–22.

52. Ibid., 29.

53. See Susan Glaspell, *Trifles and a Jury of Her Peers* (New York: Feminist Press, 1992).

54. Jordan, *Tales of the City Room,* 28.

55. Jordan, *Three Rousing Cheers,* 122.

56. Ibid., 119.

57. Ibid., 120–21. Journalist, editor, and author Julian Ralph (1853–1903) was recognized as one of the best reporters at Charles A. Dana's *New York Sun.* In 1895, two years after the Borden trial, Ralph went to work as the London correspondent for William Randolph Hearst's *New York Journal.* See Julian Ralph, *The Making of a Journalist* (New York: Harper & Bros., 1903).

58. Nearly two decades later, Jordan added another narrative twist when she retold the fictional Helen Brandow story, without even changing the accused murderer's name, as an episode in a different reporter-heroine's life. In this version, which appeared in *May Iverson's Career* (1914), Brandow does not confess to May, the newspaperwoman who interviews her in jail. But the visit inspires May to write her first short story, imagining what she would have done if Brandow *had* confessed to her. The story leads May's co-workers to assume she has suppressed Brandow's confession—just as Jordan's co-workers had. But Jordan does not allow this recycled story to stand as a fictional corrective to the previous furor, for she adds a final scene in which May apologizes to Brandow, and the now exonerated woman whispers, "Tell me, before we part—*how did you know?*" See chapter 5, "The Case of Helen Brandow," in Jordan, *May Iverson's Career,* 94–119.

59. See Seltzer, *Bodies and Machines,* for a provocative analysis of the "body-machine complex" in turn-of-the-century fiction.

60. F. O. Matthiessen singles out these changes in his study of James's revisions to *Portrait,* noting that James uses "the device of interrelating her appearance with her career"("The Painter's Sponge," 582).

61. The phrase "steel pen" is even more dehumanizing when we recognize that it could also refer to an enclosure; Gilbert associates Henrietta with both a metal writing device and a metal cage or prison.

62. In James, *Complete Stories, 1898–1910.* Citations are given parenthetically in the text.

63. One critic calls the tale of Maud and Howard "one of the strangest, most attractive, and happiest of James's love stories." See Howard, "Henry James and 'The Papers,'" 51. Although Henrietta, too, gets a marriage proposal at the end of *Portrait,* she remains defined by her role as a journalist. The novel does not celebrate Henrietta's match with Mr. Bantling—Isabel is rather disappointed in it herself—but it may be the most promising marriage in the book. The incongruity between Henrietta's romantic success and her transformation into an unpleasant publicity machine indicates the incoherence of James's 1908 revisions to her character; the depth of his hostility toward her undermines the original plot structure.

64. Henry James, "Flickerbridge," in *Complete Stories,* 439. "The Papers" is also published in this collection (542–638).

65. My reading is indebted to Mathews's more detailed discussion of this passage ("Fishwife," 204–5).

5. From News to Novels

1. Howells, *Fennel and Rue,* 6.

2. Crane based *The Red Badge of Courage* on someone else's reporting; the story

was derived from *Century Magazine*'s series on Civil War battles. See Sundquist, "The Country of the Blue," 367.

3. On journalism as a distinguishing feature of American fiction, see Fishkin, *From Fact to Fiction*, 5–7. On journalism and realism, see Ziff, *The American 1890s*, 164. On journalism and naturalism, see Howard, *Form and History in American Literary Naturalism*, 155. On journalism and modernism, see Robertson, *Stephen Crane*, 177–210. On the uses of professional neutrality for writers, see Wilson, *Labor of Words*. On the interdependence of modernism and mass culture, see Strychacz, *Modernism, Mass Culture, and Professionalism*.

4. Even Alan Trachtenberg's provocative discussion of the reporter as a performer cites only newsmen; see *The Incorporation of America*, 125–26.

5. Gale's novel competed on best-seller lists with Sinclair Lewis's *Main Street* and was declared by the *New York Times* "not one whit" less accomplished than Edith Wharton's *Age of Innocence* (June 1, 1921). On the beginning of Gale's reporting career, see Lynch, Introduction, and Burt, "Rediscovering Zona Gale, Journalist." The main character of Gale's first book, *Romance Island*, a romance novel published in 1906, was a newspaper reporter.

6. Ben-Zvi, "'Murder, She Wrote'" and *Susan Glaspell*; Bryan, "Stories in Fiction and in Fact"; and Ozieblo, *Susan Glaspell*. See also Bryan and Wolf, *Midnight Assassin*.

7. On Lane and Ferber, see Campbell, "'Written with a Hard and Ruthless Purpose.'"

8. Porter also won a Pulitzer Prize, in 1966, for her *Collected Stories*.

9. For an overview of Slesinger's life, see Sharistanian, afterword to *The Unpossessed*. On Gellhorn, see Moorehead.

10. Notable examples include Neith Boyce, who wrote for the self-consciously literary *Commercial Advertiser* in the 1890s; Pauline Hopkins, who wrote for the *Colored American Magazine* at the turn of the century; Alice Dunbar-Nelson, who produced some of her wittiest commentary as a columnist for African American newspapers such as the *Pittsburgh Courier* and the *Washington Eagle* in the 1920s; Charlotte Perkins Gilman, who wrote and edited her own feminist journal from 1909 to 1916; Mary Heaton Vorse, who wrote labor journalism and edited *The Masses;* Theresa Malkiel, who wrote for the New York socialist newspaper *Call* and published a novel, *The Diary of a Shirtwaist Striker*, in 1910; Dorothy Day, who started out as a reporter in Chicago, went to work for the *Call* in 1916, and founded the *Catholic Worker* in 1933; Josephine Herbst, who began her career writing for radical papers such as the *Daily Worker* and published her first novel in 1928; and Jessie Redmon Fauset, who wrote for the *Crisis,* the official organ of the NAACP. On the literary community fostered in the 1890s by papers such as the *Commercial Advertiser*, where writers opposed their colleagues in mainstream news, see Stansell, *American Moderns*, 18–39. On Boyce and Vorse, see ibid., 19–32. On Dunbar-Nelson, see Hull, *Color, Sex, and Poetry;* on both Dunbar-Nelson and Fauset, see Batker, *Reforming Fictions*. On Hopkins, see Wallinger, "Pauline E. Hopkins as Editor and Journalist." On Malkiel, see Basch, intro. to *The Diary of a Shirtwaist Striker*, esp. 49–62. On Day, see Roberts, "Journalism for Justice."

11. Hurst, for instance, covered a strike for the *Pittsburgh Sun-Telegraph* in January 1928, and in 1935 she reported on the trial of Bruno Hauptmann, accused kidnapper and killer of the Lindbergh baby, for the North American Newspaper Alliance. Kroeger, *Fannie*, 238, 326.

12. Day, *The Long Loneliness*, 53. See also Miller, *Dorothy Day*.

13. Gottlieb, "Grit Your Teeth," 58; Shuman, *Practical Journalism*, 149–50. In a 1909 *Collier's* article complaining about the difficulties of being a newspaperwoman, Anne Eliot, a former reporter on a Chicago daily, notes that her byline and picture

were frequently printed alongside her stories, and that her physical beauty was an aid to her career. See Eliot, "Experiences of a Woman Reporter."

14. Ferber, *A Peculiar Treasure*, 116.

15. Ferber, *Half Portions,* back cover.

16. "Few literary figures have so readily acknowledged, even boasted, about their journalistic background as much as Edna Ferber," observes John Stevens in a summary of Ferber's career ("Edna Ferber's Journalistic Roots," 497).

17. Ferber, *A Peculiar Treasure*, 108–9, 116, 124.

18. Ibid., 117. Ferber repeatedly maintains that newspaper work taught her to be a writer: "I learned to read what lay behind the look that veiled people's faces, I learned how to sketch in human beings with a few rapid words, I learned to see, to observe, to remember; learned, in short, the first rules of writing" (ibid., 111). Recalling her Appleton reporting days, Ferber insists that she "wouldn't swap that year and a half of small-town newspaper reporting for any four years of college education" (ibid., 111).

19. Ibid., 149–50. Gale herself is a striking example of a former newspaperwoman who enjoyed a long career as a fiction writer. See Burt, "Rediscovering Zona Gale" esp. 457–58.

20. "Her place in American letters is somewhat uncertain," a reference book entry on Ferber observes diplomatically. Pingatore, "Edna Ferber," 315. See also Shaughnessy, *Women and Success in American Society in the Works of Edna Ferber;* and Gilbert, *Ferber.*

21. For a detailed reading of Ferber as a worker, see Wilson, *White Collar Fictions,* 56–94.

22. Ferber, *Peculiar Treasure,* 117.

23. Christopher Wilson characterizes Ferber's fiction as a "modernization of sentimental domesticity" (*White Collar Fictions,* 58). See Berlant, "Pax Americana," on sentimentality, mass culture, and national identity in Ferber's *Showboat.*

24. *New York Times,* April 17, 1968.

25. Ferber, *Peculiar Treasure,* 111, 143, 153.

26. Ferber, *Peculiar Treasure,* 121; see also 134 and 147. According to her own report, Ferber became a newspaper reporter at least two years before Michelson's serial began appearing in the *Saturday Evening Post* in January 1905, but Michelson's heroine nonetheless shaped how Ferber thought about her own journalism career. For more on Michelson's novel, see chapter 4.

27. Ferber, *Peculiar Treasure,* 153.

28. Ibid., 147.

29. Ibid., 147.

30. Writing the society column was a "hated" duty: "To this I had to write a chatty lead, done in the butterfly manner. A search of the old Crescent files would here reveal some of the worst writing in the history of the newspaper profession." Even decades after her reporting career was over, Ferber still took the opportunity to denigrate "the newspaper girlies" who had sneered at her because she worked harder than they did. Ibid., 126–28.

31. Ibid., 154–55. Even the convent-educated reporter Elizabeth Jordan, who was teased for her formal manners, suggested that managing sexual aggression was a common problem for newspaperwomen. Jordan, *Three Rousing Cheers,* 128–31. She also dramatizes the problem in her 1914 novel *May Iverson's Career,* which tracks a young woman's successful path from aspiring nun to reporter and author. One of the most powerful episodes occurs when May, on assignment, is sexually assaulted by an elderly Wall Street millionaire in his office. When May tells her editor, he voices out-

rage and vows to "make this town ring with that story." This scene, captioned with the editor's vow, is depicted on the novel's frontispiece in an illustration by James Montgomery Flagg. Yet May's big news is never told. As a fellow reporter immediately observes, the editor cannot publish such a story, and the millionaire escapes censure. The threat is meaningless bluster. Jordan, *May Iverson's Career,* 40.

32. The exact nature of Ferber's illness is unclear; it may have been severe anemia or a nervous breakdown. See Ferber, *Peculiar Treasure,* 124, 143, and 159–60; and Gilbert, *Ferber,* 422–23.

33. Ferber, *Dawn O'Hara,* 17.

34. Ibid., 48–49. Beatrice Fairfax was a well-known columnist; some of her coverage of the Thaw trial is discussed in chapter 3.

35. Ibid., 158–59.

36. For an analysis of the novel and its reception, see Kenaga, "Edna Ferber's *Cimarron,* Cultural Authority, and 1920s Western Historical Narratives."

37. Ferber, *Peculiar Treasure,* 330.

38. Kenaga, "Edna Ferber's *Cimarron,*" documents a likely historical parallel for this incident (184–85).

39. Ferber, *Cimarron,* 290.

40. Slote, *The Kingdom of Art,* 3.

41. Willa Cather, "Escapism" (1936), in *Willa Cather on Writing,* 24.

42. Cather occasionally acknowledged her experience at newspapers and magazine offices, as in a 1915 interview with a Nebraska newspaper: "'I found that newspaper writing did a great deal of good for me,' she said, 'in working off the purple flurry of my early writing." Ethel M. Hockett, "The Vision of a Successful Fiction Writer," *Lincoln Daily Star,* October 24, 1915. In a different context, Elizabeth Shepley Sergeant (herself a journalist) remarked that she did not "commiserate" with Cather "for her journalistic past" because she had seen "how much [Cather] was able to learn and absorb from this environment and how little 'superior' to it she felt." Quoted in Thompson, *Influencing America's Tastes,* 131. But such comments—from Cather or her companions—are unusual.

43. In "The Art of Fiction" (1920), Cather insisted that "the dazzling journalistic successes of twenty years ago, stories that surprised and delighted by their sharp photographic detail," were only a diversion from true art (101). The care with which she distinguished literary work from mass-market literature indicates how strenuously she tried to protect writing as an art form separate from and superior to the consumer culture she saw as synonymous with the newspaper-reading public. "If the novel is a form of imaginative art, it cannot be at the same time a vivid and brilliant form of journalism," she wrote in 1922 in "The Novel Demeuble" (37).

44. See Slote, *The Kingdom of Art;* Curtin, *The World and the Parish;* Bennett, *The World of Willa Cather;* Downs, *Becoming Modern;* Byrne and Snyder, *Chrysalis;* and Benson, "Willa Cather at the *Home Monthly.*" For a discussion (and critique) of how Cather's notion of literary value relied on a masculinist model of journalistic objectivity, see Sawaya, *Modern Women, Modern Work,* chap. 4.

45. Cather, *Willa Cather on Writing,* 42.

46. For biographical details, see Woodress, *Willa Cather,* 72, 73, and 96. The speech, "How to Make a Newspaper Interesting," was delivered January 31, 1896. See summary in Slote, *Kingdom of Art,* 27. The speech itself is apparently not available; scholars have searched for it without success.

47. Woodress, *Willa Cather,* 89.

48. Ibid., 9, 134, 103. Even a critic who insists that Cather did "no regular re-

porting at all" acknowledges that she wrote "an occasional factual piece." Weales, "Willa Cather, Girl Reporter," 687.

49. Woodress, *Willa Cather*, 130–31.

50. Letter dated December 13, 1908, in Jewett, *Letters of Sarah Orne Jewett*, 247–50. Edith Lewis writes that Jewett's advice "became a permanent inhabitant" of Cather's thoughts (*Willa Cather Living*, 67).

51. Woodress, *Willa Cather*, 89.

52. Even a 1999 book-length study of her journalism admits, "Cather's days at the office are hard to glimpse; the routine of her professional life is hidden." Downs, *Becoming Modern*, 51.

53. Jewett, *Letters*, December 13, 1908.

54. The story's narrator reports on a fire that has killed guests and destroyed a New York City luxury hotel, while also telling the story of an Italian laborer killed while building the hotel. In its movement from a big-city news event (the hotel fire) to a tale of foundations built by immigrant workers (the Italian laborer's death, caused by his employer's cost-cutting methods), "Behind the Singer Tower" shows Cather moving toward the subject and method of her most significant fiction, which would concern itself not with the bold strokes of news events but with contemplative stories of origins and intimate histories. The story also suggests, however, that journalism was holding back Cather's artistic vision rather than propelling it forward. Woodress calls it "an uncharacteristic and mediocre story" (*Willa Cather*, 215). For a discussion of how muckraking conventions influenced "Behind the Singer Tower," see Downs, *Becoming Modern*, 131–32. In another story, "Ardessa" (1918), set in the office of a magazine called *The Outcry*, Cather again criticizes journalistic practices. On "Ardessa" and Cather's relation to journalistic objectivity, see Sawaya, *Modern Women, Modern Work*, 88–92.

55. O'Brien, *Willa Cather*, 125. In a discussion of Cather and professional journalism, Sawaya extends this argument, suggesting that Cather's attempts at social critique—especially her attacks on consumer capitalism—were hampered because she relied on a "normative white masculine professionalism" that stigmatized women (*Modern Women, Modern Work*, 82).

56. Downs, *Becoming Modern*, 58.

57. On Cather's cross-dressing, see O'Brien, *Willa Cather*, 96–116. See also Woodress, *Willa Cather*, 69–70.

58. Downs, *Becoming Modern*, 50.

59. Lewis, *Willa Cather Living*, 37.

60. Cather, "When I Knew Stephen Crane," 772.

61. Cather briefly cross-dressed as a young male reporter for this recollection of Crane, further effacing her status as a female reporter. Initially she published the piece under the name "Henry Nicklemann," a male pseudonym she frequently used, but three weeks later it appeared in another publication under her own name. Ibid., 771.

62. Ibid., 774.

63. Ibid., 777.

64. O'Brien, *Willa Cather*, 161–63.

65. While Cather was writing *My Antonia*, she read a passage from Henry James's *Notes on Novelists* in which James insists that the artist has one law and the reporter another. "With this comment [Cather] fully agreed," Elizabeth Shepley Sergeant recalls in her memoir. "She had not altogether banished the reporter in her last book. Now she aimed at a more frugal, parsimonious form and technique." Schroeter, *Willa*

Cather and Her Critics, 120–21. James's fascination with—and repulsion by—what he called "newspaperized" writing has been well documented, as has his influence on Cather's artistic vision. See chapter 4 for more on James's view of women in journalism.

66. Downs, *Becoming Modern,* 16.

67. Schwind, "The Benda Illustrations to *My Antonia.*"

68. Cather, *My Antonia,* 144.

69. Schwind interprets this image as a "new-world Madonna" ("The Benda Illustrations," 62).

70. Cather, *My Antonia,* 203.

71. Cather, "Coming, Aphrodite!" 369. Subsequent references are given parenthetically in the text.

72. Raymont, "From the Avant-Garde of the '30s."

73. Barnes was born in 1892, Ferber in 1885, and Cather in 1873.

74. "Most descriptions of her in this period have her tall and dashing and strange," writes Andrew Field (*Djuna,* 14).

75. For an astute discussion of Barnes's refusal of "natural" gender categories, see Bockting, "The Great War and Modern Gender Consciousness."

76. Levine, "'Bringing Milkshakes to Bulldogs,'" 32.

77. Stansell, *American Moderns,* 153.

78. An exception is Katherine Biers's study of Barnes's crime journalism. Biers analyzes the relation between visual culture and spectatorship in mass-market newspapers and argues that Barnes's "many portraits of public spectacles" reveal a troubling dynamic, common in sensation journalism, through which crowds constitute themselves around public violence. Biers concludes by suggesting that Barnes was caught between "being a newspaper reporter who gives readers the facts and a sensational woman who communicates with her simple and visual-minded audience only through a picture" ("Djuna Barnes Makes a Specialty of Crime," 250). Barnes, I suggest, *inherited* this position from newspaperwomen like Bly, whose journalism collapsed the division between being a reporter (transmitting facts) and being a woman (appearing as a sensational body).

79. On Barnes's literary style, see Kaup, "The Neobaroque in Djuna Barnes."

80. Djuna Barnes, "A Visit to the Haunt of the I.W.W.'s," in *New York,* 198. As with the stunt reporters and sob sisters discussed in chapters 1 and 3, Barnes's name often appeared in headlines for her stories.

81. For instance, Barnes proclaims: "When a man subscribes to God, he subscribes to an inner conviction; when a man subscribes to revolt, he subscribes to a conviction that gastritis has forced upon him. . . . The strongest of leveling forces is the stomach. Stomach trouble is the emetic that looses redemption." Ibid., 199–200.

82. Gallegher, "Vision and Inversion in *Nightwood,*" esp. 298–99.

83. Green, "Spectacular Confessions," 76.

84. Especially misleading is the observation of the early Barnes biographer Andrew Field, who incorrectly noted that "certainly no other woman journalist was doing the sort of things that she was prior to World War I" (*Djuna,* 54). For an overview of Barnes's journalism, see Plumb, *Fancy's Craft,* 19–33; for another analysis, see Levine, "'Bringing Milkshakes to Bulldogs.'"

85. Barnes wrote for the *New York Press, New York World Magazine, New York Morning Telegraph, New York Tribune,* and *New York American,* and as a syndicate writer for Newspaper Enterprise Association. Herring, *Djuna,* 76.

86. Barnes later said that this incident helped to drive her away from the newspaper business. O'Neal, "Reminiscences," 357.

87. Barbara Green argues that Barnes "transforms the celebrity interview into a mocking critique of the impossible position of the girl reporter," and rightly points out that "for Barnes, many of her interviews ultimately turn on the question, 'What is *she* really like?'" ("Spectacular Confessions," 76). For related discussions of how Barnes toyed with her position as interviewer, see Broe, intro. to *Silence and Power,* esp. 10–11; and Bombaci, "'Well of Course, I *Used* to Be Absolutely Gorgeous *Dear.*'"

88. Barnes, "The Girl and the Gorilla," 181 (first published October 18, 1914); and Barnes, "My Adventures Being Rescued," in *New York,* 185–89 (first published November 15, 1914). For the rescue story, Barnes attended a firefighters' recruiting school, climbed into a window about a hundred feet above the pavement, and was "saved" as if she were trapped in a burning building.

89. Barnes's lover at the time, Ernst Hanfstaengl, thought the plane was unsafe, so he offered to pay her the twenty-five dollars the story would have earned. She refused the assignment—a good decision, since the plane crashed, killing everyone on board. Herring, *Djuna* 68.

90. O'Neal, "Reminiscences," 357.

91. In 1922, when she started reporting from Paris for *McCall's,* Barnes wrote mostly about fashion. She used pseudonyms, signing some of her journalism "Lydia Steptoe," apparently to save her real name for art, but she also kept using "Djuna Barnes" for some journalism. Herring, *Djuna,* 78. After 1922, when Barnes joined the expatriates in Paris, she became increasingly uneasy with her journalism and used the pseudonym to distance herself from it. Plumb. *Fancy's Craft,* 24.

92. Herring, *Djuna,* 77. Along similar lines, Cheryl Plumb cites a letter in which Barnes calls her magazine prose "utterly wasteful" (*Fancy's Craft* 19).

93. A friend noted that Barnes was proud of never having written anything "for popular consumption." O'Neal, "Reminiscences," 350. This claim tells us more about Barnes's values than her actual literary career, however; within three years of her start in journalism, she was publishing drama and fiction regularly in the *New York Morning Telegraph Sunday Magazine,* a venue certainly designed for popular consumption.

94. Herring, *Djuna,* 83–84.

95. Plumb, *Fancy's Craft,* 33.

96. Herring, *Djuna,* 75.

97. An early supporter said that she used journalism to free herself from the need to please art dealers and critics. Bruno, "In Our Village," 142.

98. Plumb, *Fancy's Craft,* 33; Herring, *Djuna,* 78.

99. Herzig, "Roots of the Night"; Levine, "'Bringing Milkshakes to Bulldogs'"; Plumb, *Fancy's Craft.*

100. Messerli, "The Newspaper Tales of Djuna Barnes," esp. 9–17.

101. Herzig, "Roots of the Night," 268.

102. On Barnes's news writing as an avant-garde blurring of writer and subject, see Nel, *The Avant-Garde and American Postmodernity,* 23. On Barnes's interest in the grotesque, see Levine, "'Bringing Milkshakes to Bulldogs,'" esp. 28–30. On Barnes's news writing as an attempt to gain access to the uncanny, see Bombaci, "'Well of Course,'" esp. 175. On Barnes's gender-bending, see Green, "Spectacular Confessions."

103. For background on the forcibly fed woman as an icon of militant feminism, see Green, "Spectacular Confessions."

104. Barnes, "How It Feels to Be Forcibly Fed." The article was originally published in *New York World Magazine,* September 6, 1914.

105. Nel, *The Avant-Garde,* 26; Broe, intro., 10.

106. Carl Herzig argues that Barnes's more aggressive stunts, such as the force-

feeding incident, were "unusual cases" because she "relinquished her control entirely," whereas most of her writings reflect a tension between maintaining critical distance and "surrendering herself to the moment" ("Roots of the Night," 257). As I suggested in chapter 1, however, this very tension characterized stunt reporting itself. Thus I read the force-feeding as more typical, and more emblematic.

107. Nancy Bombaci argues that Barnes uses stunt journalism to escape commodification, as part of her search for "an uncanny, pre-verbal otherness that cannot be commodified, but experienced" ("'Well of Course,'" 177). Even Green's brilliant analysis of the force-feeding story, which reads Barnes's "gesture of making public the private experience of the female body" as inherently radical, overlooks the gesture's debt to women's sensation journalism ("Spectacular Confessions," 71).

108. Barnes, "How It Feels to Be Forcibly Fed," 174–75. Subsequent citations are given parenthetically in the text.

109. Green, "Spectacular Confessions," 80.

110. Nelly [sic] Bly, "Visiting the Dispensaries," *New York World*, December 2, 1888.

111. This set of eight poems and five illustrations was published by Guido Bruno as part of his chapbook series. See Barnes, *The Book of Repulsive Women and Other Poems*.

112. Djuna Barnes, *Ladies Almanack*, 19. On lesbian writers and artists in Barnes's Paris, see Benstock, *Women of the Left Bank*.

113. Martyniuk, "Troubling the 'Master's Voice,'" discusses how Barnes's art engages and unsettles readers. For the censored image, see ibid., 72.

114. Broe, intro., 14.

115. On censorship of *Nightwood*, see also Gilmour, "Obscenity, Modernity, Identity"; and Cheryl Plumb's introduction to Barnes, *Nightwood*.

116. Levine and Urquilla, "Djuna Barnes," 14.

117. Smith, "A Story Beside(s) Itself," reads *Nightwood* as an expression of Freudian melancholia, an attempt to address the unspeakable losses of lesbians and others whose voices have been excluded from the dominant society.

118. See Chisholm, "Obscene Modernism." *Nightwood*, Chisholm concludes, "works like a Trojan horse, constructed out of a vast battery of obscene materials and inserted into a juridical, sexological, and theological discourse where it clears explosive queer space for radically rethinking the history of sexuality" (195). For another discussion of the political dimensions of *Nightwood*'s surrealism, see Hubert, "The Word Separated from the Thing." For a more thorough analysis of Barnes's disruption of urban-guide narratives, see Scott Herring, chap. 4 of "Queer Slumming" (unpublished manuscript).

119. Seitler, "Down on All Fours," argues for the significance of the human-beast hybrid in *Nightwood*. Concluding that "through its bestialization the body becomes increasingly sexualized and racialized at once" (554), Seitler suggests that Barnes unsettled the racist assumptions of early-twentieth-century degeneration theory even while she portrayed sexual perversity as racially marked.

120. Barnes, *Nightwood*, 139.

121. Ibid., 136.

122. "Nellie Bly's Odd Letters," *New York World*, May 27, 1888.

Epilogue

1. *Dance, Fools, Dance* (MGM, 1931); *Meet John Doe* (Image Entertainment, 1941); *Woman of the Year* (MGM, 1942). Glenda Farrell also starred as newspaper-

woman Torchy Blane in a series of B-movies from 1937 to 1939. The first Torchy Blane film was *Smart Blonde* (Warner Brothers, 1937); Jane Wyman took over the role of Torchy in the last film in the series, *Torchy Plays with Dynamite* (Warner Brothers, 1939). Farrell also played a tough-talking reporter who gets suspicious about the source of a wax sculptor's amazingly lifelike figures in the horror classic *The Mystery of the Wax Museum* (1933).

2. *Mr. Deeds Goes to Town* (Columbia, 1936).

3. *His Girl Friday* (Columbia, 1940).

4. The play was made into a film of the same title in 1931.

5. For an analysis of newspaperwomen on film which argues that, from the late 1970s on, Hollywood representations of female reporters regressed, see Good, *Girl Reporter.*

6. In *I Love Trouble* (Touchstone, 1994), we learn that Sabrina Peterson, the reporter-heroine played by Julia Roberts, once entered a Pillsbury baking contest under an assumed name and won the prize without using any Pillsbury products; we also learn that she went undercover as a hooker. In *Never Been Kissed* (1999), reporter Drew Barrymore stages a desperate bid for her lover in a baseball stadium packed with thousands of spectators. In a 2002 remake of *Mr. Deeds* (Columbia), Winona Ryder recreates the original Babe Bennett's damsel-in-distress prank; in *How to Lose a Guy in Ten Days* (Paramount, 2003), Kate Hudson plays a magazine columnist who conducts an elaborate dating stunt. And in *The Life of David Gale* (Universal, 2003), Kate Winslet proves a condemned man's innocence by reenacting a brutal killing with herself as the victim.

7. The sitcom adapted Candace Bushnell's 1997 bestseller of the same title. The book, in turn, was based on the confessional newspaper columns Bushnell began publishing in the *New York Observer* in 1994.

8. The billboard—sans graffiti—appears in the show's opening credits.

9. *Sex and the City* (HBO, 2000), episode six from the first season, titled "Secret Sex."

10. Not all critics agree, of course, on the sitcom's liberating potential. For a range of critical approaches to the show, see the essays collected in *Reading Sex and the City,* ed. Akass and McCabe. See also Arthurs, "*Sex and the City* and Consumer Culture."

Bibliography

Abramson, Phyllis. *Sob Sister Journalism.* New York: Greenwood, 1990.

Akass, Kim, and Janet McCabe, eds. *Reading Sex and the City.* New York: I. B. Tauris, 2004.

Ammons, Elizabeth. *Conflicting Stories: American Women Writers at the Turn into the Twentieth Century.* New York: Oxford University Press, 1992.

Arthurs, Jane. "*Sex and the City* and Consumer Culture: Remediating Postfeminist Drama." *Feminist Media Studies* 3, no. 1 (2003): 83–97.

Atherton, Gertrude. *Patience Sparhawk and Her Times.* [1897]. Upper Saddle River, N.J.: Literature House, 1970.

Auerbach, Jonathan. *Male Call: Becoming Jack London.* Durham: Duke University Press, 1996.

Baker, Houston A., Jr. "Critical Memory and the Black Public Sphere." In *The Black Public Sphere.* Chicago: University of Chicago Press, 1995. 7–37.

Baldasty, Gerald L. *The Commercialization of News in the Nineteenth Century.* Madison: University of Wisconsin Press, 1992.

Barnes, Djuna. *The Book of Repulsive Women and Other Poems.* Ed. Rebecca Longraine. New York: Routledge, 2003.

——. "The Girl and the Gorilla." In *New York.* Ed. Alyce Barry. Los Angeles: Sun & Moon Press, 1989. 180–84.

——. "How It Feels to Be Forcibly Fed." In *New York.* Ed. Alyce Barry. Los Angeles: Sun & Moon Press, 1989. 174–79.

——. *Nightwood: The Original Version and Related Drafts.* [1936]. Ed. Cheryl J. Plumb. New York: Dalkey Archive Press, 1995.

Barth, Gunther. *City People: The Rise of Modern City Culture in Nineteenth-Century America.* New York: Oxford University Press, 1980.

Basch, Françoise. Introduction. In *The Diary of a Shirtwaist Striker* by Theresa Malkiel. Ithaca: ILR Press, 1990.

Batker, Carol J. *Reforming Fictions: Native, African, and Jewish American Women's Literature and Journalism in the Progressive Era.* New York: Columbia University Press, 2000.

Baym, Nina. "Revision and Thematic Change in *The Portrait of a Lady.*" In *The Portrait of a Lady by Henry James.* Norton Critical Edition. Ed. Robert D. Bamberg. New York: W. W. Norton and Co., 1995. 620–34.

Beard, George Miller. *A Practical Treatise on Nervous Exhaustion.* New York, 1881.

Beasley, Maurine. *The First Women Washington Correspondents.* Washington, D.C.: George Washington University, 1976.

——. "A 'Front Page Girl' Covers the Lindbergh Kidnapping: An Ethical Dilemma." *American Journalism* 1 (summer 1983): 63–74.

——. "The Muckrakers and Lynching: A Case Study in Racism." *Journalism History* 9, nos. 3–4 (autumn–winter 1982): 86–91.

——. "Women in Journalism: Contributors to Male Experience or Voices of Feminine Expression? How Historians Have Told the Stories of Women Journalists." *American Journalism* (winter 1990): 39–54.

Beasley, Maurine H., and Sheila J. Gibbons. *Taking Their Place: A Documentary History of Women and Journalism.* 2nd ed. State College, Pa.: Strata Publishing, 2003.

Beasley, Maurine, and Sheila Silver. *Women in Media: A Documentary Source Book.* Washington, D.C.: Women's Institute for Freedom of the Press, 1977. 28–29.

Beasley, Maurine, and Stacy Spaulding. "Crime, Romance, and Sex: Washington Women Journalists in Recent Popular Fiction." *Media Report to Women* 32, no. 4 (2004): 6–12.

Bederman, Gail. *Manliness and Civilization: A Cultural History of Gender and Race in the United States, 1880–1917.* Chicago: University of Chicago Press, 1995.

Beizer, Janet. *Ventriloquized Bodies: Narratives of Hysteria in Nineteenth-Century France.* Ithaca: Cornell University Press, 1994.

Belford, Barbara. *Brilliant Bylines: A Biographical Anthology of Notable Newspaperwomen in America.* New York: Columbia University Press, 1986.

Bell, Ian F. A. *Henry James and the Past.* New York: St. Martin's Press, 1991.

Bennett, Mildred R. *The World of Willa Cather.* [1951]. Lincoln: University of Nebraska Press, 1989.

Benson, Peter. "Willa Cather at the Home Monthly." *Biography: An Interdisciplinary Journal* 4, no. 3 (summer 1981): 227–47.

Benstock, Shari. *Women of the Left Bank: Paris, 1900–1940.* Austin: University of Texas Press, 1987.

Ben-Zvi, Linda. "'Murder, She Wrote': The Genesis of Susan Glaspell's *Trifles.*" In *Susan Glaspell: Essays on Her Theater and Fiction.* Ed. Linda Ben-Zvi. Ann Arbor: University of Michigan Press, 1995. 19–48.

——. *Susan Glaspell: A Life.* New York: Oxford University Press, 2005.

Berlant, Lauren. "Pax Americana." In *Cultural Institutions of the Novel.* Ed. Deidre Lynch and William B. Warner. Durham: Duke University Press, 1996. 399–422.

Berlant, Lauren. "Poor Eliza." *American Literature* 70, no. 3 (September 1998): 635–68.

Bergmann, Hans. "Panoramas of New York, 1845–1860." *Prospects* 10 (1985): 119–37.

Bernheimer, Charles, and Claire Kahane. Introduction. In *In Dora's Case: Freud—Hysteria—Feminism.* New York: Columbia University Press, 1985. 1–32.

Biers, Katherine. "Djuna Barnes Makes a Specialty of Crime: Violence and the Visual in Her Early Journalism." In *Women's Experience of Modernity, 1875–1945.* Ed. Ann L. Ardis and Leslie W. Lewis. Baltimore: Johns Hopkins University Press, 2003. 237–53.

Birken, Lawrence. *Consuming Desire: Sexual Science and the Emergence of a Culture of Abundance, 1871–1914.* Ithaca: Cornell University Press, 1988.

Bisland, Elizabeth. *A Flying Trip around the World.* New York: Harper and Brothers, 1891.

Black, Winifred. "Corpse-Laden Waters Lit by Funeral Pyres: Winifred Black Crosses the Dismal Bay of Death to the Desolate City of Disaster." *San Francisco Examiner,* September 15, 1900, 1.

——. "Rambles through My Memories." *Good Housekeeping* (February 1936): 214.

Blake, Lillie Devereux. *Fettered for Life or Lord and Master: A Story of To-Day.* New York: Feminist Press, City University of New York, 1996.

Bledstein, Burton J. *The Culture of Professionalism: The Middle Class and the Development of Higher Education in America.* New York: Norton, 1976.

Block, A. J. "Sexual Perversion in the Female." *New Orleans Medical and Surgical Journal* 22, no. 1 (1894): 1–7.

Blumin, Stuart M. "Explaining the Metropolis: Perception, Depiction, and Analysis in Mid-Nineteenth-Century New York City." *Journal of Urban History* 11, no. 1 (November 1984): 9–38.

Bly, Nellie. *Nellie Bly's Book: Around the World in Seventy-two Days.* New York: Pictorial Weeklies Company, 1890.

Bockting, Margaret. "The Great War and Modern Gender Consciousness: The Subversive Tactics of Djuna Barnes." *Mosaic* 30, no. 3 (September 1997): 21–38.

Bok, Edward. "Is the Newspaper Office the Place for a Girl?" *Ladies' Home Journal* (February 1901): 18.

Bombaci, Nancy. "'Well of Course, I *Used* to Be Absolutely Gorgeous *Dear*': The Female Interviewer as Subject/Object in Djuna Barnes's Journalism." *Criticism* 4, no. 2 (spring 2002): 161–85.

Bordin, Ruth. *Frances Willard: A Biography.* Chapel Hill: University of North Carolina Press, 2001.

Borus, Daniel H. *Writing Realism: Howells, James, and Norris in the Mass Market.* Chapel Hill: University of North Carolina Press, 1989.

Boughner, Genevieve Jackson. *Women in Journalism: A Guide to the Opportunities and a Manual of the Technique of Women's Work for Newspapers and Magazines.* New York: D. Appleton and Co., 1926.

Brady, Kathleen. *Ida Tarbell: Portrait of a Muckraker.* New York: Seaview/Putnam, 1984.

Brand, Dana. *The Spectator and the City in Nineteenth-Century American Literature.* Cambridge: Cambridge University Press, 1991.

Braxton, Joanne. Introduction. In *The Work of the Afro-American Woman* by Mrs. N. F. Mossell. New York: Oxford University Press, 1998. xxvii–xliii.

Brazelton, Ethel M. Colson. *Writing and Editing for Women: A Bird's-Eye View of the Widening Opportunities for Women in Newspaper, Magazine, and Other Writing Work.* New York: Funk & Wagnalls, 1927.

Brian, Denis. *Pulitzer: A Life.* New York: J. Wiley, 2001.

Briggs, Laura. "The Race of Hysteria: 'Overcivilization' and the 'Savage' Woman in Late-Nineteenth-Century Obstetrics and Gynecology." *American Quarterly* 52, no. 2 (June 2000): 246–73.

Brodhead, Richard H. *Cultures of Letters: Scenes of Reading and Writing in Nineteenth-Century America.* Chicago: University of Chicago Press, 1993.

Broe, Mary Lynn. Introduction. In *Silence and Power: A Reevaluation of Djuna Barnes.* Ed. Mary Lynn Broe. Carbondale: Southern Illinois University Press, 1991. 3–23.

Brown, Mary Jane. *Eradicating This Evil: Women in the American Anti-lynching Movement, 1892–1940.* New York: Garland, 2000.

Brundage, W. Fitzhugh, ed. *Under Sentence of Death: Lynching in the South.* Chapel Hill: University of North Carolina Press, 1997.

Bruno, Guido. "In Our Village." *Bruno's Weekly* 1 (October 21, 1915): 142.

Bryan, Patricia L. "Stories in Fiction and in Fact: Susan Glaspell's 'A Jury of Her Peers' and the 1901 Murder Trial of Margaret Hossack." *Stanford Law Review* 49 (July 1997): 1293–1364.

Bryan, Patricia L., and Thomas Wolf. *Midnight Assassin: A Murder in America's Heartland.* Chapel Hill: Algonquin Books, 2005.

Bullock, Penelope L. *The Afro-American Periodical Press, 1838–1909.* Baton Rouge: Louisiana State University Press, 1981.

Burt, Elizabeth V. "Pioneering for Women Journalists: Boston's Sallie Joy White." *American Journalism* 18, no. 2 (2001): 39–63.

——. "Rediscovering Zona Gale, Journalist." *American Journalism* 12, no. 4 (fall 1995): 444–61.

Burt, Elizabeth V., ed. *Women's Press Organizations, 1881–1999.* Westport, Conn.: Greenwood Press, 2000.

Byrne, Kathleen, and Richard C. Snyder. *Chrysalis: Willa Cather in Pittsburgh, 1896–1906.* Pittsburgh: Historical Society of Western Pennsylvania, 1980.

Cahoon, Haryot Holt. "Women in Gutter Journalism." *The Arena* 17 (December 1896–June 1897): 568–74.

Cairns, Kathleen A. *Front-Page Women Journalists, 1920–1950.* Lincoln: University of Nebraska Press, 2003.

Campbell, Donna. "'Written with a Hard and Ruthless Purpose': Rose Wilder Lane, Edna Ferber, and Middlebrow Regional Fiction." In *Middlebrow Moderns: Popular American Women Writers of the 1920s.* Ed. Lisa Botshon and Meredith Goldsmith. Boston: Northeastern University Press, 2003. 25–44.

Campbell, W. Joseph. *Yellow Journalism: Puncturing the Myths, Defining the Legacies.* Westport, Conn.: Praeger, 2001.

Carby, Hazel V. *Reconstructing Womanhood: The Emergence of the Afro-American Woman Novelist.* New York: Oxford University Press, 1989.

Carey, James. "The Communications Revolution and the Professional Communicator." *Sociological Review Monograph* 13 (1969): 22–38.

Cather, Willa. "The Art of Fiction." *Willa Cather on Writing: Critical Studies on Writing as an Art.* Lincoln: University of Nebraska Press, 1988: 101–4.

——. "Coming, Aphrodite!" In *Willa Cather: Stories, Poems, and Other Writings.* Ed. Sharon O'Brien. New York: Library of America, 1992. 357–96.

——. "Escapism." [1936]. In *Willa Cather on Writing: Critical Studies on Writing as an Art.* Lincoln: University of Nebraska Press, 1988. 24.

——. *My Antonia.* [1918]. Boston: Houghton Mifflin, 1988.

——. "The Novel Demeuble." In *Willa Cather on Writing: Critical Studies on Writing as an Art.* Lincoln: University of Nebraska Press, 1988. 33–43.

——. "When I Knew Stephen Crane." In *The World and the Parish: Willa Cather's Articles and Reviews, 1893–1902.* Ed. William M. Curtin. Vol. 2. Lincoln: University of Nebraska Press, 1970.

Chalaby, Jean K. *The Invention of Journalism.* New York: St. Martin's, 1998.

Chambers, Deborah, Linda Steiner, and Carole Fleming. *Women and Journalism.* London: Routledge, 2004.

Chapman, Mary, and Glenn Hendler, eds. *Sentimental Men: Masculinity and the Politics of Affect in American Culture.* Berkeley: University of California Press, 1999.

Chapman, Robert, L. ed. *Dictionary of American Slang.* 3rd ed. New York: Harper-Collins, 1995.

Chisholm, Dianne. "Obscene Modernism: *Eros Noir* and the Profane Illumination of Djuna Barnes." *American Literature* 69, no. 1 (March 1997): 167–206.

Clark, Suzanne. *Sentimental Modernism: Women Writers and the Revolution of the Word.* Bloomington: Indiana University Press, 1991.

Clymer, Jeffory A. *America's Culture of Terrorism: Violence, Capitalism, and the Written Word.* Chapel Hill: University of North Carolina Press, 2003.

Colbert, Ann Mauger. "Literary and Commercial Aspects of Women's Editions of Newspapers, 1894–1896." In *Blue Pencils and Hidden Hands: Women Editing Periodicals, 1830–1910.* Ed. Sharon M. Harris with Ellen Gruber Garvey. Boston: Northeastern University Press, 2004. 20–38.

Conn, Peter. *The Divided Mind: Ideology and Imagination in America, 1898–1917.* New York: Cambridge University Press, 1983.

Coultrap-McQuin, Susan. *Doing Literary Business: American Women Writers in the Nineteenth Century.* Chapel Hill: University of North Carolina Press, 1990.

Crawford, Emily. "Journalism as a Profession for Women." *Contemporary Review* 64 (September 1893): 366–67.

Crouchett, Lorraine J. "Delilah Leontium Beasley." In *Black Women in America: Business and Professions.* Ed. Darlene Clark Hine. New York: Facts on File, 1997. 42–43.

Curtin, William M., ed. *The World and the Parish: Willa Cather's Articles and Reviews, 1893–1902.* Lincoln: University of Nebraska Press, 1970.

Danky, James P., and Maureen E. Hady, eds. *African American Newspapers and Periodicals: A National Bibliography.* Cambridge: Harvard University Press, 1998.

Davidson, Sue. *Getting the Real Story: Nellie Bly and Ida B. Wells.* Seattle: Seal Press, 1992.

Davis, Elizabeth Lindsay. *Lifting as They Climb*. Washington, D.C.: National Association of Colored Women, 1933.

Davis, Rebecca Harding. *Earthen Pitchers*. [1874]. Reprinted in *A Rebecca Harding
Davis Reader*. Ed. Jean Pfaelzer. Pittsburgh: University of Pittsburgh, 1995.

Davis, Richard Harding. *Gallegher and Other Stories*. New York: Charles Scribner's
Sons, 1893.

Davis, Simone W. "The 'Weak Race' and the Winchester: Political Voices in the
Pamphlets of Ida B. Wells-Barnett." *Legacy* 12, no. 2 (1995): 77–97.

Day, Dorothy. *The Long Loneliness: The Autobiography of Dorothy Day*. New York:
Harper & Brothers Publishers, 1952.

Den Tandt, Christopher. *The Urban Sublime in American Literary Naturalism*. Urbana: University of Illinois Press, 1998.

Denning, Michael. *Mechanic Accents: Dime Novels and Working-Class Culture in America*. New York: Verso, 1987.

Dettmar, Kevin J. H., and Stephen Watt. "Introduction: Marketing Modernisms."
In *Marketing Modernisms: Self-Promotion, Canonization, and Rereading*. Ed. Kevin
J. H. Dettmar and Stephen Watt. Ann Arbor: University of Michigan Press,
1999. 1–13.

Dicken-Garcia, Hazel. *Journalistic Standards in Nineteenth-Century America*. Madison: University of Wisconsin Press, 1989.

Dickinson, Susan E. "Women in Journalism." In *Woman's Work in America*. Ed.
Annie Nathan Meyer. New York: Henry Holt and Company, 1891. 128–38.

Diggs-Brown, Barbara. "Ida B. Wells-Barnett: About the Business of Agitation."
In *A Living of Words: American Women in Print Culture*. Ed. Susan Albertine.
Knoxville: University of Tennessee Press, 1995. 132–50.

Dobson, Joanne. "Reclaiming Sentimental Literature." *American Literature* 69
(1997): 263–88.

Doctorow, E. L. *Ragtime*. New York: Plume, 1974.

Doreski, C. K. *Writing America Black: Race Rhetoric in the Public Sphere*. Cambridge:
Cambridge University Press, 1998.

Downs, M. Catherine. *Becoming Modern: Willa Cather's Journalism*. Selinsgrove, Pa.:
Susquehanna University Press, 1999.

Dray, Philip. *At the Hands of Persons Unknown*. New York: Random House, 2002.

Dreiser, Theodore. "Nigger Jeff." In *The Best Short Stories of Theodore Dreiser*. Cleveland: World Publishing Co., 1956. 157–82.

Dudley, John. *A Man's Game: Masculinity and the Anti-aesthetics of American Literary
Naturalism*. Tuscaloosa: University of Alabama Press, 2004.

Dunbar-Nelson, Alice. *The Works of Alice Dunbar-Nelson*. Vol. 2. Ed. Gloria T. Hull.
New York: Oxford University Press, 1988.

Dyer, Richard. *White*. New York: Routledge, 1997.

Edel, Leon. *Henry James: A Life*. New York: Harper & Row, 1985.

Eliot, Anne. "Experiences of a Woman Reporter." *Collier's* 43 (August 21, 1909):
9–11, 22.

Emery, Michael C., Edwin Emery, and Nancy L. Roberts. *The Press and America:
An Interpretive History of the Mass Media*. 9th ed. Boston: Allyn & Bacon, 2000.

Fallows, Alice Katherine. "The Journalistic Career of Evelyn." *Harper's Bazaar*
(April 1905): 360–70.

Faue, Elizabeth. *Writing the Wrongs: Eva Valesh and the Rise of Labor Journalism.* Ithaca: Cornell University Press, 2002.

Ferber, Edna. *Cimarron.* Garden City, N.Y.: Doubleday, 1930.

——. *Dawn O'Hara: The Girl Who Laughed.* New York: Grosset and Dunlap, 1911.

——. *Half Portions.* Urbana: University of Illinois Press, 2003.

——. *A Peculiar Treasure.* [1939]. Garden City, N.Y.: Doubleday and Co., 1960.

Field, Andrew. *Djuna: The Life and Times of Djuna Barnes.* New York: G. P. Putnam's Sons, 1983.

Fishkin, Shelley Fisher. *From Fact to Fiction: Journalism and Imaginative Writing in America.* Baltimore: Johns Hopkins University Press, 1985.

Fox, Richard Wightman. *Trials of Intimacy: Love and Loss in the Beecher-Tilton Scandal.* Chicago: University of Chicago Press, 1999.

Fraser, Nancy. "Rethinking the Public Sphere: A Contribution to the Critique of Actually Existing Democracy." In *Habermas and the Public Sphere.* Ed. Craig Calhoun. Cambridge: MIT Press, 1993. 109–42.

Frazer, Elizabeth. "The Sob-Lady." [1915]. In *Breaking the Ties That Bind: Popular Stories of the New Woman, 1915–1930.* Ed. Maureen Honey. Norman: University of Oklahoma Press, 1992. 37–52.

Furman, Necah Stewart. *Caroline Lockhart: Her Life and Legacy.* Seattle: University of Washington Press, 1994.

Gale, Zona. *Romance Island.* New York: Bobbs-Merrill, 1906.

Gallegher, Jean. "Vision and Inversion in *Nightwood.*" *MFS: Modern Fiction Studies* 47, no. 2 (summer 2001): 279–305.

Gandal, Keith. *The Virtues of the Vicious: Jacob Riis, Stephen Crane, and the Spectacle of the Slum.* Oxford: Oxford University Press, 1997.

Gates, Henry Louis, Jr. "The Trope of a New Negro and the Reconstruction of the Image of the Black." In *The New American Studies.* Berkeley: University of California Press, 1991.

Ghiglione, Loren. *The American Journalist: Paradox of the Press.* Washington, D.C.: Library of Congress, 1990.

Gilbert, Julie Goldsmith. *Ferber: A Biography.* Garden City, N.Y.: Doubleday and Co., 1978.

Gilman, Mildred. *Sob Sister.* New York: Jonathan Cape and Harrison Smith, 1931.

Gilmour, Leigh. "Obscenity, Modernity, Identity: Legalizing *The Well of Loneliness* and *Nightwood.*" *Journal of the History of Sexuality* 4 (April 1994): 603–24.

Glazener, Nancy. *Reading for Realism: The History of a U.S. Literary Institution, 1850–1910.* Durham: Duke University Press, 1997.

Goldsby, Jacqueline Denise. "After Great Pain: The Cultural Logic of Lynching and the Problem of Realist Representation in America, 1882–1922." Ph.D. diss., Yale University, 1999.

Good, Howard. *Acquainted with the Night: The Image of Journalists in American Fiction, 1890–1930.* Metuchen, N.J.: Scarecrow, 1986.

——. *Girl Reporter: Gender, Journalism, and the Movies.* Lanham, Md.: Scarecrow Press, 1998.

Gottlieb, Agnes Hooper. "Grit Your Teeth, Then Learn to Swear: Women in Journalistic Careers, 1850–1926." *American Journalism* 18, no. 1 (winter 2001): 53–72.

——. "Networking in the Nineteenth Century: Founding of the Woman's Press Club of New York City." *Journalism History* 21 (winter 1995): 156–63.

——. "Women Journalists and the Municipal Housekeeping Movement: Case Studies of Jane Cunningham Croly, Helen M. Winslow, and Rheta Childe Dorr." Ph.D. diss., University of Maryland, 1992.

Graham, Katharine. *Personal History.* New York: Vintage, 1998.

Green, Barbara. "Spectacular Confessions: 'How It Feels to Be Forcibly Fed.'" *Review of Contemporary Fiction* 13, no. 3 (1993): 70–88.

Grob, Gerald N. *Mental Institutions in America: Paradox of the Press.* Washington, D.C.: Library of Congress, 1990.

Groneman, Carol. "Nymphomania: The Historical Construction of Female Sexuality." *Signs* 19, no. 2 (winter 1994): 337–67.

Gunning, Sandra. *Race, Rape, and Lynching: The Red Record of American Literature, 1890–1912.* New York: Oxford University Press, 1996.

Habegger, Alfred. *Gender, Fantasy, and Realism in American Literature.* New York: Columbia University Press, 1982.

Habermas, Jürgen. *The Structural Transformation of the Public Sphere: An Inquiry into a Category of Bourgeois Society.* Trans. Thomas Burger. Cambridge: MIT Press, 1993.

Hahm, Yeonjin. "Henry James and the Devouring Publicity of Life: The Figure of the Journalist in *The Bostonians.*" *English Language and Literature* 47, no. 4 (2001): 1063–78.

Hale, Grace Elizabeth. *Making Whiteness: The Culture of Segregation in the South, 1890–1940.* New York: Vintage, 1998.

Hall, Jacqueline Dowd. *Revolt against Chivalry: Jessie Daniel Ames and the Women's Campaign against Lynching.* Rev. ed. New York: Columbia University Press, 1993.

Halttunen, Karen. *Confidence Men and Painted Women: A Study of Middle-Class Culture in America, 1830–1870.* New Haven: Yale University Press, 1982.

Hamblen, Abigail Ann. "Henry James and the Press: A Study of Protest." *Western Humanities Review* 2, no. 2 (1957): 169–75.

Hardt, Hanno, and Bonnie Brennen, eds. *Newsworkers: Toward a History of the Rank and File.* Minneapolis: University of Minnesota Press, 1995.

Harger, Charles Moreau. "Journalism as a Career." *Atlantic Monthly* 107, no. 2 (February 1911): 218–24.

Harker, Jaime. "'Pious Cant' and Blasphemy: Fanny Fern's Radicalized Sentiment." *Legacy* 18, no. 1 (2001): 52–64.

Harris, Trudier. *Exorcising Blackness: Historical and Literary Lynching and Burning Rituals.* Bloomington: Indiana University Press, 1984.

Hendler, Glenn. *Public Sentiments: Structures of Feeling in Nineteenth-Century American Literature.* Chapel Hill: University of North Carolina Press, 2001.

Henry, Susan. "'Reporting Deeply and at First Hand': Helen Campbell in the Nineteenth-Century Slums." *Journalism History* 11, nos. 1–2 (spring–summer 1984): 18–25.

Herring, Phillip. *Djuna: The Life and Work of Djuna Barnes.* New York: Viking, 1995.

Herzig, Carl. "Roots of the Night: Emerging Style and Vision in the Early Journalism of Djuna Barnes." *Centennial Review* 31 (summer 1987): 255–69.

Hochman, Barbara. *Getting at the Author: Reimagining Books and Reading in the Age of American Realism.* Amherst: University of Massachusetts Press, 2001.

Hockett, Ethel M. "The Vision of a Successful Fiction Writer." *Lincoln Daily Star,* October 24, 1915.

Hoeller, Hildegard. *Edith Wharton's Dialogue with Realism and Sentimental Fiction.* Gainesville: University Press of Florida, 2000.

Holt, Thomas C. "Afterword: Mapping the Black Public Sphere." In *The Black Public Sphere.* Chicago: University of Chicago Press, 1995. 325–28.

Honey, Maureen, ed. *Breaking the Ties That Bind: Popular Stories of the New Woman, 1915–1930.* Norman: University of Oklahoma Press, 1992.

Howard, David. "Henry James and 'The Papers.'" In *Henry James: Fiction as History.* Ed. Ian F. A. Bell. Totowa, N.J.: Barnes and Noble, 1984. 49–64.

Howard, June. *Form and History in American Literary Naturalism.* Chapel Hill: University of North Carolina Press, 1985.

———. *Publishing the Family.* Durham: Duke University Press, 2001.

Howells, William Dean. *Criticism and Fiction.* Ed. Clara Marburg Kirk and Rudolph Kirk. New York: New York University Press, 1959.

———. *Fennel and Rue.* New York: Harper & Brothers, 1908.

———. *A Hazard of New Fortunes.* New York: Oxford University Press, 1990.

———. *A Modern Instance.* Toronto: Penguin Books, 1984.

Hoyt, Eleanor. "The Newspaper Girl." *Current Literature* 34 (March 1903): 292.

Hubert, Susan J. "The Word Separated from the Thing: *Nightwood*'s Political Aesthetic." *Midwest Quarterly* 46, no. 1 (autumn 2004): 39–48.

Hughes, Helen MacGill. [1940]. *News and the Human Interest Story.* New Brunswick, N.J.: Transaction Books, 1981.

Hull, Gloria T. *Color, Sex, and Poetry: Three Women Writers of the Harlem Renaissance.* Bloomington: Indiana University Press, 1987.

Hurst, Fannie. *Anatomy of Me: A Wonderer in Search of Herself.* Garden City, N.J.: Doubleday and Co, 1958.

———. "Sob Sister." [1916]. In *Every Soul Hath Its Song.* New York: Harper & Brothers, 1916. 310–45.

Jacobson, Marcia. *Henry James and the Mass Market.* Tuscaloosa: University of Alabama Press, 1983.

James, Henry. *The Complete Notebooks of Henry James.* Ed. Leon Edel and Lyall H. Powers. New York: Oxford University Press, 1987.

———. "Flickerbridge" and "The Papers." In *Henry James: Complete Stories, 1898–1910.* New York: Library of America, 1996. 421–40 and 542–638.

———. *The Portrait of a Lady.* Norton Critical Edition. Ed. Robert D. Bamberg. New York: W. W. Norton and Co., 1995.

———. *The Portrait of a Lady.* New York: Signet Classic, 1995.

Jewett, Sarah Orne. *Letters of Sarah Orne Jewett.* Ed. Annie Fields. New York: Houghton Mifflin, 1911. Sarah Orne Jewett Text Project, 1997–99. http://www.public.coe.edu/~theller/soj/let/let-frm.htm.

Jordan, Elizabeth Garver. *May Iverson's Career.* New York: Harper & Brothers, 1914.

———. *Tales of the City Room*. [1898]. Freeport, N.Y.: Books for Libraries Press, 1970.

———. *Three Rousing Cheers*. New York: D. Appleton-Century Co., 1938.

Juergens, George. *Joseph Pulitzer and The New York World*. Princeton: Princeton University Press, 1966.

Kaplan, Amy. "'The Knowledge of the Line': Realism and the City in Howells's *A Hazard of New Fortunes*." *PMLA* 101, no. 1 (June 1986): 69–81.

———. *The Social Construction of American Realism*. Chicago: University of Chicago Press, 1988.

Kaplan, Richard L. *Politics and the American Press: The Rise of Objectivity, 1865–1920*. Cambridge: Cambridge University Press, 2002.

Kasson, John F. *Rudeness and Civility: Manners in Nineteenth-Century America*. New York: Hill and Wang, 1990.

Kaup, Monica. "The Neobaroque in Djuna Barnes." *Modernism/Modernity* 12, no. 1 (winter 2005): 85–110.

Kenaga, Heidi. "Edna Ferber's *Cimarron*, Cultural Authority, and 1920s Western Historical Narratives." In *Middlebrow Moderns: Popular Women Writers of the 1920s*. Ed. Lisa Botshon and Meredith Goldsmith. Boston: Northeastern University Press, 2003. 167–202.

Kerber, Linda K. *No Constitutional Right to Be Ladies: Women and the Obligations of Citizenship*. New York: Hill and Wang, 1998.

Kevles, Daniel J. *In the Name of Eugenics: Genetics and the Uses of Human Heredity*. New York: Alfred A. Knopf, 1985.

Knight, Denise D., ed. *Nineteenth-Century American Women Writers: A Bio-Bibliographical Critical Sourcebook*. Westport, Conn: Greenwood Press, 1997.

Kochersberger, Robert C., Jr. *More Than a Muckraker: Ida Tarbell's Lifetime in Journalism*. Knoxville: University of Tennessee Press, 1994.

Korobkin, Laura Hanft. *Criminal Conversations: Sentimentality and Nineteenth-Century Legal Stories of Adultery*. New York: Columbia University Press, 1998.

Koven, Seth. *Slumming: Sexual and Social Politics in Victorian London*. Princeton: Princeton University Press, 2004.

Kroeger, Brooke. *Fannie: The Talent for Success of Writer Fannie Hurst*. New York: Random House, 1999.

———. *Nellie Bly: Daredevil, Reporter, Feminist*. New York: Random House, 1994.

Lancaster, Paul. *Gentleman of the Press: The Life and Times of an Early Reporter, Julian Ralph of The Sun*. Syracuse: Syracuse University Press, 1992.

Langford, Gerald. *The Murder of Stanford White*. New York: Bobbs-Merrill, 1962.

Langston, Carrie. "Women in Journalism." *Atchison Blade* 10 (September 1892): 1.

Larson, Magali Sarfatti. "The Production of Expertise and the Constitution of Expert Power." In *The Authority of Experts: Studies in History and Theory*. Bloomington: Indiana University Press, 1984.

Leider, Emily Wortis. *California's Daughter: Gertrude Atherton and Her Times*. Stanford: Stanford University Press, 1991.

Lessard, Suzannah. *The Architect of Desire: Beauty and Danger in the Stanford White Family*. New York: Dial, 1996.

Levine, Lawrence. *Highbrow/Lowbrow: The Emergence of Cultural Hierarchy in America.* Cambridge: Harvard University Press, 1988.

Levine, Nancy J. "'Bringing Milkshakes to Bulldogs': The Early Journalism of Djuna Barnes." In *Silence and Power: A Reevaluation of Djuna Barnes.* Ed. Mary Lynn Broe. Carbondale: Southern Illinois University Press, 1991. 27–34.

Levine, Nancy J., and Marian Urquilla, eds. "Djuna Barnes." *Review of Contemporary Fiction* 13, no. 3 (1993): 7–15.

Lewis, Edith. *Willa Cather Living: A Personal Record.* New York: Alfred A. Knopf, 1953.

Lingeman, Richard. *Theodore Dreiser: At the Gates of the City, 1871–1907.* New York: G. P. Putnam's Sons, 1986.

Litwack, Leon. *Without Sanctuary: Lynching Photography in America.* Santa Fe: Twin Palms Publishers, 2000.

Logan, Shirley Wilson, ed. *With Pen and Voice: A Critical Anthology of Nineteenth-Century African American Women.* Carbondale: Southern Illinois University Press, 1995.

London, Jack. "Amateur Night." In *The Complete Stories of Jack London.* Ed. Earle Labor, Robert C. Leitz III, and I. Milo Shepard. Stanford: Stanford University Press, 1993. 711–23.

Looby, Christopher. "George Thompson's 'Romance of the Real': Transgression and Taboo in American Sensation Fiction." *American Literature* 65, no. 4 (December 1993): 651–72.

Lowell, Joan. *Gal Reporter.* New York: Farrar & Rinehart, 1933.

Lubow, Arthur. *The Reporter Who Would Be King: A Biography of Richard Harding Davis.* New York: Charles Scribner's Sons, 1992.

Lunbeck, Elizabeth. *The Psychiatric Persuasion: Knowledge, Gender, and Power in Modern America.* Princeton: Princeton University Press, 1994.

Lutz, Tom. "Men's Tears and the Roles of Melodrama." In *Boys Don't Cry? Rethinking Narratives of Masculinity and Emotion in the United States.* Ed. Milette Shamir and Jennifer Travis. New York: Columbia University Press, 2002.

Lynch, Diane. Introduction. In *Miss Lulu Bett and Birth* by Zona Gale. Oregon, Wis.: Waubesa Press, 1994. 5–12.

MacFarlane, Fenella. "Lucy Wilmot Smith." In *Black Women in America: The Early Years, 1619–1899.* Ed. Darlene Clark Hine. New York: Facts on File, 1997. 163–64.

Margolis, Anne Throne. *Henry James and the Problem of Audience.* Ann Arbor: UMI Research Press, 1985.

Marks, Jason. *Around the World in Seventy-two Days: The Race between Pulitzer's Nellie Bly and Cosmopolitan's Elizabeth Bisland.* New York: Gemittarius Press, 1993.

Martyniuk, Irene. "Troubling the 'Master's Voice': Djuna Barnes's Pictorial Strategies." *Mosaic* 31, no. 3 (September 1998): 61–81.

Marzolf, Marion. *Up from the Footnote: A History of Women Journalists.* New York: Hastings House, 1977.

Mathews, Carolyn. "The Fishwife in James's Historical Stream: Henrietta Stackpole Gets the Last Word." *American Literary Realism.* 33, no. 3 (spring 2001): 188–208.

Mathews, Mitford M., ed. *A Dictionary of Americanisms on Historical Principles.* Vol. 2. Chicago: University of Chicago Press, 1951.

Matthiessen, F. O. "The Painter's Sponge and the Varnish Bottle." In *The Portrait of a Lady* by Henry James. Norton Critical Edition. Ed. Robert D. Bamberg. New York: W. W. Norton and Co., 1995. 577–96.

Mayberry, Susanah. *My Amiable Uncle: Recollections from Booth Tarkington.* West Lafayette, Ind.: Purdue University Press, 1983.

McGlashan, Zena Beth. "Women Witness the Russian Revolution: Analyzing New Ways of Seeing." *Journalism History* 12 (1985): 54–61.

McGovern, Constance M. *Masters of Madness: Social Origins of the American Psychiatric Profession.* Hanover, N.H.: University Press of New England, 1985.

McMurry, Linda O. *To Keep the Waters Troubled: The Life of Ida B. Wells.* New York: Oxford University Press, 1998.

Messerli, Douglas. "The Newspaper Tales of Djuna Barnes." In *Smoke and Other Early Stories* by Djuna Barnes. College Park, Md.: Sun & Moon Press, 1982. 7–19.

Michelson, Miriam. *A Yellow Journalist.* New York: D. Appleton and Co., 1905.

Miller, Elise. "The Marriages of Henry James and Henrietta Stackpole." *Henry James Review* 10, no. 1 (winter 1989): 15–31.

Miller, Monica L. "W. E. B. DuBois and the Dandy as Diasporic Race Man." *Callaloo: A Journal of African American and African Arts and Letters* 26, no. 3 (summer 2003): 738–65.

Miller, William D. *Dorothy Day.* San Francisco: Harper & Row, 1982.

Mindich, David T. Z. *Just the Facts: How 'Objectivity' Came to Define American Journalism.* New York: New York University Press, 1998.

Mitchell, S. Weir. *Characteristics.* New York: The Century Company, 1892.

Moers, Ellen. *The Two Dreisers.* New York: Viking, 1969.

Mooney, Michael MacDonald. *Evelyn Nesbit and Stanford White: Love and Death in the Gilded Age.* New York: William Morrow, 1976.

Moorehead, Caroline. *Gellhorn: A Twentieth Century Life.* New York: Henry Holt and Company, 2003.

Mossell, Mrs. N. F. [Gertrude Bustill]. *The Work of the Afro-American Woman.* [1894]. New York: Oxford University Press, 1998.

Mott, Frank Luther. *American Journalism: A History, 1690–1960.* 3rd ed. New York: Macmillan, 1962.

Nel, Philip. *The Avant-Garde and American Postmodernity: Small Incisive Shocks.* Jackson: University Press of Mississippi, 2002.

Nord, David Paul. *Communities of Journalism: A History of American Newspapers and Their Readers.* Urbana: University of Illinois Press, 2001.

Nostwich, T. D. "Historical Commentary." In *Theodore Dreiser: Journalism.* Vol 1. *Newspaper Writings, 1892–1895.* Philadelphia: University of Pennsylvania Press, 1988. 335–46.

O'Brien, Sharon. *Willa Cather: The Emerging Voice.* New York: Oxford University Press, 1987.

Odem, Mary E. *Delinquent Daughters: Protecting and Policing Adolescent Female Sexuality in the United States, 1885–1920.* Chapel Hill: University of North Carolina Press, 1995.

O'Farrell, Mary. *Telling Complexions: The Nineteenth-Century English Novel and the Blush.* Durham: Duke University Press, 1997.

O'Neal, Hank. "Reminiscences." In *Silence and Power: A Reevaluation of Djuna Barnes.* Ed. Mary Lynn Broe. Carbondale: Southern Illinois University Press, 1991. 348–60.

Ozieblo, Barbara. *Susan Glaspell: A Critical Biography.* Chapel Hill: University of North Carolina Press, 2001.

Penn, I. Garland. *The Afro-American Press and Its Editors.* [1891]. Ann Arbor: University Microfilms International, 1981.

Perkins, Kathy A., and Judith L. Stephens, eds. *Strange Fruit: Plays on Lynching by American Women.* Bloomington: Indiana University Press, 1998.

Perrucci, Robert. *Circle of Madness: On Being Insane and Institutionalized in America.* Englewood Cliffs, N.J.: Prentice-Hall, 1974.

Pingatore, Diana R. "Edna Ferber." In *The Oxford Companion to Women's Writing in the United States.* New York: Oxford University Press, 1995. 315–16.

Pittenger, Mark. "A World of Difference: Constructing the 'Underclass' in Progressive America." *American Quarterly* 49, no. 1 (March 1997): 26–65.

Pizer, Donald. *The Novels of Theodore Dreiser: A Critical Study.* Minneapolis: University of Minnesota Press, 1976.

Plumb, Cheryl J. *Fancy's Craft: Art and Identity in the Early Works of Djuna Barnes.* Selinsgrove, Pa.: Susquehanna University Press, 1986.

Ponce de Leon, Charles L. *Self-Exposure: Human-Interest Journalism and the Emergence of Celebrity in America, 1890–1940.* Chapel Hill: University of North Carolina Press, 2002.

Ralph, Julian. *The Making of a Journalist.* New York: Harper & Bros., 1903.

Raymont, Henry. "From the Avant-Garde of the '30s, Djuna Barnes." *New York Times,* May 24, 1971.

Reagan, Leslie J. *When Abortion Was a Crime: Women, Medicine, and Law in the United States, 1867–1973.* Berkeley: University of California Press, 1997.

Rhodes, Jane. *Mary Ann Shadd Cary: The Black Press and Protest in the Nineteenth Century.* Bloomington: Indiana University Press, 1998.

Roberts, Nancy L. "Journalism for Justice: Dorothy Day and the Catholic Worker." *Journalism History* 10 (1983): 2–9.

Robertson, Cara W. "Representing 'Miss Lizzie': Cultural Convictions in the Trial of Lizzie Borden." *Yale Journal of Law and the Humanities* 8, no. 2 (summer 1996): 351–416.

Robertson, Michael. *Stephen Crane, Journalism, and the Making of Modern American Literature.* New York: Columbia University Press, 1997.

Rooks, Noliwe. *Ladies' Pages: African American Women's Magazines and the Culture That Made Them.* New Brunswick, N.J.: Rutgers University Press, 2004.

Ross, Ishbel. *Ladies of the Press.* [1936]. New York: Arno Press, 1974.

Royster, Jacqueline Jones. Introduction. In *Southern Horrors and Other Writings: The Anti-lynching Campaign of Ida B. Wells, 1892–1900.* New York: Bedford/St. Martin's, 1997.

Salmon, Richard. *Henry James and the Culture of Publicity.* New York: Cambridge University Press, 1997.

Salpeter, Harry. "Fannie Hurst: Sob-Sister of American Fiction." *Bookman* (August 1931): 612–15.

Sanchez-Eppler, Karen. *Touching Liberty: Abolition, Feminism, and the Politics of the Body.* Berkeley: University of California Press, 1993.

Sawaya, Francesca. *Modern Women, Modern Work: Domesticity, Professionalism, and American Writing, 1890–1950.* Philadelphia: University of Pennsylvania Press, 2004.

Scharnhorst, Gary. "'It has served the truth without fear and without favor': Kate Field and *Kate Field's Washington.*" In *Blue Pencils and Hidden Hands: Women Editing Periodicals, 1830–1910.* Ed. Sharon M. Harris with Ellen Gruber Garvey. Boston: Northeastern University Press, 2004. 248–64.

———. "James and Kate Field." *Henry James Review* 22, no. 2 (spring 2001): 200–206.

Schechter, Patricia A. *Ida B. Wells-Barnett and American Reform, 1880–1930.* Chapel Hill: University of North Carolina Press, 2001.

———. "Unsettled Business: Ida B. Wells against Lynching, or, How Antilynching Got Its Gender." In *Under Sentence of Death: Lynching in the South.* Ed. W. Fitzhugh Brundage. Chapel Hill: University of North Carolina Press, 1997. 292–317.

Schiller, Dan. *Objectivity and the News: The Public and the Rise of Commercial Journalism.* Philadelphia: University of Pennsylvania Press, 1981.

Schilpp, Madelon Golden, and Sharon M. Murphy. *Great Women of the Press.* Carbondale: Southern Illinois University Press, 1983.

Schocket, Eric. "Undercover Explorations of the 'Other Half,' Or the Writer as Class Transvestite." *Representations* 64 (fall 1998): 109–33.

Schroeter, James. ed. *Willa Cather and Her Critics.* Ithaca: Cornell University Press, 1967.

Schudson, Michael. *Discovering the News: A Social History of American Newspapers.* New York: Basic Books, 1978.

Schwind, Jean. "The Benda Illustrations to *My Antonia:* Cather's 'Silent' Supplement to Jim Burden's Narrative." *PMLA* 100, no. 1 (January 1985): 51–67.

Seitler, Dana. "Down on All Fours: Atavistic Perversions and the Science of Desire from Frank Norris to Djuna Barnes." *American Literature* 73, no. 3 (summer 2001): 526–60.

Seltzer, Mark. *Bodies and Machines.* New York: Routledge, 1992.

Sharistanian, Janet. Afterword. In *The Unpossessed: A Novel of the Thirties.* New York: Feminist Press, 1984. 359–86.

Shaughnessy, Mary Rose. *Women and Success in American Society in the Works of Edna Ferber.* New York: Gordon Press, 1977.

Showalter, Elaine. *The Female Malady: Women, Madness, and English Culture, 1830–1980.* New York: Pantheon, 1985.

Shuman, Edwin L. *Practical Journalism: A Complete Manual of the Best Newspaper Methods.* New York: D. Appleton and Co., 1905.

Siegel, Adrienne. *The Image of the American City in Popular Literature, 1820–1870.* Port Washington, N.Y.: Kennikat Press, 1981.

Simmons, Charles A. *The African American Press: A History of News Coverage during National Crises, with Special Reference to Four Black Newspapers, 1827–1965.* Jefferson, N.C.: McFarland and Co., 1998.

Slote, Bernice. *The Kingdom of Art: Willa Cather's First Principles and Critical Statements, 1893–1896*. Lincoln: University of Nebraska Press, 1966.

Smith, Lucy Wilmot. "Some Female Writers of the Negro Race." *The Journalist*, January 26, 1889. Reprinted in *Women in Media: A Documentary Sourcebook*. Ed. Maurine Beasley and Sheila Silver. Washington, D.C.: Institute for Freedom of the Press, 1977. 38–44.

Smith, Victoria L. "A Story Beside(s) Itself: The Language of Loss in Djuna Barnes's *Nightwood*." *PMLA* 114 (March 1999): 194–206.

Sofer, Naomi Z. " 'Carrying a Yankee Girl to Glory': Redefining Female Authorship in the Postbellum United States." *American Literature* 75, no. 1 (March 2003): 31–60.

Solomon, Martha M., ed. *A Voice of Their Own: The Woman Suffrage Press, 1840–1910*. Tuscaloosa: University of Alabama Press, 1991.

Snorgrass, William. "Pioneer Black Women Journalists from the 1850s to the 1890s." *Western Journal of Black Studies* 6, no. 3 (fall 1982): 150–58.

Stansell, Christine. *American Moderns: Bohemian New York and the Creation of a New Century*. New York: Metropolitan Books, 2000.

Stead, W. T. "Young Women in Journalism." *Review of Reviews* 6 (November 1892): 451–52.

Steele, Janet E. "The Nineteenth-Century *World* Versus the *Sun:* Promoting Consumption (Rather than the Working Man)." *Journalism Quarterly* 67, no.3 (autumn 1990): 592–601.

Steinem, Gloria. *Outrageous Acts and Everyday Rebellions*. New York: Holt, Rinehart, and Winston, 1983.

Steiner, Linda. "Gender at Work: Early Accounts by Women Journalists." *Journalism History* 23, no. 1 (spring 1997): 2–12.

Stevens, John. "Edna Ferber's Journalistic Roots." *American Journalism* 12, no. 4 (fall 1995): 497–501.

Stokes, Mason. *The Color of Sex: Whiteness, Heterosexuality, and the Fictions of White Supremacy*. Durham: Duke University Press, 2001.

Streitmatter, Rodger. "African American Women Journalists and Their Male Editors: A Tradition of Support." *Journalism Quarterly* 70, no. 2 (summer 1993): 276–86.

———. *Raising Her Voice: African American Women Journalists Who Changed History*. Lexington: University Press of Kentucky, 1994.

Strychacz, Thomas. *Modernism, Mass Culture, and Professionalism*. New York: Cambridge University Press, 1993.

Sumpter, Randall S. "Sensation and the Century: How Four New York Dailies Covered the End of the Nineteenth Century." *American Journalism* 18, no. 3 (summer 2001): 81–100.

Sundquist, Eric J. "The Country of the Blue." In *Documents of American Realism and Naturalism*. Ed. Donald Pizer. Carbondale: Southern Illinois University Press, 1998. 366–85.

———. *To Wake the Nations: Race in the Making of American Literature*. Cambridge: Belknap Press of Harvard University Press, 1993.

Tarkington, Booth. *The Gentleman from Indiana*. [1899]. New York: Charles Scribner's Sons, 1915.

Tate, Claudia. *Domestic Allegories of Political Desire: The Black Heroine's Text at the Turn of the Century.* New York: Oxford University Press, 1992.

Terborg-Penn, Rosalyn. "African American Women's Networks in the Anti-lynching Crusade." In *Gender, Class, Race, and Reform in the Progressive Era.* Ed. Noralee Frankle and Nancy S. Dye. Lexington: University of Kentucky Press, 1991. 148–61.

Terrell, Mary Church. *A Colored Woman in a White World.* [1940]. New York: Humanity Books, 2005.

——. "Lynching from a Negro's Point of View." *North American Review* 178 (June 1904): 853–68.

Thompson, George. "Romance of the Real: Transgression and Taboo in American Sensation Fiction." *American Literature* 65, no. 4 (December 1993): 651–72.

Thompson, Stephanie Lewis. *Influencing America's Tastes: Realism in the Works of Wharton, Cather, and Hurst.* Gainesville: University Press of Florida, 2002.

Tichi, Cecelia. *Exposes and Excess: Muckraking in America, 1900–2000.* Philadelphia: University of Pennsylvania Press, 2004.

Tolnay, Stewart, and E. M. Beck. *A Festival of Violence: An Analysis of Southern Lynchings, 1882–1930.* Urbana: University of Illinois Press, 1992.

Trachtenberg, Alan. "Experiments in Another Country: Stephen Crane's City Sketches." In *American Realism: New Essays.* Ed. Eric J. Sundquist. Baltimore, Md.: Johns Hopkins University Press, 1982.

——. *The Incorporation of America: Culture and Society in the Gilded Age.* New York: Farrar, Straus and Giroux, 1982. 138–54.

Travis, Jennifer. "The Law of the Heart: Emotional Injury and Its Fictions." In *Boys Don't Cry? Rethinking Narratives of Masculinity and Emotion in the United States.* Ed. Milette Shamir and Jennifer Travis. New York: Columbia University Press, 2002. 124–40.

Tucker, David M. "Miss Ida B. Wells and Memphis Lynching." *Phylon: The Atlanta University Review of Race and Culture* 32, no. 2 (summer 1971): 112–22.

Umphrey, Martha Merrill. "Media Melodrama! Sensationalism and the 1907 Trial of Harry Thaw." *New York Law School Law Review* 43 (1999–2000): 715–39.

U.S. Bureau of the Census. Sixteenth Census of the United States: 1940. Population: Comparative Occupation Statistics for the United States, 1870–1940. Washington: United States Government Printing Office, 1943.

Wade-Gayles, Gloria. "Black Women Journalists in the South, 1880–1905: An Approach to the Study of Black Women's History." In *Black Women in American History.* Ed. Darlene Clark Hine. Vol 4. New York: Carlson, 1990. 138–52.

Wagner, Wendy. "Black Separatism in the Periodical Writings of Mrs. A. E. (Amelia) Johnson." In *The Black Press: New Literary and Historical Essays.* Ed. Todd Vogel. New Brunswick, N.J.: Rutgers University Press, 2001. 93–103.

Wallinger, Hanna. "Pauline E. Hopkins as Editor and Journalist." In *Blue Pencils and Hidden Hands: Women Editing Periodicals, 1830–1910.* Ed. Sharon M. Harris with Ellen Gruber Garvey. Boston: Northeastern University Press, 2004. 146–72.

Ward, Stephen J. A. *The Invention of Journalism Ethics: The Path to Objectivity and Beyond.* Montreal: McGill-Queen's University Press, 2004.

Warner, Michael. *Publics and Counterpublics.* New York: Zone Books, 2002.

Warren, Joyce W. *Fanny Fern: An Independent Woman.* New Brunswick, N.J.: Rutgers University Press, 1992.

Watkins, Maurine. *Chicago.* [1927] Carbondale: Southern Illinois University Press, 1997.

Weales, Gerald. "Willa Cather, Girl Reporter." *Southern Review* 8 (1972): 681–88.

Weaver, Paul H. *News and the Culture of Lying.* New York: Free Press, 1994.

Weddon, Willah. "Michigan Woman's Press Association." In *Women's Press Organizations, 1881–1999.* Ed. Elizabeth V. Burt. Westport, Conn: Greenwood Press, 2000. 114–21.

Wells, Ida. B. *The Memphis Diary of Ida B. Wells.* Ed. Miriam DeCosta-Willis. Boston: Beacon Press, 1995.

——. *Southern Horrors and Other Writings: The Anti-lynching Campaign of Ida B. Wells, 1892–1900.* Ed. Jacqueline Jones Royster. Boston and New York: Bedford/St. Martin's, 1997.

Wells-Barnett, Ida B. *Crusade for Justice: The Autobiography of Ida B. Wells.* Ed. Alfreda Duster. Chicago: University of Chicago Press, 1970.

Whites, LeeAnn. "Rebecca Latimer Felton and the Wife's Farm: The Class and Racial Politics of Gender Reform." *Georgia Historical Quarterly* 76 (summer 1992): 368–72.

Willard, Frances Elizabeth. *Occupations for Women: A Book of Practical Suggestions for the Material Advancement, the Mental and Physical Development, and the Moral and Spiritual Uplift of Women.* Cooper Union, N.Y.: The Success Co., 1897.

Williams, Linda. "Melodrama Revised." In *Refiguring American Film Genres.* Ed. Nick Brown. Berkeley: University of California Press, 1998.

Wilson, Christopher P. *Labor of Words: Literary Professionalism in the Progressive Era.* Athens: University of Georgia Press, 1985.

——. *White-Collar Fictions: Class and Social Representation in American Literature, 1885–1925.* Athens: University of Georgia Press, 1992.

Winslow, Helen M. "Confessions of a Newspaperwoman." *Atlantic Monthly* (February 1905): 206–11.

Woodress, James. *Willa Cather: A Literary Life.* Lincoln: University of Nebraska Press, 1987.

Yezierska, Anzia. *Salome of the Tenements.* [1923]. Urbana: University of Illinois Press, 1995.

Yurick, Sol. "Sob Sister Gothic." *The Nation* 202 (February 7, 1966): 158–60. Reprinted in *Truman Capote's In Cold Blood: A Critical Handbook,* ed. Irving Malin. Belmont, Calif.: Wadsworth, 1968.

Ziff, Larzer. *The American 1890s: Life and Times of a Generation.* New York: Viking, 1966.

Index

Note: Page numbers followed by an *f* refer to figures.